Humble by Nature

Humble by Nature

Life, lambs and a dog called Badger

Kate Humble

headline

First published in 2013
by HEADLINE PUBLISHING GROUP

1

Cataloguing in Publication Data is available from the British Library

Hardback ISBN 978 0 7553 6424 4

Typeset in Baskerville by Palimpsest Book Production Ltd, Falkirk, Stirlingshire

Printed and bound in Great Britain by Clays Ltd, St Ives plc

Headline's policy is to use papers that are natural, renewable and recyclable
products and made from wood grown in sustainable forests. The logging and
manufacturing processes are expected to conform to the environmental
regulations of the country of origin.

HEADLINE PUBLISHING GROUP
An Hachette UK Company
338 Euston Road
London NW1 3BH

www.headline.co.uk
www.hachette.co.uk

For Willie Wormald

Always marvellous for his age and without whom no part of this adventure would have been possible.

Chapter 1

Itchy Feet

We didn't want to buy a farm. We only wanted a field. Or even part of a field – just a few more acres. We had thought that the four acres we got when we moved to the Wye Valley in the winter of 2007, to a house that sits on a Welsh hill overlooking English woods and fields, was enough. In fact, at the time, it seemed a daunting amount of land for which to be responsible. We had come from London and twenty square feet of terraced garden, hemmed in and over-looked on all sides, and although we had both grown up in the countryside, this was the first time in our adult lives that we had owned a piece of land that we couldn't walk around in less than a minute.

We had no connection with this part of the country and knew no one. In the minds of a lot of Londoners Wales is 'too far' – another country with not enough motorways and a language with no vowels and unpronounceable words. We had braved the 'wild west' a few times before, crossing the border at the Severn Bridge and winding through startlingly pretty countryside to places like Crickhowell and Brecon to walk in the Black Mountains and the Beacons. Having grown up in rather flat, manicured Berkshire, the wild, stark grandeur of mountain scenery was bewitching. I loved – I still love – the breathless climbs that bring you puffing and grinning (quite hard to do at the same time) to a summit that reveals another whole range of tracks and peaks and possibilities. Like our tireless mongrel Badger, I could walk all day.

In those days Wales was the place for an occasional visit; it had never crossed our minds that we might live there. But as the years went on in London it became harder and harder for me to find any good reason to carry on living there, apart from the boring, practical necessity of work. I have a theory, backed up by nothing scientific whatsoever, that if your roots are in the country, if your childhood was like mine, one that involved making camps, climbing trees, horses, bike rides with Marmite sandwiches, permanent bits of sticking plaster and scabs, swimming in rivers, it is that – that sense of space, of freedom – more than location, that eventually, inevitably draws you back.

I had moved to London when I was twenty. After leaving school I spent a number of months living in a store cupboard in a house in Oxford, working in a hospital during the day and a pub at night and at weekends to earn the money to go to Africa. I had no plans to go to university; Africa, I thought, would serve me rather better, and it did. I returned after a year with a disintegrating rucksack and a wealth of traveller's tales, with a notion that a career in television might be what I did next. With the help of a friend's brother, I moved into a squat in Camden. London became my home for the next twenty years. Ten probably would have been enough. I became increasingly restless. I married Ludo, a clever, funny and endlessly patient man who I had quietly held a candle for since I was sixteen, and we moved from our respective rented rooms to a little terraced two-up, two-down in Shepherd's Bush. Two years on, the first democratic elections were held in South Africa. Mandela had been released from his long imprisonment and everyone was expecting what only a few years before had been unthinkable and unimaginable. South Africa would have a black president.

'I have to go back!' I said to Ludo. The country was still ostensibly in the grip of apartheid but there were rumblings and mutterings, protests and marches, not just from the black community, but from whites too. Something was happening, change was coming. We could be part of that change.

'We can't,' said Ludo. 'We have a house, a mortgage, we're freelance – if we leave we might never find a job again.' At this time he was making children's programmes for ITV. I was just starting out; making a lot of tea and doing a lot of typing for very little money and not much sense that this was a career that was going to go anywhere.

The pull to go back to Africa was insistent. 'Well, I'm going.'

Given little choice, Ludo gallantly agreed to my madcap plan and we flew to Cape Town in October of 1994. Our work permits had been turned down that morning, but by then it was too late. We'd rented out our house, sold our car, said goodbye to our friends. We moved to a little rented place with no furniture in a Cape Town suburb. Our neighbours were black. The new South Africa. We tried to work, tried contacting production companies back in Britain to offer programme ideas or help if they were planning shoots in South Africa. We were spending more of our meagre savings than we were making. 'This is ridiculous,' said Ludo one morning. 'If we want to work in television we should have stayed in London. We're in Africa. Let's make the most of it.' We gave up the house, bought a Ford Cortina pick-up with a yellow 'go-faster' stripe and a gear stick that would detach itself from the rest of the car when changing between second and third, and headed north.

We left South Africa, crossing the border into the newly independent Namibia with its long, straight, dirt roads and other-worldly vegetation. We discovered an abandoned mining town almost swamped by the shifting sands of the desert. We scrambled down a vertiginous path to the bottom of Fish River Canyon, envying the soaring eagles and the sure-footed little klipspringer antelope that skipped effortlessly down an almost sheer rock face and disappeared into the shadows. We climbed giant dunes, marvelled at the cruel majesty of the Skeleton Coast and narrowly missed being swept away in a flash flood. We drove through Etosha National Park, where giraffes stalked across the landscape, lions lazed in the shade and hyena skulked at the edge of the waterholes, scattering warthogs and making the antelope snort and stamp. We travelled the length of the Caprivi Strip, pausing to let marching columns of elephants cross the road in front of us.

Passing briefly through the border with Botswana we went on into Zimbabwe and the romance of Matopos (now Matobo) National Park, the final resting place of Cecil Rhodes, and the mysterious ancient site of great Zimbabwe. On Christmas Day, camping near Lake Kariba, we were woken by a herd of buffalo filing past our tent and later got a magical glimpse of a rare wild dog as it raced across the road in front of us in pursuit of an unseen prey. In Harare we applied for visas to Mozambique, newly emerged from decades of civil war. We went to the AA office to ask how much petrol was available in Mozambique and whether we would be wise to take our own supply.

'We don't advise our members to go to Mozambique at all,' said the woman in the office.

'OK,' I said, 'but we are going, so can you tell us whether we can buy petrol there?'

'We don't advise. . .'

We climbed a mountain while waiting for our visas to come and then headed across the border to a desolate land devoid of almost all wildlife. The roads were rutted and broken, the few towns we passed through were a dilapidated jumble of disintegrating buildings, blocked drains and hastily set-up stalls selling Johnny Walker Black Label and contraband cigarettes. Food seemed in desperately short supply. We camped on beaches beside the hot brown waters of the Mozambique Channel, sweltering in our tent from the tropical heat and unforgiving humidity. We drove south and then turned to the west over the border to Swaziland and our first shower for a fortnight.

Three months and 30,000 kilometres later we were back in Cape Town where we picked up a message from Ludo's old boss. He had had a series commissioned that would go into production in a couple of months' time. He was offering us both a job. We sold the pick-up, used the proceeds to spend the two intervening months on the extraordinary island of Madagascar and returned to Shepherd's Bush, penniless but employed.

We moved house a few years later, buying an uninhabitable wreck in Chiswick and living first with one friend, then another, then, with almost all our possessions in various garages and attics and our essentials in a few plastic bags, alongside the dust and the builders in the hope that that would encourage them to get on with it. Finally they moved out and we could move in, by which time my tentative flirtation with city life was well and truly over. I didn't want to be there.

'Perhaps,' I said to Ludo, 'we could rent or buy a little place in the countryside; somewhere we could go to at weekends or between contracts?'

In the early 'Noughties' – 2003 and 2004 – little places that were within striking distance of London and did not necessitate beginning and ending every weekend with several hours in stop-start traffic on a motorway were few and far between and hundreds of thousands of pounds more than we could afford. With increasing desperation, I pored over the *Road Atlas of the British Isles*. The home counties were way beyond our financial reach, although we did go and see a tiny, thatched curiosity, a sort of medieval hobbit house, which appealed because it was so romantic and unusual. However, as Ludo pointed out, neither of us could stand up straight in any of the rooms and it looked out on a soulless cul-de-sac of modern, red-brick horrors. 'There is nothing romantic,' he opined, 'about stooping and having the sound of other people's lawn-mowers constantly whining in the background.' Valid points, both, so I turned to another page of the map book to scan the villages of Oxfordshire and Gloucestershire, Wiltshire and Dorset.

'The problem', said Ludo, as we sat in static Sunday traffic on our return from another fruitless search, 'is that the little stone shack that is in your head – the one in the middle of nowhere, with no neighbours, magnificent views and honeysuckle around the door – either doesn't exist at all, is never going to be for sale, or is half a million quid.'

It had been a particularly depressing weekend. We had 'discovered' what we thought was the perfect area – pretty villages, still with pubs and post offices, sweeping open countryside and lovely walking. 'This would do,' I said, as we walked into one particularly pretty village. The landlord at the pub was friendly; the cider local and delicious; the ham in the sandwiches home-cooked and thick-cut.

'Madonna was in here yesterday,' said the landlord nonchalantly, as he waited for Ludo's beer glass to fill.

'Really?' I said, trying not to sound incredulous. 'What was she doing in this part of the country?'

'Oh, she lives here. She and that Ritchie bloke bought a big mansion outside the village. Pops in quite regularly, actually. Likes a pint. Tiny, she is, can barely see over the bar.'

'Wow,' I said, dully, realising that our 'discovery', our

'no-one-will-have-ever-heard-of-this' place had almost certainly appeared with tedious regularity in *Hello!* magazine. 'That must have pushed the house prices up.'

'Through the roof!' said the landlord, cheerily.

Back to the map for me.

'That's where I want to be,' I said wistfully. 'Look! There are hardly any roads and most of the map is brown and green; big areas with mountains, sheep and no pop stars.'

'Wales is fine for the odd weekend,' said Ludo, as we crawled a few metres in second gear and came to a halt again, 'but we wouldn't want to do it every week. It's too far. I thought we wanted to keep the journey time to under two hours.'

'It's taken longer than that to get back from Wiltshire,' I said sulkily, and at that moment realised that all this schlepping about the countryside was a waste of time. I didn't want a 'weekend' place, which even in the ever-more unlikely event that we did find the perfect hideaway was going to be another thing to worry about, another place that would need cleaning and fixing, another lot of council tax and bills. And worse than all those things would be the interminable hell of endless Friday nights and Sunday nights spent in a traffic jam. However sweet-smelling the honeysuckle, however heart-lifting the view, I could already envisage the time when neither of us could quite face the journey, when we would make the excuse of a stressful week, or something unavoidable or unmissable that would keep us in London. The dust would start to settle, the honeysuckle would be swamped by ground elder, the gutter would leak unnoticed and our rural retreat would metamorphose from idyll to chore.

'Why don't we just move out of London altogether?' I suggested, as Ludo, with a sigh of relief, left the motorway for a brief respite from the traffic, before promptly joining another jam on Chiswick High Road.

'And do what? Neither of us wants to commute and as far as I know there aren't any television production companies in the Black Mountains. I make TV programmes. I'm freelance. I need to be in a place where there are enough possibilities of finding work. It's different for you. You could live anywhere, because when you're working, more often than not it involves you being away anyway, but it's not the same for me.'

He was right, of course. Unless either or both of us were to consider making a career change – and we were both in the unusual and privileged position of enjoying our jobs – London seemed the only obvious place to be. My hunger for the countryside would have to be slaked by walks in the Chilterns and the occasional weekend away. So we stopped searching. I refused to let myself trawl the property websites and instead tried to settle and to make the most of Big City Life. 'We live', I told myself repeatedly, 'in a great house, in a nice area, with neighbours we love and friends, a book-shop, a deli, a butcher and greengrocer all within walking distance. There's a farmers' market on Saturdays, I can go running along the river and we have an allotment. Life is good.'

And it was good. It just wasn't right.

Chapter 2

Wales, Via Ethiopia

'Phone me as soon as you get this,' said the text message from Ludo. It was April 2006 and I had spent the day underground, deep beneath the Welsh hills experiencing the dubious pleasures of caving. I was making a programme about underground Britain. We had started in a relatively tame cave system that winds beneath the rolling North Yorkshire countryside. Hours spent in dark, damp tunnels and squeezing through sometimes alarmingly tight spaces were rewarded when we emerged, muddy and ecstatic, into the open shaft of Alum Pot. With its dripping vegetation and a water-fall falling in a silvery curtain from the ground 100 feet or so above, it felt like we had walked out onto a set from *Lord of the Rings*. From North Yorkshire we had travelled south to the Mendips, and the great rushing, watery rollercoaster that is the Swildon's cave system. Challenging and a little bit frightening for a novice like myself, it was, nonetheless, exhilarating.

Well it was, until we came to Sump Number One. A narrow but high-ceilinged tunnel had led us into a chamber and what to my inexperienced eyes appeared to be a dead end. 'We carry on through there,' said Tim Fogg, my instructor and guide. He was pointing at a pool at the far end of the chamber. 'There's a short tunnel under the water, that brings you out into another chamber,' he explained in answer to my perplexed expression.

'So you . . .?'

'Get in the pool, breathe out and empty your lungs, so you sink, and make your way through the tunnel until you get to the other side. It's quite tight, but it's not smaller than anything you've done before and there's a rope to guide you and to pull yourself through with.'

'Right,' I said. 'Easy.' My heart was going like the clappers. The water was horribly cold. I put my face in and spluttered.

'Go on!' encouraged Tim. 'You'll do it easily.'

I grabbed the rope, shut my eyes tight and submerged myself in the muddy water. I pulled myself along but then WHACK! My helmet hit rock in front of me. Whack! Above me. I was trapped. There was no tunnel. 'Don't panic! Don't panic!' I said to myself, over and over again, as I tried to pull myself backwards, desperate to get back to Tim. My helmet kept bashing on the rock. I wanted to scream, I wanted someone, anyone, to realise I was helpless, stuck, lost, running out of air, and come and rescue me. Then suddenly I was out, gasping and shaking, trying incoherently to explain to Tim that there was no tunnel, that it was just rock, or a tunnel so small a goldfish couldn't get through it. Tim, ever calm, explained that the wetsuit and overalls that make up the glamorous get-up of a caver were very buoyant. 'You didn't get yourself far enough beneath the surface to find the tunnel. It's there. I promise. And you'll have no problems getting through it.' I bit my lip, nodding with a conviction I didn't feel. I lay down in the water, breathed out and sank. I felt Tim give me a helpful shove and this time I didn't hit rock, but pulled myself through, emerging the other side, relieved and triumphant until I realised the only way back was the way we'd come.

The biggest challenge of the Dan-yr-Ogof system, which snakes from the head of the Swansea Valley in an intricate series of tunnels and passages under the Brecon Beacons National Park, is a section called the Long Crawl. It is a misleading name, given that it takes what feels like a very long crawl just to get to the start of what soon becomes a long slither. The passage is so narrow it is too small to traverse on hands and knees and I inched my way along on my belly, using my elbows and toes to propel me. 'Why does anyone do this?' I asked myself, as the rock closed in, ever tighter, around me. 'And *we* know this leads somewhere. Imagine being the first person to come down here. What if they discovered after 100 metres, 200 metres, that it was too small to go any further or to turn round. Then what would they have done?'

I pressed on, deciding it was better not to give it too much more thought, until the tunnel ended, suddenly and without warning, in a sheer drop. Some thoughtful lunatic had miraculously managed to squeeze a ladder, or perhaps the component parts of a ladder all the way to this point, assemble it and screw it to the wall of the descent. I climbed down into a much higher, wider chamber and gasped. In the light of my head torch I could see the first of the glittering, delicate formations that make the long crawl so completely worth the effort. Known, appropriately, as 'straws', they are delicate hollow tubes of calcium carbonate formed by the water seeping through the dripping roof of the cave. I made my way along the tunnel until I reached a chamber that was entirely encrusted in these luminescent spikes, so that it resembled a light shop displaying hundreds and hundreds of chandeliers.

Heady with the excitement of our subterranean adventure, I dialled Ludo's number. 'Sorry, I didn't ring before,' I gabbled. 'We've just come back to the surface.' And I proceeded to give him an excited account of the day.

'How would you like to live in Wales?' he said, finally able to get a word in.

My heart stopped. 'What did you say?'

'I've been offered a job in Cardiff. How would you like to live in Wales?'

He came up to meet me at the end of the shoot and we drove from Brecon along the Heads of the Valleys Road towards Abergavenny. 'I've been looking at the map,' said Ludo, 'and I think we want to find somewhere between Chepstow, Monmouth and Usk. That way we will be in easy reach of the motorway to get to Cardiff, or to Bristol, which will be good for you, and it will only take a couple of hours to get back to London to see our friends.'

'Or for our friends to come and see us,' I said, brightly.

'Mmm,' said Ludo, a noise laden with doubt and the knowledge that most people in London think of Wales as being Very Far Away. I do remember once travelling to a filming job in Snowdonia and the drive taking longer than a flight to New York, but the scenery was so spectacular I frequently had to stop the car and phone Ludo to tell him. It is certainly true that bits of Wales are Very Far Away, even from other bits of Wales, because of its gloriously chaotic topography and lack of roads that allow for speeds of anything over thirty miles an hour. But like Dan-yr-Ogof's Long Crawl, the rewards almost always outweigh the dearth of high-speed motorways and service station Little Chefs. And Chepstow and the Wye Valley, deemed in the eighteenth century to be the very epitome of author William Gilpin's idea of the picturesque, are really only separated from Bristol by the turbid waters of the River Severn and the relinquishing of a fairly hefty sum of cash for the toll bridge.

Ludo's BAFTA-winning triumph, *The Choir*, had prompted the BBC to offer him a job. He had made many series for the BBC, but had stayed stubbornly within the independent sector, suspecting that big corporation life wasn't really for him. But now an opportunity presented itself that would not only be professionally challenging and exciting but would also allow us to leave London. 'It's only temporarily,' Ludo warned. 'Just a year's contract. But we can get tenants into the house in London, rent down here and see if we like it.'

It sounded simple enough, but there was one, not inconsiderable, complication. The BBC wanted Ludo to start in a month. In a week I was leaving for a major diving expedition in the Pacific. I would be living on a boat and largely out of contact for six weeks. For Ludo to be able to accept the job, we had to at least find a house before I left. And even if we managed to do that, Ludo would have to find a tenant for our house, pack everything up, organise and supervise the move without any help at all. 'We can do it!' I said, racing down Monmouth High Street to another estate agent. We had seen a couple of houses to rent already that afternoon but they hadn't been quite right. We had stipulated unfurnished without realising that, unlike London where unfurnished tends to mean 'we'll leave you the curtains, a cooker and the white goods, but you'll need to bring your own sofa', in Wales unfurnished means 'stripped of pretty much everything that can be removed'. In one house, the estate agent opened a door with a flourish and announced: 'The kitchen!' There were a couple of bits of Formica attached to the walls and that was it. 'We would literally have to bring the kitchen sink,' muttered Ludo.

I paused in my mad dash down the hill and turned back to see why Ludo wasn't keeping up with me. He was walking, rather slowly, down the pavement, apparently deep in thought. 'Quick!' I was about to shout, 'we've only got five minutes before they shut!' But then I saw the look on his face. I walked back up the hill and stood in front of him. 'We can't do this,' he said, his face grey with tension, his shoulders hunched. And much as I wanted to seize him by the hand and jump up and down and say, 'We can, we can!' I knew that I would be lying; because it wouldn't be 'we'. In a couple of days I would be off to the other side of the world, leaving him to deal with everything on his own. It wasn't fair, and I knew it. If we were going to try living in Wales we had to be able to give it the best chance. We shouldn't just rush to move into the first available place and live like refugees, camping with our few bits of furniture, cooking on a Primus stove with sheets over the windows in lieu of curtains.

I tried to offer some reassurance. 'If the BBC want you now, they will want you in a year.' Ludo looked at me doubtfully. 'Come on,' I continued, 'we've got no kids, so we can move without all that worry of trying to find schools which puts a lot of people off. You've got loads of experience making the type of programmes they would love to see made in-house rather than by an independent, and you've got a big shiny doorstop called a BAFTA. How can they resist?'

He gave me a weak smile. 'I suppose I could ask,' he said, 'take a London job in the meantime and give us the chance to really explore where we want to be and find somewhere that maybe includes some kitchen equipment in the rent.'

The thrill of house-hunting palls quite quickly. Mercifully viewings were never available on a Sunday, so we would cram in as many as we could on a Saturday and then spend the rest of the weekend getting more familiar with an area we might, one day, call home. Armed with Ordnance Survey maps we tramped long sections of Offa's Dyke and the Wye Valley walk. We discovered that the ruin of Tintern Abbey, a victim of Henry VIII, is as captivatingly beautiful in the rain or the mist as it is in the soft, golden light of the early morning. We wandered through the arch and down the hill along Chepstow's high street, past the shops and the banks and the houses until a gap in the buildings revealed the surprisingly substantial remains of its castle, which appear to grow out of the limestone cliff on which it stands, overlooking a sweeping horseshoe bend in the River Wye. We climbed the Sugarloaf and the Skirrid, tasted the intoxicating delights of perry – cider made from pears, a local speciality – and, on the way to register with yet another estate agent in the small market town of Abergavenny, got sidetracked and gloriously diverted by its quirky art shop and gallery. 'Come on,' said Ludo, pulling at my coat, 'there's no point imagining paintings on a wall when we haven't got a wall yet.'

As Ludo gave out our details to the estate agent I stood by, reading the details of a house that wasn't for rent but would be within our price range if we sold the house in London. It was an old stone house, with roses and trees and a view of the mountains. 'It even has a paddock,' I whispered, reverentially.

'Excuse me!'

I snapped out of my reverie. 'Yes?' I said to the man, who was looking at me eagerly, his hand tightening on the handle of his plastic carrier bag.

'Are you Kate Humble?'

I'm always unsure what to do in situations like this. I find myself apologising – 'Er, yes, sorry, I am' – and blushing furiously like a hapless teenager. I did it again now.

'Really?' he said. 'Really it's you?' I nodded. 'Hold on! Please hold on!' and he dived for the door, thrusting his head outside. 'I was right, love, it IS her. Yes, yes, come in, come and see for yourself.'

A woman – I assume his wife – bustled through the door with her shopping bags and gave me a huge smile. 'So it is!' she exclaimed. 'He said he'd seen you coming out of the art shop, but I said to him, don't be ridiculous. What would Kate Humble be doing in Abergavenny?'

'We're going to live here,' I said, and as soon as the words were out of my mouth I knew it was true, that after all those restless years I'd found a place I felt happy to settle in.

'Oh, well, that's wonderful! You'll be very happy here. Good luck. Come on love,' she said to her husband, 'we mustn't miss the post office.'

'This renting lark is going to be very expensive,' I said to Ludo as we walked away from yet another house. Sitting in the middle of a field, looking out over a nicely ramshackle collection of farm buildings and more fields, it should have been perfect. Newly painted and carpeted, with more space than we could possibly dream of, it had no cooker, no fridge, no curtains – not even lampshades. 'It's crazy!' I said, shaking my head. 'We'd have to buy all the things we have in London and will be expected to leave there for our tenants, for a house that isn't even ours. Even if we went to Ikea and got the cheapest of everything it is still going to cost a fortune and what do we do with it all when we move out? If we sell it, we'll get a fraction of what we pay for it. It'll be such a waste.'

Ludo nodded in silent agreement.

'We could', I said tentatively, as if it was the first time I'd thought about it, 'perhaps look at places for sale – small places, places that we could afford to buy without selling the London house. Then if it works out, we've got a home here and if it doesn't we could maybe keep it for weekends or let it out.'

Ludo sighed. 'I'll do the maths and see what we can afford.'

I looked at the figures on the computer screen. It wasn't much but we thought we might be able find a little one- or two-bedroom cottage tucked away down a quiet lane with a bit of a garden. House prices may not have reached the ludicrous levels they had reached in London in 2006 and 2007, but the pickings in our price bracket were slim and those that we liked and could just about afford needed lots of work that we couldn't.

'We can't sell our house,' said Ludo. 'The BBC said there might be a job next year, but they couldn't promise anything, or make a firm offer. And if we sell in London now, we'll never be able to afford to go back there.' I gave him a look of stubborn determination that he knew only too well. He continued, undeterred. 'There's not much point in us moving lock, stock and barrel out here if we don't have any work. And if you get work,' he added quickly, 'which I'm sure you will continue to do, you'll be off somewhere filming blue tits or something, and I'll be left on a wet Welsh hillside all by myself, with no friends and no job.'

I couldn't argue. We may have been getting to know the area, but we still didn't know any locals.

Jennifer changed all that. I was away again, filming and ringing whooper swans in Iceland, and Ludo had gone to Wales for a couple of days with our old friend Richard. They had decided to find a new B&B, closer to the little town of Usk, and look at houses slightly further afield. I phoned Ludo from the hotel in Reykjavik to see how they had got on. 'I've fallen in love with another woman,' he announced. 'You'll fall in love with her too. She's called Jennifer, she owns the house we stayed in and she's wonderful. We're booked in to stay when you get back. Richard and I have found some houses you might like the look of . . .'

Something had happened while I had been away. Whether Richard's enthusiasm for the area made Ludo look it at afresh, or whether meeting Jennifer – who I did, indeed, love as soon as I walked into her kitchen – made him realise that moving here wasn't necessarily going to condemn him to a life of lonely isolation, I don't know, and I didn't ask in case he should re-think and change his mind. But whatever it was, it had caused a seismic shift; the estate agent details Ludo handed me as we drove back down the M4 were all for houses that we could only afford if we sold our house in London. A couple of them Ludo had already seen with Richard, most of them we would both be seeing for the first time and one Ludo had seen only from the outside because the estate agent hadn't had the keys. 'That's the one I look the look of most,' he said.

It was a pretty stone cottage with an ugly conservatory ('we can always get rid of that'), five acres of land and a trout pond. I looked at the picture. It seemed extraordinary to me that we might be able to swap life in a Victorian terrace, with neighbours on all sides and the constant roar of traffic, for this. By the time we got to the Severn Bridge I had mentally moved in. From the floor plan I'd worked out where I'd put our sofa and which bedroom would be ours and I was already transforming the small room behind the kitchen into my dream, book-lined hideaway, with wood-burning stove and a dog or two spreadeagled on the furniture.

Later that weekend, just before our appointment to see the cottage, my phone rang. It was the estate agent.

'I'm afraid we're going to have to cancel the viewing because the property has been sold,' he said.

'What do you mean, sold? It can't have been! It wasn't even under offer.'

I was indignant, furious that someone might have had the nerve to buy 'my' cottage. We were at the end of our third day of non-stop viewing and we'd seen nothing that felt right, nothing that had that inexplicable, intangible quality that made it feel like home. We were exhausted and a little dispirited but we hadn't quite been despairing because there was always the cottage-with-the-trout-pond, which we had left, on purpose, until last. Now 'somebody from London' had come along and paid over the asking price to ensure it was taken off the market. 'Bloody Londoners!' I yelled as I hung up the phone, making Ludo laugh and remind me that that was exactly what we were too.

'Not for long,' I muttered under my breath.

'Oh-my-God-have-you-seen-this?' I garbled, heart racing.

'Yes,' said Ludo wearily. 'Look at the price. We can't afford it.'

We had gone back to the little computer shop on the Usk high street to sit at its lone computer and begin another mindless trawl around the Rightmove website, looking at anything in the area that was for sale. I had put in £5,000,000 as the top price. Ludo raised his eyebrows. 'Now you're just being silly.'

'It's worth looking out of our price range just to see if there is something we've missed. People are willing to negotiate, you know.'

'No one is going to drop their price by over four million quid . . .'

The house was stone, with strangely tall chimneys, standing out against the blue sky of the photograph. I clicked on the details. A seventeenth-century Welsh farmhouse, four bedrooms, a barn, four acres.

'I'm going to call the estate agent.'

'There's no point.'

But I was already dialling.

'It's got to be close to here,' I said, squinting at the OS map as we bumped down another narrow lane. I had impressed on the estate agent that our budget fell well short of the asking price; that by allowing us to view it, she was either saying that the owners were willing to negotiate – a lot – or that they didn't mind a couple of nosy parkers coming to have a poke around with no intention of buying. 'See you at ten o'clock on the fifteenth,' she said. We would have to wait for another week before we could go and see it because the owners were on holiday – 'But', I said to Ludo, 'we could always go and have a look from the outside, just to get an idea . . .'

The car turned off a lane onto a forestry track. It was midsummer. The beech and oak trees cast thick, dappled shade over the rutted gravel road. We kept going, climbing through the woods, our Mini juddering and bouncing over the potholes.

Ludo broke the silence. 'What are you thinking?'

I was looking out at the trees, imagining this as the way I would always have to come to get home and wondering how to describe the route to people who had never been here before.

'I'm writing directions to our friends.'

He smiled, swinging the car around another switch-back and upwards towards the first glimpse of stone through the thick summer foliage. We stood, our backs to the house, looking out, over the patchwork of woods and fields, over the valley, the river hidden by the dips and curves of the voluptuous landscape.

'Can you imagine ever living anywhere else?' I asked.

'No,' said Ludo, 'I can't.'

The next few months were exhausting; an emotional fairground ride that lurched us from one extreme of feeling to another. Our first offer on the house was turned down, and we had to think hard and fast about whether we could afford to offer more. Every envelope was covered in scribbled sums, equations and hypotheses, as we agonised and rationalised the pros and cons of giving up or pressing on. In the end we phoned the estate agent, offering our absolute, full-stretch limit. We waited. One day; two days. Nothing, no word. It was agonising. I felt hamstrung, unable to think or concentrate on anything else. Finally, on the afternoon of the third day we got our answer. 'They've accepted your offer.'

I was jubilant. This was it. The unattainable was suddenly within grasp. Home would no longer be a place of pavements, parking metres, traffic fumes and wailing sirens. We wouldn't wake every morning to the revving diesel engine of our neighbour's van which he always managed to park outside our house and not his own. There'd be birdsong and crowing cockerels instead of thumping car stereos and the appalling, ear-splitting trumpet playing of the kid who lived over the back fence. 'We've got to sell our house first, remember,' warned Ludo, but I had no qualms. This was 2007. Houses in London were selling almost before they went on the market, certainly before any details were published. Sure enough, ours sold in three days for above the asking price to a bloke who wanted it as a buy-to-let. It was ridiculous, but we didn't care. We were moving to Wales.

A couple of weeks later we drove west to see the house again, partly to reassure ourselves that it really was as special as we remembered it, and partly to spend a bit of time with the owners learning about things like septic tanks and how their slightly eccentric heating system worked. Ludo talked boilers, electricity supplies and water tanks with the man of the house, while his wife showed me the garden, agreed to leave all the downstairs curtains and asked if I'd mind looking after their chickens and possibly their cat until they got settled. We came out of the kitchen door to see Ludo and her husband standing by our car. Ludo had a strange expression on his face. I gave him an enquiring look.

He didn't speak, but the husband did. 'It's just . . . we might have changed our minds. We might not want to sell after all.'

I looked at him, aghast, speechless. 'But you can't,' I said, trying to keep the desperation out of my voice. 'You can't. We only sold our house because of this, because you agreed, you accepted our offer.' He said nothing. His wife, looking awkward and embarrassed, broke the silence that hung heavy in the air. 'It's fine. Of course we're selling. It'll be fine. Don't worry. It's fine, really.'

We sat, shell-shocked and numb, in the pub at the bottom of the hill. 'I think he wants more money,' said Ludo, gloomily. 'I think it's a ruse to make us pay more.' I wasn't convinced. They had taken on the house when it had been pretty much a ruin, with crumbling walls and only part of a roof. They'd rebuilt it, raised a family there; I suspected it was more an emotional response to the realisation that the house would no longer be their home, but somebody else's. It didn't really make any difference which one of us was right; suddenly there was a thick blanket of doubt hanging heavy over our new life.

The estate agent was all cheer on the following Monday. 'Everything go well?' she asked, breezily.

'Err, not exactly,' I said and told her what had happened.

'Well, they haven't said anything to me. It'll all be going ahead, don't worry.'

But as the weeks went by and we exchanged with the buyer of our London house, our solicitor was getting increasingly restless. 'They haven't sent back any of the paperwork. We can't proceed with the exchange until the documents are signed and returned.'

I phoned the estate agent who promised to chase them up. 'They'll go in the post this afternoon,' she reassured me, but they never materialised. More phone calls, more reassurance, still nothing.

'At this rate we're going to be homeless,' said Ludo. Completion had been set for our sale in mid December, barely six weeks away, and still we hadn't had the paperwork to allow us to exchange on the Welsh house. I had to press on as if we were definitely moving, finding removal firms who could come up with a way of getting our stuff up a very steep, narrow lane and then forestry track which no full-size truck would be able to manage. I needed to order things like a fridge and cooker because the buy-to-let man wanted to buy all our kitchen goods. Then there were the letters to write to the utilities companies and the final bills to pay. All this while I was also making frantic preparations for a filming trip which would take me to a remote region of Ethiopia, leaving a month before our moving date and returning, thanks to a last-minute change of plan, on the very day of the move.

'You do understand,' I said to the producer, 'that I absolutely have to be back on that day, as that is the day we're moving house?' I was assured that I would definitely be back early on that morning.

Ludo was also desperately busy, finalising the edit of a programme for delivery that day. He would almost certainly be working late. So our plan was that our friend Richard would pick me up from the airport and we'd race down the motorway to be at the Welsh house in time to greet the removal van. Ludo would finish everything off in London and come down that night. But that was only if the sale had gone through by then and still there was no sign we were going to exchange.

My bag was packed and by the front door. I'd packed up most of my office too, and was sitting amidst a pile of cardboard boxes checking the enormous list I'd left for Ludo of people to ring, orders to confirm and letters to post as soon as the exchange happened. The phone rang. 'The exchange has gone through, with the completion date set for 14 December 2007. Congratulations.' I had no time to celebrate or take a last look around my old home. The taxi was outside waiting to take me to the airport. I slammed the front door, posted my key through the letter box and left London. The next time I saw Ludo would be in our new home in Wales.

The middle of nowhere is an overused phrase and really, is there anywhere that is nowhere? I was in the middle of somewhere, but somewhere remote, inaccessible, hot and dusty with very little means of contacting the outside world. The Danakil region of Ethiopia is famed for its inhospitable landscape and climate and, according to Wilfred Thesiger, who travelled there in 1930, a tribe of people who will remove your testicles first and ask questions later. I spent a month there, trying to learn and understand how people live and survive in this, the harshest of environments. Perhaps because of my lack of testicles I had found the Danakil tough and uncompromising, but ultimately hospitable, though it was a difficult, sometimes heartbreaking few weeks, with little sleep and a diet of Vache Qui Rit processed cheese and the occasional goat. Much as I love Africa and all the conflicting emotions it evokes, I was desperate to get back to the UK and to the start of a new life.

I stood on the edge of a dusty airstrip, ears alert, eyes squinting in the harsh sunlight, scanning the vast, empty African sky for the first sight of the little plane that would take me on the first stage of the journey from the Ethiopian desert to the green, wooded hills of the Wye Valley. The afternoon wore on. My flight from Addis Ababa was not until the evening, but we all knew the small plane we were expecting wouldn't fly after sunset and the lengthening shadows told us time was running out. The producer made a call, shouting into the Sat phone to make himself heard over the static. 'It's not coming,' he said. 'Some technical hitch or something. They'll leave as soon as the sun comes up tomorrow. There is a daytime flight back to London, but you won't be back until late that night. I'm sorry.'

It was almost midnight when Richard and I walked into the kitchen of the new house in Wales to find

Ludo, looking shell-shocked and surrounded by piles of cardboard boxes. Outside it was freezing, the landscape gripped by a hard December frost. Inside it wasn't much better. 'We've been left with no oil and no wood, so we've got no heating, no hot water and I can't light a fire. I did find the glasses though,' he added, passing us both hefty measures of red wine. We drank a toast to our new home, our new life, then went to bed fully clothed, surrounded by looming towers of cardboard boxes.

When we woke up the next morning the world was white and glittering as the sun crept above the trees, flooding the garden in pale, wintery gold light. My feet left tracks in the frost. I stood, hardly able to breathe, looking out over the fields – our fields! – across the woods and down into the valley. I turned to look at the house – our house! – standing grey and solid on the spot that it has stood for 300 years or more, and then walked on into the garden to marvel at the leafless trees, the frost-covered shrubs, the stone walls and the lawn. 'This is our garden,' I said to myself, just to try and see if it sounded true. It sounded incredible and even to my own ears, a little mad.

I let the chickens out, which we had agreed to look after, along with quite a lot of other stuff that the previous owners hadn't quite got round to moving out. The barn was full of machinery, rubbish and boxes and boxes of old copies of *Interiors* magazine. The hens, accompanied by their handsome cockerel, stalked doubtfully out of their house onto the frozen grass. I chipped the ice out of their water bowl and re-filled it, scattered feed, guessing how much they might need, and opened the back of the hen house. It was thick with muck, but in the corner was an egg. I picked it up and looked at it as if I'd never seen an egg before. The shell was smooth, dark brown and still warm. I had got up, gone outside and collected breakfast. Not a nasty, over-sweet muffin and a ruinously expensive coffee in a cardboard cup, but a proper, healthy home-produced breakfast that didn't involve queuing, shouting over the noise of a milk frother or making the brain-scrambling decision to go for 'tall' or 'vente'. To thank the hens for the egg, I cleaned out the hen house, sprinkling the floor with fresh wood shavings and putting a handful of straw in the nest box, before heading back to the kitchen to unearth the kettle.

It was, I thought, a nigh-on perfect way to start a day.

Chapter 3

A Dog Called Badger

The New Year was heralded by rain, lots of it. By the middle of January, when we had been living in Monmouthshire for four weeks, we realised it had been raining, without let up, for two of them. A woman in front of me in the little post office-cum-shop-cum-pub at the bottom of the hill asked how we were getting on.

'Oh, fine,' I said. 'Could do with a bit of sunshine, though.'

'You'll never make it through the winter,' she said

sagely, as she paid for her stamps and wrapped her anorak tightly around her to face the deluge.

But in spite of the weather we had made progress. We no longer needed to use the porch as a fridge, we'd found someone to sell us some firewood to keep us going until we could cut some of our own and the oil truck had managed to negotiate the hairpin bend that is the final hurdle before reaching the house, so we now had the twin luxuries of heating and hot water. We were still woefully short of furniture, principally book shelves, but we'd repainted some of the more lurid rooms – egg-yolk yellow is not a restful colour in any circumstances – and most importantly we'd met our neighbour.

Back in December, a few days after we had moved in, I had been out again in the frozen garden, feeding the chickens and planning an assault on the vegetable patch as soon as it thawed, when I heard the noise of a chainsaw. It was coming from the other side of the hedge that is the boundary between our land and the farm our house used to belong to. At some point back in the sixties the family who were then farming this bit of Monmouthshire decided that living in a newly built, all-mod-cons bungalow would be preferable to roughing it in an old-fashioned stone house with leaky windows and damp. Our house was abandoned, left to disinte- grate, until it was sold, more-or-less derelict with a few steep acres of north-facing land, to the people we bought it from. The farm had since changed hands and the current owners – the Parrys – were using their land to produce organic beef for a supermarket.

There had been no love lost between the Parrys and the previous owners of our house. We never quite got to the root of the problem, but part of it, at least, seemed to involve water. The mains water for the house actually came from the farm. It was metered, as all water usage is in this part of Wales, and the Parrys would send a bill for the water used. At some stage the owners of our house had tried to connect themselves to the mains, bypassing the farm – but claimed Mr Parry wouldn't give them access to allow them to connect the pipe. The problem, which was raised when we were in the already teeth-pulling process of trying to buy the house, became so contentious that our solicitor advised us to pull out of the sale. It turned out, after a few phone calls to Welsh Water, to be a lot of fuss about nothing, easily resolved, but it had clearly been one of many sources of contention between the neighbours. Having heard nothing to make me think we were going to be made welcome, I wondered about the wisdom of introducing myself to a man armed with a chainsaw.

'You must be Mr Parry,' I said, stretching out my hand.

He nodded, turning off the saw, but didn't say anything.

'I'm Kate Humble. We've just moved in here.'

'We know who you are,' he said, gruffly.

'Right,' I said, a little awkwardly, trying to judge how this was going. The silence lengthened. 'Not promising,' I thought, trying to hold my 'I may be on the telly, but I'm quite normal' smile.

Eventually he spoke. 'We saw you in the *Farmers Weekly* last week,' he said.

I had presented the *Farmers Weekly* annual awards that year. It is a high point of the farming year, a black-tie event held in a grand London hotel to which farmers from all over the country come for a night of well-deserved revelry. *Farmers Weekly* had run an article listing that year's winners and reporting that the event had been hosted by 'TV presenter Kate Humble, who wore Wellington boots with her dress'.

Mr Parry gave a half-smile. 'If you want to meet the locals, I suggest you come to the carol service on Christmas Eve. Everyone will be there.'

The tiny local church sits in the middle of a field, a short climb up behind Mr Parry's house, following a footpath which winds up through the cow pasture to an old stone stile by the church gate. The frost was gone, and we walked through the dusk in thick drizzle. We climbed the stile into the church field, which had been thoughtfully floodlit by the headlamps of a couple of Land Rovers. Inside, the church was packed, damp waxed jackets steaming in the light of the candles and gas lamps. The church has no electricity supply and is all the more magical for it. As our eyes grew accustomed to the flickering light, we could see that every window-sill and every pew was decorated with holly, ivy and pine from the local woods and hedgerows. There is no organ, so the vicar's wife accompanied the carols on her cello with a man we now know as Bob on the clarinet. 'It's like we've stepped into a Thomas Hardy novel,' I whispered to Ludo, as we squeezed ourselves in at the back. After the service, home-made mince pies were handed out and paper cups were generously filled with mulled wine by a jovial man who introduced himself as Euan.

'Come to dinner!' he boomed. 'We live three fields that way. We can introduce you to a few of the natives.'

Just after Christmas a figure appeared at the kitchen door with a sack. It was Mr Parry. 'I've brought you some turnips. I plant them for the cattle, but I thought you might like some.'

It was clearly a test. Did this city-dwelling telly-type even know what a turnip looks like?

'Fantastic,' I said. 'I love turnips, especially mashed. They make you fart though, don't they?' His eyebrows shot up. 'Thank you, Mr Parry.'

'Rhys,' he said, with a smile. 'Let me know when you want some more.'

It may have been pouring with rain that January, but Ludo wasn't starting his new job until February and I didn't have any filming commitments until the spring so we made the most of the time, not just to unpack boxes and endlessly trawl the junk shops for bits of furniture, but to explore the enticing, if sodden, countryside around the house. It is the greatest luxury to be able to walk straight across a field or into a wood from your kitchen door. We walked for miles with our increasingly soggy OS map, discovering a seemingly endless network of paths, tracks and lanes; perfect, as I pointed out to Ludo, for a dog.

This was familiar territory. I had long fantasised about having a dog. I had grown up with a series of much-loved and indulged tabby cats, but secretly thought the farm dogs that lived next door were rather more fun and pretended they were mine. Wooed, as they were, by my unwavering devotion and bits of sandwich, the dogs were just as happy to let me believe they did indeed belong to me, but at the end of the day, when I was called home for supper, the dogs stayed on the farm and the illusion was shattered. Ludo grew up with dogs and I knew wanted one as much as I did, but, being far more practical, recognised that our lives in London were not conducive to having a dog. But we didn't live in London any more and we had a proper garden and fields and woods beyond that. 'OK,' said

Ludo, 'let's go to the local rescue centre, have a look and find out what the procedure is. But remember, they might think that two people who work most of the time are not suitable potential owners.'

Animal rescue centres are gloomy places. However dedicated the staff, or clean and shiny the facilities, there is no escaping the fact that you are going to see rows and rows of caged creatures that have been abandoned, or mistreated, or are simply unwanted. We walked along the enclosures, past Staffies and Rottweilers, yappy little terriers and sad-eyed, grey-muzzled old faithfuls – dogs of every shape, size, colour and age. 'It's impossible,' I whispered to Ludo. 'How do you even begin to choose?'

Ludo stopped suddenly. 'This is your dog, right here,' he said, looking into a kennel where a small, scruffy black and white mongrel was jumping up and down repeatedly, as if to say 'Pick me! Pick me!'

'You're right,' I said. 'He's the one.'

Elaine, the centre manager, looked at us questioningly. 'You're really interested in Junior? He's been with us for months. No one wants him.'

'Why not?' I asked, imagining she was going to reveal that behind his cartoon-like cuteness lurked a savage, straight-for-the-jugular killer.

'Too bouncy.'

Ludo and I looked at each other. A too-bouncy dog! Who could resist? 'What's his history?'

'Not very happy, I'm afraid,' said Elaine, gravely. 'He was rescued from a flat where he was shut in a room and, from what we can gather, was rarely fed or let out. All the white parts of his coat were stained yellow with urine and he weighed under half what he does now and he's still underweight. The officer who went to pick him up said he was the thinnest dog he'd ever seen that was still alive. Do you want to meet him properly?'

Out of his kennel he seemed very small and rather fragile, no longer a joyous bouncy little thing full of life. He stood nervously at the end of his lead, refusing to make eye contact and unwilling to be stroked. He walked tentatively behind us as we followed Elaine to a fenced-in exercise paddock full of dog toys in various stages of disintegration. I picked up a bald tennis ball and threw it for him. He scampered delightedly after it and dropped it back at my feet. Half an hour later, our arms were aching but he was showing no sign of tiring. Clearly this was a dog that loved to play but had no idea of how to respond to any sort of affection. 'What do you think?' asked Elaine, as we let him back into his kennel.

Our response was unequivocal. 'We'll take him!' we chorused.

Three weeks later the day came when we could pick him up. We'd had the requisite home check, registered with a local vet and enrolled in dog-training classes. Clutching a brand-new collar and lead I followed Elaine round to his kennel. We'd been to visit him several times, and on Elaine's advice, taken things from home that would smell of us. I gathered up my old sweatshirt, a towel and a pair of Ludo's socks.

'We're going to change his name,' I confessed.

'That's OK. We don't know what he was called before, so we just called him Junior for our records.'

The name issue had dominated conversation for the last few weeks. Ludo thought we should call him Horatio, or Montgomery, or Julius Caesar – 'Something like that, to make him feel magnificent.'

'You'll just give him a complex,' I countered, 'like parents who insist that calling their child Dodecahedron will make him stand out in the playground and become a future captain of industry, when in fact all they've done is fast-tracked him to the nearest addiction clinic.'

'That's not the same thing at all,' said Ludo, grumpily.

'Fine. Try standing outside the back door and yelling "Horatio" at the top of your lungs and see what a good idea it seems then.'

We walked to the car and I opened the boot. The dog-formerly-known-as-Junior just stood looking bewildered. I lifted him in and drove him to his new home. Over the course of the journey he climbed from the boot to the back seat, cautiously moved to the front seat, and then inched onto my lap, where he sat, one ear up, one ear down, surveying the landscape over the top of the steering wheel. 'Horatio!' I said softly. Nothing. 'Agamemnon!' Not a stir. 'I think we should call you Badger. It may not make you feel magnificent but it won't make me feel like a prat if I lose you on a walk.'

We had no idea how much, if any, training he had had, so for his first week we kept him on a lead. I'd bought one of those extendable ones but he seemed nervous about wandering far and stayed close to my side. I thought it would be a good idea to walk him to all the nearby houses and introduce him, in case he did run off and someone found him. We went to see Rhys and Judith at the farm, who were very complimentary, and then on across the fields to our other neighbours, most of whom I had not yet met. We discovered not only that we had some very hospitable neighbours, but two of them also had black and white dogs called Badger. Clearly, I was not the only one to think it was a good, solid, no-nonsense sort of a name. Ludo, when I told him, just looked pained and said, 'I told you we should have called him Hercules.'

It was obvious from the start that Badger was not very brave and had had little experience of the great outdoors. Pigeons flapping through the woods made him jump; he ignored rabbits and had no idea at all how to get over a stile. He avoided cows and sheep and was blindly terrified of horses. Although he didn't want to be touched, nor did he want to be out of our sight, so we let him walk off the lead and he would scamper a few steps ahead before stopping and checking we were still behind him. He was perfectly happy in the car, as long as he wasn't in the boot, but on the front seat. He had boundless energy and wanted to play all the time. We had, like over-indulgent parents, bought him a selection of toys, which he would place carefully at our feet, looking up at us expectantly from under his hopelessly unruly eyebrows. If he had ever been house-trained he'd forgotten and for a dog who had been starved almost to death we thought he would be a voracious eater, but he was quite the opposite, picking at his food and dropping most of it on the kitchen floor. Offer him a bit of frankfurter, however, as advised by the woman who ran the dog-training classes, and he would do anything. He soon became the star pupil.

For many months Badger's tail hung, not quite tucked between his legs, but low down, as if he was permanently expecting the worst. Gradually, as time went on, and he got a bit braver and felt a bit more secure, his tail started to rise, even tentatively to wag. He was – and remains – neurotic and adorable, and it only took a matter of days before we couldn't imagine life without him.

Chapter 4

Roger, Gary, Lawrence And Bertie

I grew up in Berkshire. We lived in a Victorian house down a deeply rutted, pot-holed lane with puddles so deep they threatened to entirely submerge Mum's Austin Metro. Next door was a farm where horses were bred and trained and I spent most of my childhood and teenage years there, mucking out stables, grooming horses and cleaning tack. I was permanently filthy, covered in horsehair, straw and muck, with grimy fingernails and the accompanying whiff of horse. My mother, always immaculate, must have wondered how she had managed to raise such an uncouth tyke, but I couldn't have been happier. I loved being outside all day, loved the rather mindless physical toil, loved the daily proximity to animals that, although not exactly wild, were certainly more challenging and dynamic than the family cat. Now that we had moved to Wales I could begin to feel part of the outdoors again, be attuned enough to my surroundings that I would recognise the first, barely perceptible signs of a season changing. I had missed the satisfying state of exhaustion that comes, never from a session at the gym, but only from a day of hand-blistering manual labour and I looked forward to having the impetus to get up in the morning whatever the weather. To be truly content, I realised, I needed the routine that comes with keeping animals.

The chickens that had been left in our care by the previous owners of our house had given me that routine. Every morning I would get up and, before doing anything else, go outside to let the chickens out, feed them and collect the eggs. There is something rather soothing about starting a day with a simple task, a bit of light toil in the open air, and although a chicken may not express its affection in quite the same way as a dog, I liked to believe they were quite pleased to see me. The arrival of Badger had coincided with the departure of the chickens, which had been reclaimed by their rightful owners. They were loaded, clucking with the indignity of it all, into a cardboard box and driven away in the boot of the car. I felt bereft. 'We should go and see the lady at the bottom of the hill,' Ludo suggested. 'I think she sells chickens. She's certainly got a lot of them.'

Janet and Trevor's garden is a homage to their

passions. Trevor, with his magnificent handlebar moustache, spends much of the day under the bonnet of a Land Rover. He appears to have an endless collection in various stages of disintegration, and there is always one parked on the home-made blocks in front of their cottage. The garden beyond Trevor's workshop is Janet's domain, a poultry paradise, where chickens of every conceivable type peck contentedly amongst the fruit trees and guinea fowl lurk in hedges. I explained to Janet that we had just moved in and had little experience of looking after chickens. 'Start with three,' she said, as we walked through her maze of pens, 'then you won't get overwhelmed by eggs and you'll have one small hen house to clean out. Any idea what type you want?'

'I don't really know any types,' I confessed, 'apart from Buff Orpingtons, which seem to be everyone's favourite.'

Janet rolled her eyes. 'Lovely looking, lots of fluffy golden feathers, useless at laying, you might as well have a ginger cat.' Oh.

We went back the following morning to pick up our three new hens. With Janet's help we'd chosen a Welsummer, which she described as a good 'utility' breed. They have rich, rather regal plumage, and strut about looking a bit like the poultry equivalent of Henry VIII. But for all their pomp, they lay well and produce large, dark terracotta-coloured eggs. Janet also suggested we take a Cream Legbar, another useful, easy-to-keep breed which lays powder-blue eggs, and we liked the look of a funny little black hen which Janet said was a bit of a mongrel, but mainly Black Araucana. 'She's a little bit wild, but a good layer. The eggs are a sort of greenish-blue. It's good to have three hens that lay different coloured eggs because it is easy for you to tell which one is laying.'

'How much do we owe you?' I asked, having no idea of the cost of a chicken that isn't wrapped in plastic and in a supermarket chill cabinet.

'I charge £10 a bird, but there's a discount for locals.'

We were delighted; the discount was one thing, but being considered a local after just a few weeks was even more pleasing.

We kept the hens shut in their new house for the first day, before they were allowed out to explore their new surroundings. That short amount of time would be enough, said Janet, to make the chickens realise that this was their new home and to return to it to roost when the light started to fade. Also on Janet's advice we had rigged up electric netting around the field. We knew it worked because we had both inadvertently tested it. The woods that surround our house on two sides provide perfect habitat for foxes so the chicken field, if we weren't careful, could all too easily become a walk-through take-away for an opportunistic fox. 'We've got our first livestock,' I said to Ludo, as we stood in the field watching the hens contentedly pecking at insects in the grass. It is, I have now discovered, very easy indeed to stand in a field looking at chickens and for time to pass, rapidly and unnoticed, in a deeply pleasurable, rather therapeutic way.

'They do look a bit lost in that big field,' said Ludo, after a bit.

'Well,' I replied. 'Paul wondered if we might want a cockerel.'

Paul lives across the valley and had spent the last couple of weeks with us fixing up a dilapidated outbuilding – transforming it with a couple of old telegraph poles and some recycled corrugated iron from a leaky wreck to a sturdy, invaluable shed. 'He has a smallholding,' I added, admiringly, 'and he said he has two cockerels that keep fighting and wants to find a home for one of them.'

'They crow.'

'Well, yes, but the Parrys' house isn't exactly next door and our bedroom is at the other end of the house, so he'll be out of earshot.' Ludo looked doubtful. I ploughed on. 'And anyway, Paul said hens like to have a cockerel with them. It makes them feel protected.' There is some truth in this, and of course, although a well-looked-after hen will happily lay eggs with or without the presence of a cockerel, the eggs won't be fertile unless a cockerel has been involved, but I wasn't thinking about any of that. I was getting the livestock bug and Ludo had sussed me.

'Well, I suppose one extra chicken won't make a huge difference, but we're not getting any more animals after that,' he said, firmly.

Inevitably, when Paul brought over the cockerel, a splendid fellow with a bright red Mohican-like comb and a fountain of tail feathers, who we called Roger, he happened to mention he also had a gander – 'very quiet, lovely temperament, can give you a couple of geese to go with him for a tenner' – that also needed a home and would be more than happy in the field with the chickens. 'You'll get goose eggs for about two or three months – they usually start to lay on Valentine's Day – and they are very low maintenance. Good guard animals too. They make a huge racket if someone or something they don't know comes into the garden.'

So with Paul's help we set about excavating what had been an old pond and increased our livestock count once more. Three months after our move to Wales we were the proud owners of a dog, three chickens, a cockerel called Roger, a gander called Gary and two geese. 'That,' said Ludo, 'really is it.'

Spring had come. The woods were full of anemones and celandines. The wild garlic and bluebells were pushing their first green shoots through the thick leaf litter, the buds on the beech trees were beginning to unfurl and the mornings were a riot of birdsong. I bumped into the woman I'd met in the post office at the beginning of the year, the one who had foretold we wouldn't last the winter. She looked surprised to see me. 'Still here then?'

'Yes,' I nodded. 'We love it.'

'You'll be here forever then,' she prophesised and this time I was happy to believe her.

I did, however, worry constantly about our land, about wasting it by not using it properly. One dog and a handful of poultry was not going to make much of an impression on four acres and I would lie awake for hours fretting about what to do with all the grass that was suddenly shooting up as the spring sun warmed the soil and days lengthened. To make matters worse it had struck me, during one of those dark, wakeful nights, that land wasn't really something that could be owned. Ludo and I were merely caretakers; we had taken on a legacy in the form of four steep, challenging acres in an area famed for its natural beauty and the responsibility felt almost too weighty to bear. Grassland needs managing. Without it, it becomes rank and useless, but the right management can have miraculous results, transforming a field into a meadow; turning something which has little value for wildlife into a bucolic haven for untold numbers of animals and birds. A wildflower meadow is achieved by a careful mix of mowing, grazing and leaving in peace. Mowing was, we had discovered, not possible because our land was too steep, even for the alpine tractor belonging to a neighbour. 'You'd just end up somersaulting down the slope and piling into the trees at the bottom,' he said, rather more graphically than required. 'Grazing is your only option. There's a woman down the road that has Exmoor ponies that are ideal for helping to manage land like this. She lends them out, but I think they are all booked out for this grazing season. Sheep?'

We had talked about sheep but realised we didn't really know anything about how to keep them. 'Don't they just go lame, get infested with maggots, find a way to escape or if all else fails, die, for no particular reason?' asked Ludo as we mulled over the small ads in the back of our newly discovered favourite magazine, *Country Smallholding*. I had to agree that sheep seemed a bit beyond our realm of experience and what we needed was something easy, familiar and low maintenance – in other words, the four-legged equivalent of a lawn mower. 'Donkeys!' I exclaimed. 'That's what we need. The perfect solution. There's always a donkey somewhere that needs rescuing.'

By happy chance there were two donkeys in need of adoption at the farm down the road. The farm is the base for a charity that takes in unwanted and sometimes horribly mistreated horses and ponies, and the occasional donkey. They don't sell their animals, but people with the right experience and land are able to adopt an animal, taking on full responsibility for its welfare and paying all the costs for its upkeep. It is hard not to lose your heart to a donkey. They always manage to look slightly hangdog and a little bit grumpy, their ears are far too big for the rest of them and they have a slightly ungainly look as if they have been put together with parts that don't quite fit. They are quite often bad tempered, will just as often wake you up very early in the morning with a resounding, unapologetic HEE-HAAAW and yet still, inexplicably, manage to be lovable. Or perhaps it is just me that has a soft spot for the hairy, cantankerous and big-eared.

Lawrence was the smaller and grumpier of our two adopted donkeys. He was a rather unusual pinky-grey colour, as if he'd gone in the wash with something he shouldn't. His coat was long and thick and he remained resolutely hirsute, even when the onset of summer would make him moult enough hair to stuff several mattresses. He loved ginger biscuits and when he was feeling affectionate – which was rare – or could smell the biscuits about your person he would walk up and rest the entire, not inconsiderable weight of his head on your shoulder and look deeply and lovingly into your eyes until he got the biscuit or got bored or both.

Bertie – bigger, dark grey, with vast ears and a mane like a scrubbing brush – was, by contrast, sweet-natured and affectionate but hopelessly, impossibly greedy. It was his greed that almost certainly contributed to the fact that he had laminitis, a horrible condition that affects a bone inside the hoof and causes frequent, painful lameness. Once an animal has laminitis it is impossible to get rid of. A laminitic horse or donkey has to be kept away from rich spring grass and allowed to graze only for a limited time each day. Poor Bertie was on a constant diet that even the most faddy Hollywood A-lister would have found hard to stick to. 'Not much good for keeping the grass down, then,' said Ludo, pointedly. 'But don't even think about getting any more animals,' he added hastily, before I could come up with another four-legged, grass-munching idea. 'We have more than enough.'

Chapter 5

Two Smallholders (One Reluctant)

'OH MY GOD!' shouted Ludo, rapidly winding down the window. 'WAS THAT YOU?'

'No it bloody wasn't,' I retorted, furiously winding down my window to let the hot, metallic air of the motorway blast into the car.

'Can something that small really produce a smell like that?'

'Well, obviously it can,' I said, indignantly, 'because it wasn't me.'

Euan, the generous pourer of mulled wine after the carol service, had made good his promise of an invitation to dinner. Suspecting that the evening would not be an entirely sober affair, we had taken advantage of a warm April evening to walk across the fields to his house. We ate kitchen supper with him and wife Laura and another local couple called James – known universally as Jambo – and Kirsty. We had departed in the early hours of the morning, adamant that we didn't need the torch we had forgotten, leaving a table laden with empty bottles and clutching a bit of paper on which Kirsty had written a phone number. 'I'll phone them in the morning to say to expect your call,' she called as we waved fond farewells and started our ungainly stagger home. Amazingly we didn't lose the phone number and Kirsty, despite a surfeit of wine, remembered her promise, so it seemed churlish not to go ahead with what had seemed an excellent idea in the drunken heat of the moment. I telephoned the number Kirsty had given me and found myself arranging to collect the two KuneKune piglets that were now in a dog crate in the boot of the car, farting their way merrily down the M4.

Neither Ludo nor I had ever seen or indeed heard of a KuneKune. Having agreed to buy two of them (pigs need company, I was told, cleverly, by the owner of the piglets), I did some hasty research and discovered, a little late in the day, that they are not great for meat, unless you like fat and lots of it. They are a rare breed pig that come originally from New Zealand and were favoured by the Maoris, who clearly liked more crackling than chop. In common with many of the breeds classed as rare these days like the Gloucester Old Spot, Berkshire and Tamworth, they fell out of favour when leaner, faster-growing commercial breeds came on the scene, producing pork for more modern tastes with less fat, and many will argue, less flavour. Rare-breed pork is much more readily available now but I have never seen KuneKune on a menu. 'We'll breed them and sell the piglets,' I said to Ludo when he once again questioned the wisdom of having two pigs that we had to feed every day with no hope of them ever feeding us. 'People love them. They don't grow too big, they're nice natured and they're not nearly as destructive as other pigs.'

Ludo pulled a face. Pigs are natural born diggers, using their powerful snouts to upend clods of turf to get at roots and insects. Put a large-breed pig into a beautiful field of lush green grass and it will look like a World War I battlefield in twenty-four hours. KuneKunes are unusual in that they are supposed to enjoy grazing rather than rooting, and it is true, they won't systematically tear up the ground in the dramatic plough-like fashion of the bigger breeds of their species. However, as we discovered when we wanted to turn a rather brambly, weedy corner of a paddock into a vegetable patch, they are every bit as effective as a rotavator and provide fertiliser as part of the bargain.

The piglets, after another protracted debate over names, became known as Duffy and Delilah. Ludo favoured Merthyr and Tydfil; thank God we don't have children. After briefly earning their keep by saving us the cost of hiring a rotavator, they, like the donkeys, settled into a life of ease with no threat at all that they would end up as Sunday lunch. Ludo returned to full-time work, commuting daily to the BBC in Cardiff, and I was back to the peripatetic life of a television presenter. The big difference was that between leaving London a few months before and now was that we had become, somewhat unwittingly and – in Ludo's case, a little reluctantly – smallholders. In common with many smallholders we had no training at all and just threw ourselves into learning as we went along in a somewhat haphazard way, hoping that the basic maxim that every living thing needs food, water and shelter would carry us through.

For the next year we didn't buy any more animals, although I was given some Aylesbury ducks by one of the keepers at Longleat where I was filming *Animal Park*. Our chickens hatched their first chicks and soon we had a dozen hens, and during spring and summer had more eggs than we knew what to do with. I'm not a great baker, but we made a lot of omelettes and lemon tarts, took eggs to people we were having dinner with, and pressed boxes of them on friends who came to stay. Eventually we ended up selling them at the local farm shop and received the greatest compliment when after a few weeks the owner told us she had a regular customer who asked her to phone when our eggs came in, because they were particularly delicious. For about two months from late February 2009 we had goose eggs, which would also be snapped up at the farm shop. The Aylesbury ducks also started to produce eggs: large and white with porcelain-like shells. A boiled duck egg is a well-documented delight, but poached, on toast, with Marmite, it is the breakfast of kings.

The pig-rotavated vegetable patch was also proving productive, although dishearteningly, not to the same extent that our London allotment had. Growing vegetables in London's benign climate, with the help of a few sacks of horse manure from Ealing Riding Stables, gave us the sadly false impression that either vegetable growing is easy or that Ludo and I were naturally brilliant at it. Here in Wales, 180 metres above sea level, on a windy hill, the growing season is noticeably shorter and things like butternut squash, which we had grown all too successfully in London, proved impossible to produce. But our rhubarb flourished, as did the runner beans, and thanks to Delia Smith we made our first chutney – a delicious, spicy green tomato one to use up the pounds and pounds of tomatoes that had failed to ripen.

All of which makes it sound rather easy and effortless, which of course, a lot of the time, it wasn't. Bertie the donkey had an unerring ability to go hopping lame with his laminitis on a morning when one of us was away and the other in a tearing hurry to get somewhere. Both donkeys had a health check by the vet and needed their teeth seeing to – a protracted and, needless to say, expensive procedure involving sedatives and an enormous rasp. One Saturday, Delilah decided that she was dying. She refused all food and lay looking pathetic in the straw until the vet, called out at great expense on a weekend, arrived, whereupon she made a miraculous recovery and ran away at the first sight of a syringe. Roger, our faithful cockerel, died of old age, hastened I suspect, by his bully of a son, Gregory. Magpies discovered the hen house and raided eggs and then the chickens more or less stopped laying. Not only that, they seemed increasingly unwilling to go in their house at night. The culprit proved to be red mite. Microscopic and rapacious, red mite thrive in warm weather, infesting the deepest, darkest crevices of the hen house, lying in wait for their feathery dinner to come back into the house so they feast on the poor bird's blood. Left unmolested, red mite will breed and feast, breed and feast until the hen house is crawling with dark, creeping organisms no bigger than poppy seeds and the chickens have been sucked, almost literally, of their life blood and begin to die.

The fight back has to be two-pronged and planned as meticulously as any military campaign. First, catch all the hens and dowse them liberally with a sort of noxious, mite-killing powder. Then clear out all the bedding from the houses, scrub them, spray them with something Chemical Ali might have been proud of and leave them shut up until every remaining mite has gasped its last. Drifts of them can then be joyfully swept up with a dustpan and brush, new bedding put back in and the hens return to their laying without fear of losing several pints of blood.

It sounds simple enough, but it does depend on the temperament of your chickens. Our hens, luxuriating in their own private quarter of an acre of orchard, protected by fox-zapping netting, are more jungle fowl than domestic hen, free to come and go, roost and wake up as they please. They find being shut into their houses enough of an affront; add to that the indignity of being manhandled and rubbed down with poisonous powder and there is all-out rebellion. In the middle of the night before the planned Mite Wipeout, we crept out into the orchard and slid the doors shut on all the hen houses. The following morning we were greeted by four still-closed houses and Gregory and some of his hens parading the perimeter fence. Whether they had been hiding in a hedge when we shut them all in, or Gregory is, in fact, a feathered Houdini, I don't suppose we'll ever know. What I do know is that the chase that ensued was anything but dignified. We were out-run, out-witted and out-manouevred in every way possible. The evasion tactics were varied and 100 per cent effective. One hen, supple as a limbo dancer, somehow squeezed herself under the gate and went to ground in the garden. Another simply disappeared. It was like a magic trick, but less entertaining. Gregory, all strut and tail feather, went down fighting. Chickens are not famed for their intelligence, but Gregory had us sussed. He resisted being gently persuaded into the feed shed, eluded being shepherded into a corner, disregarded rugby tackles, shouts of abuse and finally death threats. As we raced around the field, dripping sweat and cursing, Gregory put on his finest display of dodging, weaving and squawking before finally taking cover in the prickliest of hedges. With much swearing and a certain amount of blood-loss – ours not his – we finally managed to extricate him and dose him with mite powder before he was released with much shaking of tail-feathers and affronted clucking. Only then could we turn our attention to the hens that had stayed in the houses, but which proved to be equally uncooperative and ungrateful. Two long hours later the first prong of the attack was more or less complete. At this point the disappearing hen reappeared and the one that went AWOL in the garden sauntered back under the gate.

Although neither edible nor strictly practical, we did decide that the time had come to get Badger a companion. We had always planned to have two dogs, but Badger was so mentally scarred by the appalling neglect he had suffered at the hands of his previous owners, the RSPCA advised we keep him on his own until he had settled down and grown in confidence.

Despite the fact that I had resisted naming him after a Roman general or a mythical warrior he had become magnificent, in his own unique way. Badger had decided that he wasn't really a dog at all, but a human being trapped in the body of a mongrel. In the eighteen months we had had him he had learned how to jump over stiles, become a master at catching a Frisbee in mid air and had developed a curious and endearing fascination with feet – human feet, ideally without socks. He had spent plenty of time in the company of other dogs and remained resolutely uninterested in them. When we had other dogs to stay, he would ignore them, happily letting them sprawl in his basket or chew his toys, as long as he could be curled up between me and Ludo watching an episode of *The West Wing*.

But then something happened that turned Badger's world upside down. Princess Tallulah Tinkerbell, a neighbouring whippet of unsurpassed elegance and refinement, came on heat. Badger, who had barely given Tallulah a passing glance before, suddenly redis-covered his canine side. He gazed at her with lovelorn admiration and his adoration was not unnoticed. Tallulah decided Badger was her perfect bit of scruff and together they could act out their very own version of *Lady and the Tramp*. Badger, neutered, but nonetheless drunk on pheromones and befuddled by Tallulah's shameless flirting, finally understood what she was after and for the next couple of weeks they were, almost literally, inseparable. But it was not to last. Like many a mismatched relationship, Tallulah soon lost interest and Badger had to go back to lone nights in front of the telly. The time had come for him to have a girlfriend he could call his own.

Match-making, as all Jane Austen fans know, can be

a game fraught with embarrassment and trauma. We needed help and we had the perfect person to go to. David Newall is an old friend who had recently become director of the Dogs Trust. He had met Badger on several occasions, knew his history and realised that finding the perfect match would require a certain amount of expertise. Enter Rachel, a dog trainer and specialist in dog behaviour working at the Dogs Trust just down the road from us. 'I've picked out three dogs that I thought might be suitable,' said Rachel when we met, 'but now I've met Badger I don't think any of them are right.' What was she saying? Did she think our sweet-natured, scruffy-but-harmless mongrel might turn into a crazed killer when faced with a Pekinese he'd never met before? 'He's a sensitive little thing.' Ah. Namby-pamby mummy's boy, that's what's she saying. Think my Badger can't handle a girl with a bit of spirit? She was, of course, right. The springer spaniel was just too springy, the luscious lurcher left him for dust and the Labradoodle, a gorgeous, bouncy blonde, made him cower behind my knees. 'He needs a young dog, probably a bit smaller than him, and one that doesn't feel the need to be dominant.' Was Rachel prescribing that my Badger end up with the canine equivalent of a Stepford Wife? 'We'll keep looking,' she said. 'Sadly, dogs are coming in all the time. It probably won't take long.'

Sure enough, barely a week went by before Rachel called to say that Bella had been brought in. 'We think she might be perfect,' said Rachel. 'If she's any breed at all she's a border terrier, possibly mixed with Jack Russell. She's very sweet natured and she hasn't come from a bad home. Her owner sadly died and there was no one in the family who could take her. It says on her notes that her favourite things are Rich Tea biscuits and toast.'

Bella won Ludo over in a flash. She sped across the room like a little brown missile and flung herself into his arms. Badger, who was looking desperately out of the window as if planning his escape, turned, gave her a look of withering disdain and went back to his gazing. It didn't look promising. Rachel suggested we take them outside and let them run riot in the field. Badger immediately went in search of a stick or a ball or something that wasn't another dog and Bella, refusing to accept Badger's rebuttal, scampered joyfully along beside him. She didn't bully him but she wasn't going to let herself be ignored either. 'He's not giving me many clues,' said Rachel, 'but even if it isn't love at first sight, he seems quite relaxed with her. I think it could work.'

Bella came home with us a week later. She sat in the boot merrily shredding the *A-Z of Great Britain* while Badger lay on the front seat in a state of denial. It took him a while to come round to the idea that she was not a passing whim, but a permanent fixture. However he soon realised that, with her wiry Mohican hair-do, feisty attitude and uncouth habit of snoring and farting in tandem, she would never live up to the standards the haughty, beautiful Tallulah had led him to expect.

We'd certainly progressed. In little over two years since we'd moved to Wales we'd acquired two dogs, we had livestock and we were producing food. Not much food, as Ludo was at pains to point out, because far too many of our animals were, in his view, more decorative than useful. Lawrence and Bertie provided nothing much beyond a bit of manure for the vegetable patch and Duffy and Delilah, by now fully grown, had become pigs of great character and comedy value, but had not, as yet, produced anything either saleable or edible. 'The time has come, girls!' I announced when I went to feed them one summer morning. 'You're going to have start earning your keep.'

It was Adam Henson, friend, colleague and farmer, who I phoned for advice about breeding. Adam, as well as being *Countryfile*'s farming expert, is a full-time tenant farmer in Gloucestershire, taking over the land and the tenancy from his father who farmed it before him. As well as growing arable crops and raising sheep and cattle for meat, the farm is home to the Cotswold Farm Park. Adam's father, Joe Henson, had always had an interest in Britain's traditional farm animals – Galloway cattle, the local Cotswold sheep, Guernsey goats – but with this interest came the realisation that many of these breeds were teetering on the brink of extinction. He became one of the founder members of the Rare Breeds Survival Trust and in 1971 did something no one had done before. He opened up part of his farm to the public to showcase these rare breeds. Adam has continued his work championing and supporting these breeds and the Cotswold Farm Park has become hugely and deservedly popular. Interestingly, Adam, in common with many of his profession, didn't just step into the job when his father retired. Farmers, I was surprised to learn, train to be farmers. Most of them, even if they are born into farming families and have grown up knowing nothing else, will go to agricultural college or to gain experience on other farms. Adam went to college in Devon and on graduating went to work on various sheep and arable stations in Australia and New Zealand.

Treating red mite and other simple ailments is one thing, but for livestock management which goes beyond the checking/feeding/watering routine, it is invaluable to have an expert who is happy to hand out advice on anything from what to do with a chicken with a prolapse to how to treat a limping lamb. Adam, in answer to my queries about how to go about breeding Duffy and Delilah, had the perfect solution. The following week he was due to drive to Hereford to pick up a young KuneKune boar from a breeder. 'I'll be driving practically past your door,' he said. 'I can pick up your sows on the way back.' So Duffy and Delilah left Wales for an extended stay in the Cotswolds in order to have sex and be admired by the public.

The gestation period for a pig is three months, three weeks, three days. Adam's boar had obviously found Duffy and Delilah to his liking and it wasn't long before Adam phoned me to say that he was pretty sure both of them were 'in pig'. The resulting piglets were adorable. KuneKunes are hairy and come in all sorts of colours. Duffy is unashamedly ginger with black patches; Delilah predominantly black with cream patches. Adam's boar was a rich, dark brown and the piglets – all thirteen of them – formed a patchwork quilt of black and white, brown, russet and auburn as they lay spread-eagled in the straw, bellies taut and round and full of milk.

My grand plan to sell the piglets for a healthy profit proved only partly successful. The piglets may have been adorable, multi-coloured and conceived in the smartest of surroundings, but only the gilts, the female piglets, sold. The money they raised only just about covered what we owed Adam for bed, board and stud fees. No one wanted the boars. I returned from Adam's farm with five piglets we didn't have room for. It was a salutary lesson. Instead of coming home triumphantly waving a cheque that proved Duffy and Delilah were earning their keep, I came back with five extra mouths to feed. We had started out with two not terribly useful pigs and now we had seven.

We were rescued by our friend and neighbour, Stafford. Stafford farms sheep and cattle a few miles down the road from us and agreed, in return for a couple of oven-ready piglets, that he would house them in one of his barns and feed them until they reached slaughter weight. 'How are those piglets of yours?' called a lorry driver from his cab as I walked past him on the farm road a few weeks later, the romance between Adam's boar and my sows having been documented on *Countryfile*, which is presumably why the driver knew all about my porcine adventures. 'They're in the freezer!' I shouted back. The poor man nearly drove his truck into the hedge. The piglets did make absolutely wonderful sausages – kilos and kilos of them, and they were all the more delicious, I suspect, because they were the first meat we had had a hand in producing. With enough pork to keep us going for several years, we decided Duffy and Delilah could live out the rest of their days in matronly splendour.

Inspired by a long weekend in a cottage in Snowdonia, we did decide to look into the possibility of getting more chickens, but not for eggs. The owners of the cottage we were staying in lived next door and generously showed us around their smallholding. They had hens, a few sheep, but in a run behind their house they had some large white chickens that looked altogether more substantial than your average laying bird. 'They're Ross Cobbs,' said the man, 'table birds. We get them as day-old chicks and grow them on. They have to be kept under a heat lamp until they get their feathers and then we let them out into the field. Once you've eaten a bird you've raised yourself, you'll realise that no supermarket chicken is ever going to be able to compete.'

We have a free-range poultry farm a few miles from us, run by a delightful couple called Daryn and Elaine Williams. I went to buy some chicken from them and tentatively mentioned that we might have a go at raising some ourselves. Daryn couldn't have been more helpful, despite the fact that if we were successful we wouldn't be buying chicken from him any more. He gave me the name of his supplier and said that I could add my order to his and pick them up from the farm when he got all his delivered.

We started with just half a dozen. Daryn handed me a small cardboard box. I lifted the lid to find six, bright-eyed, cheeping, fluffy, yellow chicks looking for all the world as if they'd just escaped from an Easter card. I resolutely shut the lid, hardened my heart and took them home. They thrived under their heat lamp on a diet of chick crumb, quickly feathering up and turning from little yellow pom-poms into white, dinosaur-like creatures with outsize feet and no manners.

'It's two kilos!' I exclaimed delightedly to Ludo, who was holding on to the bag that was perched precariously on the kitchen scales. In it was one of our chicks, now full grown, heavy breasted, with thighs like a shot putter. They were ready.

We had been reading up on how to dispatch the birds when the time came and we weren't entirely sure that we had the means to do the job properly. Ludo had killed chickens before with a quick, sharp pull that breaks the neck and causes instant death, but only hens that were already sickly and weak. These table birds were big, strong and in their prime. The accepted way to kill a bird for the table is to stun it first, using an electric shock, and then slit its throat, allowing the blood to drain so it doesn't taint the meat. Then they are eviscerated, head and feet removed and plucked. 'Bring them up here,' said Daryn, 'then you'll know they've been killed quickly and humanely and we can put them through the plucker for you too. Takes hours if you have to do it by hand when you've never done it before.'

I looked at the six birds, plucked and plump, sitting in Daryn's chiller. 'You've done a good job with those,' he said.

'I feel a real wimp not killing them myself.'

'Well don't,' he said, kindly. 'You've given them a good life. Be a shame to muck it all up because you don't know how to kill them properly. If you stress them, or don't drain the blood you'll taint the meat and they'll taste horrible. We're happy to do them. Now you go and enjoy them.'

The meat was like nothing I'd tasted before. Firm and full of flavour it was a whole different texture and taste, even from a free-range supermarket bird. It felt like a real achievement, not just being responsible for producing the food on our plates, but knowing that our little patch of Wales wasn't going to waste. We had found a way to use our land to do something that had a tangible benefit, yet fitted with our working lives and didn't completely dominate our free time. I no longer fretted about it; I relished it and the connection it gave me with the seasons, the weather, the natural world. I was content. I couldn't wish for more. But then, in July 2009, came a phone call that changed everything.

Chapter 6

Testicles, Brazilians And A Lamb Called Humble

'Humble? Ausden.' Lisa Ausden is a highly experienced producer at the BBC. We knew each other a bit, but had never actually worked together. 'Now then. *Lambing Live*.'

'Oh God,' I breathed, 'you've heard about it, have you? Isn't it a terrible idea?'

'Be that as it may,' said Lisa, crisply, 'it's commissioned, I'm the executive producer and you're the presenter. We're making it.'

'Christ,' I said.

'Exactly. How much do you know about sheep?'

It transpired over the next hour that neither of us knew anything at all about sheep apart from the fact you can make jumpers out of their wool and the rest tastes pretty good with mint sauce. But the more we talked, the more we realised the *Lambing Live* had the potential to be far from a terrible idea; that the subject matter was fascinating and could, if handled well, give a much broader insight into not just sheep, but farming – an industry which has a pivotal role to play in rural Britain and which also has an impact on every single person in the country, whether we are aware of it or not. 'You need to go and be a trainee shepherd,' said Lisa, 'learn every part of the job from whatever happens first to when the lambs start being born. We just need to find a family who is willing to take you on and then agree to be on live television during the busiest and most important part of their year. Shouldn't be hard . . .'

There are not many men, in my albeit limited experience, who when they meet you for the first time, ask you to bend down and fondle a large pair of testicles. I had driven from home, leaving behind the gentle rolling slopes of the Wye Valley and heading through increasingly rugged Welsh countryside to the town of Builth Wells, home of the Royal Welsh Showground. It was the day of the annual ram sale and it was here I was to meet Jim Beavan, the man who was to be my mentor over the next few months, for the first time. Jim is tall, broad, with a closely shaven head and a beard that makes him look, as one viewer was to observe during his five nights of live broadcasting, 'like that bloke from ZZ Top'. He had come to the sale to buy two new rams, or 'tups' as he calls them, to take back to his farm for the upcoming lambing season. He shook me by the hand, eyes twinkling with mischief, and said, 'I've seen a couple I like the look of. Come and see what you think.'

I had never, until that day, been in close proximity to a ram, let alone considered appropriate the tickling of its nether regions, but, as I was to discover, if you are in the business of buying or selling rams, testicle fondling is not only acceptable, but a regular – and necessary – occurrence. As Jim put it in his unequivocal way, 'There's no point buying one that's not much good in the ball department. You want them to be evenly sized, and no lumps or bumps.'

The two rams he was hoping to bid for were not animals I would ever describe as handsome. Jim's ewes are confusingly known as mules, simply because they are a mix of two breeds. It is common for commercial sheep farmers to have these cross-bred ewes which combine the advantages of both breeds. Jim's flock of 900 ewes is made up of predominantly Welsh mules – Welsh sheep crossed with Suffolk sheep. The Welsh are hardy and self-sufficient, the Suffolks good, prodigious lambers. The combination should result in a ewe that will have at least two lambs but also be able to look after herself.

Jim chooses his rams with meat in mind. Sheep farmers breed sheep for different reasons. Some for breeding stock to sell on; others, like Jim, for producing meat. A few will go to the family butcher shop in their local town of Abergavenny, but the majority get sold to dealers who pay by weight and condition. The right tup can make a real difference to the success and profitability of a lambing season.

Jim had chosen Charollais rams; thick-set, rather belligerent-looking creatures, heavy-browed, broad-faced, with short, tight fleeces but the sort of hind quarters that made me want to start peeling potatoes and breaking out the redcurrant jelly. 'That's what to look at next,' said Jim, his eyes getting twinklier by the second. 'Once you're satisfied he's got a good pair of balls you want to check that he's good and strong in the hind quarters. He's got a lot of standing up to do.'

All the rams were to be sold that day by auction. The first of Jim's chosen rams went for well over Jim's budget and over a thousand guineas. Livestock and horses are often still sold in 'guineas' – the equivalent of £1.05 – although obviously paid for in pounds. I had no idea what a sheep cost, but I would never have guessed it would be as much as that. 'That's nothing,' said Jim, 'I've seen tups here go for forty, fifty grand. Most expensive one ever sold went for over 200 grand.'

Jim got his second ram at a price within his budget and another from the same breeder for slightly more. We went back to the pens to look at them again. Jim was pleased. He had spent a lot of money but was confident that it would pay dividends. 'They're both young animals, so they've got a good four or five years of work left in them. They'll each cover about fifty ewes this year and if we're lucky each ewe will produce twins. If the weather's kind and the market's good, they will pay for themselves in the first season.'

Jim left me to go and pay the auctioneer and I walked around the maze of pens. There were sheep of every size and description filling four or five sheds the size of aircraft hangars. There were hundreds of people – tough-looking farmers with outdoor faces and checked shirts, caps and sticks. This was clearly an important day in the sheep-farming calendar: a day for making and spending money, but also for showing off stock, catching up on news and gossiping. Something I would learn over the coming months is that farming is a lonely business. Gone are the days of Constable's *Hay Wain*, of farmers and their labourers toiling in the fields together and then gathering at the end of the day for cider and bread and cheese carried out into the sun-drenched fields by a fulsome wench with a come-hither smile. The mechanisation of farming, and the increasing difficulty of making a profit, mean that many farmers work alone and days like this are a welcome respite from an otherwise rather solitary life.

Jim returned and I helped him load the rams into his trailer. As I shook hands with the breeder, he pressed a ten-pound note into my hand. I looked at him, bemused.

'Luck money,' he said, with a smile. 'It's just a thing we all do. Give back a percentage of the money the buyer has spent with you as a way of saying thank you and good luck. Jim said you should have it as you helped him choose them. He said you're learning fast – getting a feel for it!' And with that he roared with laughter and disappeared into the crowd.

Jim's farm has been in the family for four generations. He lives in a converted dairy with his wife Kate, daughter Celyn and son Sam. His mother and father, Trevor and Anne, live in the main house and his brother Hugh on the other family farm a few miles down the road. Between them they have about 900 ewes on 500 acres of land. The farm is west from our house, near the market town of Abergavenny and on the edge of the Black Mountains. 'Not a bad place to work,' I muttered to myself as I swung my car into the farmyard, narrowly missing a couple of hens and sparking a cacophony of honking from what Kate fondly called 'our three gay ganders'.

My task that day was to help Jim prepare 300 ewes to go to the tup. I had learned that the gestation period of a sheep was five months and that Jim planned to spread his lambing season out over several months. Some of his ewes were already with the tups and, he hoped, in lamb. They would give birth in late January. The 300 we were dealing with that day would be ready to lamb in March, when we would be at the farm with all the trucks and satellites and paraphernalia needed to allow us to broadcast live from Jim's lambing shed. The remaining 300 would go to the tup later, to lamb in April. That way, Jim hoped to have lambs ready to sell for most of the year, a welcome source of fairly regular income in a business that at best can be hand to mouth.

I wasn't entirely sure what was required to get a ewe ready to go to the tup. I couldn't quite imagine Jim sitting in the shed with a PowerPoint presentation, giving them all a pep talk on sex education. In my ignorance, I assumed if you have a field full of ewes, all you had to do was introduce a couple of rams, shut the gate and leave them to it. That would work, but first of all you have to get the time of year right. There is a reason why we only see fields of gambolling young lambs in the early part of the year, and rarely after about May. Sheep, most breeds anyway, are seasonal breeders, only coming into oestrus as the days start to get shorter and the nights draw in. Put a ram in a field of ewes in July and nothing will happen. They will remain chaste and stand-offish until September when the shorter days trigger the release of hormones that tell a ram that now is the time to put his perfectly balanced testicles to work.

Jim likes his ewes to be in tip-top condition before they go to the tup and brings every single one of them in to give them a thorough check-up. First, it's the nether regions again. He showed me how to check the udder; if I found any hard, unyielding lumps it would mean the ewe wouldn't be able to produce the milk needed to feed her lambs. Those ewes would be marked with purple spray and sent to market for meat. Farmers have to be practical, but it doesn't mean there isn't room for sentiment. Jim was visibly upset to discover that one particular ewe had lumps in her udder. 'She's a great sheep, this one. Lambs on her own without any trouble, always has good-size twins, it's a shame,' he said, as he marked her and let her go. I was surprised, not just that he was upset about the loss of one of his sheep, but that out of 900 animals he knew her and her history. He smiled. 'You do get to know them – some of them, anyway. You spend a lot of time with them . . .'

The next job was to check their feet. The ancestors of our domesticated sheep originated in places like Western Iran, Turkey and Syria – dry, stony lands, a far cry from the soft, lush, grassy fields of Wales. Some breeds have less trouble with their feet than others, but anyone who keeps sheep will know that foot trimming is a regular task and that sheep seem to spend as much time on three legs as they do on four. The foot is split into two 'toes', each with a horny covering, the equivalent of our fingernails, and like our fingernails, they grow. If not worn down by rough ground and trimmed regularly they can cause a sheep to go lame. Warm, wet weather can cause foot rot, where the inside of the foot does literally rot and the foot needs to be trimmed back, the rotten material removed and the sheep injected or sprayed with antibiotic. And then there's scald, a sort of ovine athlete's foot. Long, wet grass can cause irritation, inflammation and sores between the toes and have a sheep hopping about looking very sorry for itself indeed. The one small blessing is that sheep are tough and respond very quickly to treatment. Once treated, ewes that were standing on three legs, holding one leg clear of the floor, will leap across the yard and out into the field almost without sign of a limp.

Jim had his shearing machine rigged up in the barn too, although all the ewes had been sheared earlier in the year. 'It's for tailing them,' said Jim. I looked at him uncomprehendingly. 'Some people call it dagging. Basically taking all the shitty wool off their tails and back ends. Want them nice and clean for my new tups!' So that was how I spent my first morning on Jim's farm; giving 300 ewes a pedicure and a Brazilian. Trevor, Jim's dad, came to watch as I clipped the particularly mucky tail of one of the ewes, trying to feel the contours under the shears, dreading I might nick her and draw blood.

'You're doing a good job,' said Trevor generously. 'Have you ever clipped anything before?'

'No,' I confessed.

'Well, I'm impressed,' said Trevor. 'You can have a job if you want!' I could feel a huge smile breaking out across my sweaty, dirty face. I felt ridiculously proud and pleased. And at that moment it struck me how much this mattered. I really wanted to be good at this, to work hard to learn and be more of an asset than a burden, and most of all to earn the Beavans' trust and approval. It was an enormous undertaking on their part, to agree to take on a woman they didn't know, who had no experience of sheep or farming, and agree to let her become part of their working lives and look after and handle the livestock that is their family's primary source of income. It was a privilege and one I should absolutely make the most of. And with that, I stopped thinking about how much my back ached and how everything I was wearing was encrusted in poo and got on with shearing the next ewe.

The big day came in the middle of October 2009. After a rather wet, disappointing summer, we were being treated to the most glorious of sun-drenched golden autumns. The ewes – neat, clean and clipped – were ready. The tups were penned up in the yard when I arrived and Jim handed me a pot of what appeared to be paint and a long plastic glove, reminiscent of James Herriot and stuck calves. 'You're going to raddle them,' he announced.

'I'm going to do what to them?'

'Raddle them. In that tin is a thick oily paint. You rub it on the brisket of the tup and when he mounts the ewe he'll leave a smear of raddle on her hind quarters and you can tell if he's been doing his job or not.'

'I smear it on the what?' I asked, feeling thick.

'The brisket,' said Jim. 'This bit!' And he pointed to the lower chest area between the front legs of one of the tups. 'Go on!' he urged, as I looked at him doubtfully. I'm still never quite sure when Jim is being serious or not, but I took him at his word, took a big dollop of blue paint in my gloved hand and smeared it on the ram. The ram seemed unconcerned. I did the same to the other one. 'Perfect,' said Jim. 'Now they can go out and meet the girls.'

Jim, his wife Kate and I stood in the field, bent double with laughter as we watched the ewes take one look at the approaching rams and hightail it up the hill to get as far away from them as possible. 'How much did you pay for them?!' I asked Jim. 'I'm not sure your ewes are impressed by your choice. You might have to go and get them better-looking ones!'

'Give 'em time,' said Jim, 'they'll win them over.'

'That's how Jim courted me,' said Kate, with a laugh. 'Hung around until I gave in!'

The rams made tentative progress towards the ewes. As they got closer they started curling their lips, as if leering in anticipation. 'It's called the Flehmen response,' explained Kate. 'That curling of the lip allows them to detect whether the ewe is giving off the pheromones which tell him she is in season and ready to mate.' Suddenly one of the rams put on a burst of speed, chasing down a ewe who didn't play hard to get for very long. We let out an unruly cheer as he mounted her, leaving a tell-tale blue smear of paint on her behind when he had finished. 'That's my boy!' cried Jim. 'They'll do a grand job.' And we turned back to the farmyard, leaving them to get on with it in peace.

Autumn gave way to a bitterly cold but spectacular winter. Snow fell in big lazy flakes, covering the landscape in a thick, white blanket that lasted for weeks. The gravel track that switchbacks it way up the steep hill to our house became a slick bobsleigh run of solid ice and for several days we were unable to leave the house. Jim and Kate were flat out. All the water troughs and pipes were frozen and they were spending every daylight hour getting water and feed out to the now-pregnant ewes. I was desperate to get to the farm to help them, but I was stuck.

Finally a brief thaw allowed me off our hill and back to the farm. Jim was driving to the local abattoir that morning with a couple of last year's lambs for the family butcher shop. I had never been to an abattoir before and was a little apprehensive, but it was an important part of my training, and for the television series. 'We can't gloss over the fact that the lambs we are going to see being born will ultimately end up as meat,' said Lisa, 'and I think it is pertinent that we film the whole process.'

We all agreed, but there was a problem. Jim's local abattoir didn't want us to film there. 'It's the animal rights crowd,' explained the owner. 'We just dare not go on TV in case we get attacked.' I was stunned. This was a tiny, old-fashioned, small-scale local slaughterhouse on the edge of a small Welsh town with a butcher's shop at the front. A far cry from the huge, industrial-scale operations that have seen most little abattoirs like this one close down. What could anyone possibly object to, when all it does is provide a service – to kill animals in a humane and hygienic way to supply a market driven by consumers who want to eat meat?

'I know,' said the owner, sadly. 'We would love people to see what goes on here. We take pride in what we do. We are a small operation. The animals are kept here overnight so they are calm and stress-free after the journey, and dispatched quickly and painlessly by our slaughterman who has worked here for forty years. But we dare not take the risk.' So Jim and I unloaded his two lambs and settled them into the big, straw-filled pen outside the slaughterhouse.

'I know you're probably going to think this is a ridiculous question,' I said, 'but do you feel sad or conflicted when you bring an animal to be slaughtered?'

'You know what, Kate,' said Jim, leaning on the rails

of the pen, looking at his lambs, 'I feel proud. Look at those animals. They are healthy, fit, in the peak of condition and I bred them. They look like that because I've done my job right. I'm a farmer producing a crop and I do everything I can to make sure that my crop is the best. It's just that my crop is meat and it has to be harvested like any other.'

Although we never got permission to film in an abattoir, I did persuade the one local to me to allow me to come in and see sheep being slaughtered. I was, I admit, terrified, lying awake for much of the night before with visions of screaming animals and men, stripped to the waist, covered in blood and wielding huge knives. I imagined myself fainting, crumpling onto a blood-soaked floor with the sound of mocking laughter in my ears. I couldn't have got it more wrong.

The first thing that struck me was how quiet it was. 'It's noisier when we have pigs in,' said the manager, 'but on sheep days it is very quiet.' He led me to the door of a room where a small flock of sheep were standing being inspected by a vet. 'We have a vet on site all the time,' I was told. 'It's regulations. When we are slaughtering sheep we keep them together in their flocks. It is less stressful for them than being taken in one at a time.'

Another white-coated man walked slowly up to the flock carrying what looked like an outsize pair of tongs. He put the tongs either side of the head of one of the sheep and it instantly dropped to the ground. 'We stun them first. If we left them for a couple of minutes they would regain consciousness as if nothing had happened, but this way they can be dispatched without knowing anything about it.' As soon as the sheep dropped to the floor a chain was attached to its back legs, it was hoisted in the air and away to the next door room where the slaughterman slit its throat so quickly I didn't even see it happen. 'The blood has to be allowed to drain out because otherwise it goes into the meat and taints it.'

The sheep made its way along the processing line. The head was removed, it was gutted and skinned and within about five minutes of being stunned, it was a carcass hanging in a chill room. Everything was done quickly, quietly and respectfully, with utmost efficiency. I was both surprised and impressed, admitting to my host that I had been dreading coming, that I would find the whole thing really distressing.

'That's the problem,' he said, shaking his head. 'Most people are perfectly happy to buy and eat meat, as long as it is cut up and in a neat plastic container in a supermarket, so in their minds it has no connection with a live animal. They don't like to think that the cute, woolly lamb in a field is only there because it is destined for one of those plastic containers and they certainly don't like to consider the process the animal has to go through to get from field to plate. Many abattoirs used to be open to the public, for school trips and so on, but now we have to be so careful and because of that it looks like we've got something to hide.'

Back up at the Beavans' farm it was a big day in the sheep-rearing calendar. It was a bitterly cold January morning, snow still thick on the ground, the steeply sloping field behind the Beavans' house criss-crossed with toboggan tracks. Jim had been out checking the ewes first thing that morning. 'Look what he found!' said Kate, leading me into one of the barns. There, curled up in the straw with its mother, was a tiny newborn lamb. 'We're not expecting any of our early lambs for at least a month,' said Kate, 'so this ewe must have somehow had a bit of a sneaky encounter with a ram. It was lucky Jim found it. It was minus five this morning. Amazing how tough they are. We're going to call it Elvis, because it is Elvis's birthday today.'

'Surely,' I said, 'you don't name your lambs?'

Kate laughed. 'No, not usually, but this one's special.'

The 300 ewes we had introduced to Jim's new rams back in October were in a holding pen in the yard. Today was the day we'd find out if Jim had made a good investment and the rams had started to earn their keep. A van arrived. Kelly Atkinson, the scanner, jumped out and we helped him unload his kit. Kelly had come to scan the ewes, not just to find out if they were pregnant or not, but also to find out whether they were having a single lamb, twins or even triplets. Scanning is a relatively new thing but more and more sheep farmers are getting their flocks scanned before lambing. 'It helps so much with management,' said Jim. 'If we know a ewe is expecting triplets, we'll bring in her into the shed a bit earlier and feed her more than we would with a ewe expecting a single lamb. It doesn't mean we get any more sleep at lambing time, but it does mean we know what to expect and can look after the ewes accordingly.'

It was an impressive operation. Kelly had rigged up his scanner and a seat that allowed him to be at sheep-belly height. The ewes were channelled from the holding pen down a narrow race of hurdles, the width of one sheep, so they arrived one at a time at Kelly's holding crate. Once in, he would place his scanner on their bellies and a grey, fuzzy image would appear on the screen of his monitor. 'Twins!' he would call out, or 'Single!'

I was standing on the other side of the crate, along with Jim and a couple of pots of paint. A ewe expecting a single lamb would get a single orange spot on her back, 'one blue for two!' said Jim and triplets got two blue spots. It all happened remarkably fast. At one point, I was relieved from my painting duty to go and look at the monitor. Kelly held the scanner and said, 'There, look. There's a backbone, and the heart beating. See?'

'Not really,' I confessed. He showed me again. A slightly thicker white line amongst the scribble of other lines was the backbone. He moved the scanner slightly and said, 'Look! There's a second one. This ewe is expecting twins.' Kelly scanned all 300 ewes in a couple of hours and then handed Jim a slip of paper. 'Not bad,' he said, '198 per cent.' And with that he was off, down the icy drive to the next farm.

'What does it mean when he said you scanned at 198 per cent?' I asked Jim. 'Well,' he said, pulling at his beard in the way he always does when he's thinking, 'A ewe has two teats, so she's designed to have two lambs. If all your ewes scan to have two lambs you'd get 200 per cent. Does that make sense?' I nodded. 'But some ewes only have one lamb and some, because over the years sheep have been bred specifically to produce more lambs, have triplets or even quads, although that is quite unusual. Of our 300 ewes, about 200 are expecting twins, fifty singles and fifty triplets. Now, as I said, a ewe has only two teats, so she can't raise three lambs. We either have to bottle-feed them, or if a ewe expecting a single lamb gives birth soon after triplets have been born, I'll take the biggest and most robust of the triplets and adopt it on to the ewe with a single lamb.'

'Will she accept a lamb from another ewe?' I asked, incredulously.

'She will if the lamb isn't too big and you do what's called a wet adoption. As she is giving birth, you bring in the triplet and rub it in all the birthing fluids so it smells the same as her own lamb. After they've given birth they spend ages licking the lambs, cleaning all the fluids off them, but it is this process that also forms the bond between ewe and lamb. Present her with two lambs that smell the same and both need cleaning off, and nine times out of ten she'll accept them both. Not very bright, sheep!' he said, with a smile. 'But it's much better than having loads that need bottle-feeding every couple of hours.'

'So are you pleased with your rams? 198 per cent sounds like a pretty good percentage.'

'It is,' nodded Jim, 'and at least we know there'll be some lambs in March when you do your programme. I just hope they start lambing in time.'

In March 2010 two and a half million people tuned in to watch *Lambing Live*, as gripped and fascinated by the drama of the lambing shed as I had become. I barely slept. I wanted to be at the farm all the time. With Kate's expert instruction I delivered my first lamb, an unforgettable moment of sheer, unutterable wonder and joy.

'You can feel the feet, can't you?' she said. My tentative fingers entered the ewe and sure enough, there were the soft points of two feet, neatly packed, side by side. 'Now if you feel up the legs from the feet, if the lamb is presented right you should feel a nose and then the dome of the head.'

'I can!' I gasped, excitedly.

'OK,' said Kate, 'try and get a grip on the front legs and as the ewe pushes, gently ease the legs out.'

The legs were slick and slippery, and the space was tight, but I persevered and gradually they started to come. When both legs were clear, one gentle pull brought the lamb tumbling out onto the straw, a rather alien-looking creature, eyes closed, ears pressed against its skull, the black fleece wet and slimy with mucus. Kate showed me how to clear the area around its nose, quite hard – triggering the lamb to shake its head, sneeze and start breathing – and then to take it gently round to the ewe's head, where immediately she started to lick it. We stepped back, leaving her in peace to bond with her lamb. She got to her feet, licking and nickering; the lamb too, only seconds old, uttered a feeble first bleat.

'They're talking to each other,' whispered Kate. 'The ewe will recognise the call of her lamb, even when they are out in the field with hundreds of others.' Within just a couple of minutes the lamb was getting to its feet. It staggered, it swayed, it staggered again and then it was there, upright, for just a moment before it collapsed once more.

'We'll call her Humble, in your honour,' said Kate, giving me a congratulatory slap on the back, 'but you can't stand here watching her all day. There's another one going into labour in the corner. You've got work to do!'

It had been nine months since the telephone call with Lisa the BBC producer. What had started out as a television project, another job, had become rather more than I would ever have anticipated. I had relished every minute of the experience, even the dreadful, heart-stopping moment when I realised that a lamb I had delivered was not breathing, and wouldn't breath, whatever I did, and I felt overcome and overwhelmed with hopelessness and inadequacy and sobbed on Jim's shoulder, saying I'd killed the lamb and let him down. Jim had taken his knife and cut open the tiny, lifeless chest. 'Look!' he said, pointing at the lungs. 'They're not fully developed. It was nothing you did. This lamb would never have breathed, would never have survived. It happens, sometimes.'

But it was not just that I had found my time at the Beavans' farm fascinating. It was more that I had been given an inkling, an insight into a way of life that felt right. It was as if I'd spent forty or so years scrabbling about to find a pair of shoes that fitted and finally I'd found a pair that didn't pinch, or give me blisters, or needed breaking in. People talk about life-changing experiences and maybe I'd just had one. I just didn't know yet how much change it might bring.

Chapter 7

The Quest For A
Few More Acres

If you wait a couple of years you can buy the whole farm!' laughed our next-door neighbour Rhys as I broached the idea of him selling us the field that borders our land. At about ten or fifteen acres it would give us the space I now desperately aspired to that would allow us to graduate from being have-a-go smallholders with a couple of pet donkeys and two over-indulged sows, to doing things a bit more seriously – breeding and raising our own animals; even, perhaps, building up a small local network of people who we could sell meat to on a fairly regular basis. We were under no illusion that we could make a proper living from it – even life-long farmers like Rhys and Jim with all their land and experience find it a struggle – but I wanted to find some small way of emulating that feeling of connection between land and life that had so fired me up during the making of *Lambing Live*.

Rhys and his ever-practical wife Judith had had no end of amusement from our early forays into livestock management, but Judith loved the occasional goose egg I would bring to her back door and when I delivered one of our chickens, plucked and oven-ready for her to try, she phoned me the next day to ask if I had any more. She wanted to buy some for her freezer and knew some other people who would like some too. It felt like a breakthrough, a first tentative step towards doing something well and being recognised for it. And, confessed Rhys, they had both been deeply sceptical about *Lambing Live* and ended up watching all of it. 'You did very well,' he smiled. 'I reckon there'll be a few people around here who will offer you a job next lambing season.' I was delighted, but he still wouldn't sell me his field. 'I'll put the word out,' he said. 'There might some land about. You ask around too.'

A few days later, the phone rang. The familiar voice of Pete Davies greeted me. 'Some relations of my wife's have a council farm just down the road. They've just retired so that farm might have a field available. Do you want me to ring them and bring you up to see it?' Pete lives on a farm in the valley below us and like so many farmers does other jobs to supplement his income. Hard-working, strong and dependable, he'll drink a just-made scalding mug of sugary tea down in one and carry on. Pete has repaired or replaced almost all our fences, a back-breaking task made worse because our land is so steep that even using a quad bike – if we had one – would be perilous, so Pete had to carry all the new fence posts, wire and tools himself, and dig all the holes by hand.

One February day Pete was doing the fences and I was planting a new hedge. He was digging holes a foot or so deep for the fence posts, I was digging holes a few inches deep for my hedge plants. My progress was pathetically slow. I had a fifty-metre stretch to plant and by mid morning had done barely five. The ground wasn't hard but was full of stones, and every time I put the spade in I'd hit a stone, and then another one, and another, making me curse with frustration. Pete came to see how I was doing. Born and bred in this borderland between Wales and England he has a way of speaking and an accent that seems peculiar to this very particular part of the country. It doesn't sound Welsh, but nor is it pure Gloucestershire and the thing I love most is inanimate, sexless objects have a gender.

'Give 'im to me,' said Pete, putting his hand out for my spade.

'I've got another one,' I said, handing it over. 'I'll start digging from the other end.'

By the time I'd collected the other spade Pete had done almost as much as I had achieved all morning. 'You want to put 'im in the ground like this,' said Pete, stabbing the spade expertly into the soil, 'and then make another slit crossways. You don't need to dig a proper hole. Just a slot in the ground will be enough.' So I started at one end while Pete carried on method- ically working his way towards me. I'd love to say we met in the middle, but that would be a lie.

'Thanks, Pete,' I said, wiping a muddy forearm across my sweaty forehead, 'I'll have the whole lot planted before dark now.'

'Before you start that,' said Pete, 'I need you to come and look at the gate and what side you want me to 'ang 'im.'

On the appointed day of our meeting with the tenant farmers we drove to meet Pete on the road outside his farm and followed his truck for a few miles down narrow winding lanes. It was late spring but cold and grey, a bitter wind blowing off the Black Mountains bringing squally showers and a chill to the bones. We turned off the road, passing through metal gates into an immaculate farmyard. Cattle stood munching silage outside a red corrugated Dutch barn. Beyond were more cattle sheds, a hay store and sheep sheds, all clean, modern and in a good state of repair. Past a rather beautiful old stone barn, a remnant from an old farmyard, perhaps, was the house. Ros Edmonds came to the door and waved us in. 'It's horrible out there!' she cried. 'Come in and have some tea.'

It was April 2010. Every day there was more bad news for the economy, of entire countries teetering on the edge of bankruptcy, gloomy forecasts of double dip recessions and politicians earnestly explaining the need for more cutbacks. We were all being urged to economise, find money behind a metaphorical sofa. Cash-strapped councils were being encouraged to make ends meet by selling their assets. In rural areas like ours, council assets include council-owned farms, known as county farms. These tend to be relatively small areas of land – 50–150 acres – that were traditionally rented out to young farmers who had no land of their own.

These farms played an important role in the rural economy, keeping land productive and enabling young people to get a start in farming. In the early sixties there were over 16,000 county farms in England and Wales; now there are less than 4,000.

Over the last few years, land prices have risen dramatically. It seems many are heeding the advice of Mark Twain to 'buy land because they're not making it any more'. As stocks and shares become an ever more precarious investment option, land appears to have become an increasingly popular way for bankers to spend their bonuses. Land-owning councils are sitting on pots of gold. Small farms that, it can be convincingly argued, are too small to be really viable, will fetch a very good price, particularly if they are broken up. Sell the house with a bit of land as one lot, put planning permission on old, characterful barns and sell them as another lot, parcel up the rest of the land for people to use as pony paddocks or increase the size of their gardens, and suddenly a small farm is worth a very large amount of money indeed. It may appear to be a sensible solution in the short term, but in the long term there will be a lot of landless farmers and an awful lot of barn conversions at a time when populations are increasing and there is more and more pressure on our farmers to produce food.

Ros and Arthur Edmonds had been tenants on this farm for thirty-three years. The farm is just over 100 acres, the land flat, but high and full of stones. Arthur had bred and raised cattle and sheep and through sheer hard work and an enviable depth of knowledge and understanding, he had eked a living from that difficult land. During tough times – and with BSE and foot and mouth, there were many – Ros, who worked as a teacher too, baked cakes and made jams to sell at the WI stall in the market in the nearby town of Monmouth. Practical and realistic, they knew it was likely the farm would be sold; what they hadn't realised when they handed in their notice, was the way the council planned to sell it. As this particular farm wasn't what the council term part of their 'core estate', they sent a land agent round to value it and marked it down 'for disposal'. Auctioned off in parcels to maximise the money the council could expect to raise, it would cease to be a farm at all. The skill and care that Ros and Arthur had lavished on that land to make it productive over three decades would be dismissed with the bang of an auctioneer's hammer.

It was hard sitting in the kitchen of these two kind, hospitable people, the air heavy with sad resignation, the years of physical toil evident in the twist of Arthur's fingers, the slight stoop of his back, and not feel a sense of outrage. They hadn't been made to retire; they weren't being thrown off their land and they had already put an offer in on a house with a few acres around the corner, so that, in Ros's words, they could still keep a few sheep and one of Arthur's beloved vintage tractors. 'A farmer without a farm is like a caged animal,' she said, 'but we'll have enough land to keep him busy and I do want to keep hold of my Jacobs.'

I could see her little flock of Jacob sheep from the window. Handsome animals with horns and brown and white fleeces, they produce good meat and the wool is very popular with spinners and weavers – facts I'd learned after some intensive study of the sheep breeds of Britain. 'A good sheep for smallholders,' I thought, making a mental note. But it was more that the decision to break up the farm seemed so short-sighted, so unimaginative – and even worse, it would actively take land out of production, take away the already swiftly dwindling opportunities for young farmers to hone their skills and provide food for the nation.

'It's just stupid!' I said to Ludo as we drove back home. 'It shouldn't be allowed to happen.' Ludo gave me a look. It was a look that said, 'I don't really understand why you are so het up about this and if you start this battle and you win, which you won't, do you think we'll take on the farm? Because we can't; because one series of *Lambing Live* does not mean we know anything about farming. We want a field, remember, or a bit of a field, not a farm. We have a perfectly nice house already and we don't need a hundred acres.' I could see all this from his expression; it was as if I could hear his words. I turned away, looking resolutely out of the car window, brain whirring.

Ludo was right. We didn't want a farm, but something inexplicable was driving me to do something to stop this one being destroyed. I had no grand plan, no brilliant solution, but still I phoned the council. I asked if someone would ring me back about the farm. They didn't. I phoned again. I emailed. I kept phoning until someone told me that it was too late, the farm was to be sold, in lots, and there was nothing that would change that. Without thinking, I asked if I could take it on as a tenant. No, I was told with decreasing patience, it is going to be sold. If I wanted to be a tenant farmer I'd need to join the list. It is a long list and the wait even longer. No council farms have been rented out to new tenants in our area for the last decade. But I didn't want to be a tenant farmer on another farm; I wanted to keep this farm. It had supported Ros and Arthur and generations of farming families before them. It could still provide a living for another family, still produce food for the area; it seemed so short-sighted and such a waste to simply flog it off to become a few over-grazed pony paddocks and a housing development.

The more I was rebuffed the more resolute I became. I was not going to give up, but clearly I was going to have to be a bit more creative than just banging on about the cultural importance of county farms to someone who viewed them as nothing more than an untapped wad of cash. I needed to convince them that I had an alternative, an idea that would persuade the council that perhaps there was another way the farm could still bring in much-needed revenue, and yet still remain a farm.

It took six months. Six months of phoning, emailing and driving everyone at the council to distraction before they finally caved in and we got an appointment to see someone about the farm. In the meantime, Ludo had decided not to renew his contract with the BBC. He had gone from programme maker to manager, spending more time in meetings and dealing with staffing issues than doing the creative stuff he thrived on. Although he had enjoyed the challenge at first, it became apparent towards the end of his second year that he was not relishing the idea of going to work any more. 'Take a sabbatical,' I suggested. 'I've got enough work at the moment to support us both and you've done that for me plenty of times in the past.'

Ludo's six-month sabbatical was spent, in part, writing music, which he had always wanted to have more time to do. He rigged up a makeshift studio at home and, when not sitting at his keyboard or strum-ming a guitar, started to rediscover the joy of living in the Welsh countryside. Badger and Bella were all too happy to help him, sitting expectantly in his studio with an 'Isn't it time for a walk?' look on their faces. And, if I wasn't around, the pigs, poultry and donkeys became less of a chore to be fed and mucked out as they had been when it all had to be done in a mad rush before an hour-long commute along the motorway. He started to become a less reluctant smallholder.

When the phone call from the council eventually came we drove to the offices together. 'So what are we going to say?' said Ludo. In retrospect it is extraordinary that we hadn't thought to turn up at this first crucial meeting with any sort of document or proposal to show them we had a rock-solid, money-earning alternative to selling the farm. 'Getting a meeting' had become a sort of game. It had gone on so long I don't think either of us ever believed we would actually get that meeting and so had given no thought at all to what we would do or say if we did. So here we were, about to sit down with the newly appointed Head of Regeneration and Culture, and two people from the Farm Estates, with only the vaguest notion of what we were going to say or suggest, but knowing that one way or the other this was our greatest, possibly only, chance of saving the farm.

An hour later we walked back to the car park in a state of shock.

'Did she really say she liked the idea?'

Ludo nodded, mutely.

'What did I say?'

He laughed. 'I can't really remember, but you talked a lot and sounded very convincing.'

'Bloody hell!' It began to dawn on both of us that we were on the cusp of something potentially far bigger than we'd bargained for.

'The way I see it,' said Ludo, opening a bag of Maynard's Sours in lieu of lunch, 'we have two choices. Back out now, or go for it and see what happens, in which case we'd better try and remember what you said.'

'What do you want to do?' I asked, tentatively.

Ludo swallowed the remains of a sweet. 'I think we should give it a shot. If it doesn't work it's not the end of the world; I'll go back to directing if anyone will have me. But this feels like an opportunity we shouldn't just walk away from because it is a bit scary and we know nothing about starting or running a business – whatever that business is going to be!'

That same month Ros and Arthur left for their new home taking just the small flock of Jacob sheep, Arthur's favourite tractor and their cat. All the other livestock had already been sold and everything else – machinery, tools and general farm hardware – was sold by auction from the farm. Ludo and I were away the day of the sale but Stafford, whose farm is just down the road from Ros and Arthur, had gone, hoping to buy a trailer.

'I've never seen so many people at a farm sale,' he said. Arthur had a well-deserved reputation for looking after his machinery and keeping everything in immaculate condition and working order. 'Stuff was going pretty much for the same price as it would be new,' said Stafford, shaking his head. 'I got outbid on everything. He's very well liked, too. I think people were paying top prices as a mark of respect as well.'

A week or so later we drove up to the farm. The big metal gates at the entrance were padlocked together. The place already had a sense of abandonment, the fields and buildings eerily quiet without the mooing, baaing presence of the livestock. We needed to get a move on.

In the intervening months we had dozens more meetings with the council and the farm began, in the way that choosing the right school or the progress of a loft conversion can, to dominate our lives and become almost our sole topic of conversation. We bored our friends, had sleepless nights, subscribed to the *Farmers Guardian* and started trying to learn about single farm payments and grant schemes. Our business idea, which had started as a few disjointed phrases like 'outdoor education', 'reconnecting people with where their food comes from', 'commercial farming that works for wildlife', 'green energy', became more substantial, concrete and workable. Our main objective – and my unspoken promise to Ros and Arthur – was to keep the farm a proper working farm, and to keep it tenanted. It wasn't just Ludo's perfectly legitimate concern that we didn't know how to run a farm that made us keen for new tenants to take it on; it was more what a farm like this represented – a future for someone who did know how to farm, who'd been born to it, who had the skills and expertise to bring value to land but had no land of their own.

Fearful that our plan might and could come to nothing and the farm could still be broken up and sold at auction, we nonetheless thought it might be wise to put out a few initial enquiries to see if anyone actually wanted to be our tenants. I had assumed that given there was such a lengthy waiting list for farms, we would have people literally queuing at the gates, pleading with us to let them take it on. Andrew laughed. Andrew was the lawyer who had bravely agreed to advise us and steer the way should any sale be forthcoming. Specialising in agricultural cases, he had a weight of experience working both for councils selling farms and for people trying to buy land from councils.

A humble bee-keeper.

Opposite page: With Ludo and Badger on a rare dry day.

This page, clockwise from the top left: Badger cooling off; Me and Bella with Tim, Sarah and Dai; we've found water!; watching the tups with Jim and Kate Beavan.

Above: The farmhouse gets a facelift.
Below left: Bob Stevenson, Pig Guru!
Below right: Kate and Jim with Lass at home on their farm.

Above: Who nicked the wall? Work starts to re-build a barn.
Below: Rubble and mud, but progress…

This page: My Badger Face Welsh Mountain ram.

Opposite page, clockwise from the top left: Two Kates in Marigolds!; Me and Sarah with Stafford Bell; Tim and Sarah take a break during lambing; the tree planters and the copse they created during one of our courses; Adam Henson pays us a visit; the birth of Humble the lamb.

Feeding a lamb with Rags and Champ looking on.

'What's so funny?' I asked, affronted.

'You must be joking!' said Andrew. 'Most tenants want to take on their farm, pay their rent and be left in peace. You and Ludo are going to be on site most of the time, trying to run a business while they are trying to run a farm. You'll be bringing members of the public in, which will have a huge impact on your tenants, plus you'll be scrutinising everything they do because you want everything to be perfect and beyond rebuke. It's a tough call. You'll be lucky to find anyone!'

We drove home feeling not a little deflated. I didn't imagine, quite, that farmers would see us as heroes for championing the cause of the young and the landless, but I did hope that what we were trying to do might be viewed as something positive, something that would be good for the area and may even have an impact further afield. As we were to discover not much later, some of the local farmers thought quite the opposite, but for the moment we were blissfully unaware of the mutterings that would herald the coming storm.

The business that Andrew had pointed out would be the bane of our tenants' lives, would, we believed, be able to be pretty self-contained, based in the old farm buildings that are no longer practical for modern agriculture. The two stone barns we envisaged being our headquarters sit either side of a sort of courtyard. The courtyard is right in the heart of the farm, but separated from the modern barns which occupy a different area and would be for the exclusive use of the tenant. Our barns would be fixed up and made safe, without allowing them to lose their agricultural heritage, and would become a centre running courses for people who want to learn rural skills and animal husbandry. We imagined we would keep a few acres to create a sort of model smallholding, keeping a range of livestock suitable for small-scale production or personal use. We already had some of the teachers in mind – local experts who had helped us in our first, haphazard years take the leap from keeping an animal or two as a pet, to having animals for more practical, pragmatic reasons – to breed, sell and eat.

In my mind one area of the barn would have an apple press, for those apple-glut years, to be used by anyone in the community who wanted to make apple juice instead of endless crumbles. I also thought it would be great to have some honey-extracting equipment. Extractors can be bulky and pricey – a significant outlay for anyone with just a hive or two, so we thought if we had one at the farm, locals could use it too. We wanted to have a little shop to sell our farm produce and other stuff produced locally. We wanted school children to come and get their fingernails dirty, muck out pigs, jump in wool sacks at shearing time and help with lambing. We envisioned planting more trees, putting up bird boxes, digging a pond. We would rebuild dry-stone walls, lay hedges, install PV panels on roofs. In short, we imagined creating a utopia, an asset for the community, which would also bring in an income for us and still be a practical, viable, working farm for our hypothetical tenants. Were we dreaming? Could this vision of bucolic harmony really work, and most importantly, generate enough money to sustain itself?

A business plan would give us an idea of our level of delusion, but here we faltered. We had, by now, produced a document, which thanks to Ludo's computer wizardry, was rather beautiful and full of pictures of happy-looking farm animals and people enjoying delicious, wholesome food. 'It is very pretty,' conceded Phil

Cooper, of Venture Wales, who had become a regular at our meetings, and was there to advise us on the wherefores of setting up a new business. 'In fact, I called my colleagues in to have a look at it and we all agreed it is the prettiest business plan we've ever seen. It's a bit short on numbers, though.'

Phil was being characteristically kind. Our business plan wasn't just short of numbers, but devoid of them altogether. 'Business Plan' is a one of those strange, alien concepts, which, like handbags that cost hundreds of pounds and Jimmy Choo shoes, have no relevance or place in a life like mine. Not any more. We became obsessed with the business plan. Well, Ludo did, while I looked over his shoulder occasionally and wondered how he made his computer create all those columns. Thanks to Tony, the world's most patient accountant, we ended up with more than numbers. We had cash-flow projections! We had tables showing money in and money out! We knew the eye-watering amount we'd have to spend and what we'd have to make to avoid debtors' prison and a life of prostitution! We knew, that if all went well, without any hitches or unforeseen glitches, if our progress was smooth, building work finished on time, animals stayed healthy and people were actually prepared to pay to take part in this venture, we – the sole investors and people responsible for getting the business up and running and keeping it that way, doing everything from feeding and mucking out our livestock to doing the accounts and emptying the bins – would make a profit of £137.00 in our first year. 'No question,' said Ludo, turning from the computer screen to Tony, voice heavy with irony, 'it's all absolutely worth it.'

But however glossy and number-crunched our

business plan, and utopian and community-minded our vision, it didn't disguise the fact that we were left with one, pretty major stumbling block. The council, although still nodding and smiling and making supportive noises, had yet to officially agree to let us take on the farm. Everything we had done, months of meetings, hair-pulling, agonising and slog, was hypothetical until the moment when the Council Cabinet met to discuss with every council member whether this was the right thing to do with this particular farm.

But it appeared to be impossible to fix a date for this to happen. Anyone who has ever had any dealings with councils, and let's face it, that's most of us, knows that even Job would have been driven to jumping up and down on his mobile phone or hurling his computer out of the window. In the 'trash' section of my laptop are any number of emails, often written at 3 a.m. after lying for hours, sleepless with frustration, and liberally interspersed with irate capital letters. 'I AM NOT PREPARED TO WASTE ANY MORE TIME!' 'HOW HARD CAN IT BE?' 'WHAT DO YOU MEAN THE MEETING CAN'T BE ORGANISED THIS SIDE OF CHRISTMAS?' 'I GIVE UP!' Flounce. Ludo banned me from sending any of them. In fact he banned me from sending anything direct to the council and made me send everything to him first. If this thing ever came to fruition, it would, in no small part, be down to his rigid control of my 'outbox'.

Andrew and the lawyer for the council sent bits of paper back and forth, back and forth, trying to agree Heads of Terms. More weeks passed. Statements were drawn up. Another month gone. Business plans were polished. Finally, finally a date was set. Cabinet would meet at the end of July 2011 and, nine months after our very first meeting with the council, we would know our – and the farm's – fate.

Cabinet meetings are open to the public, so we would be allowed to attend but not speak. However, because of the unusual nature of this project, and because it had been agreed that the council would retain 30 per cent ownership of the farm as an insurance policy, so we couldn't just turn around after a couple of days and sell it to a supermarket, we were asked to come in early to answer questions and clarify anything to any councillor who wanted more information.

We were ushered in to a large chamber, with semicircular rows of banked seats, filled with intimidating faces and suits. I felt like I was being hauled up in front of the UN for war crimes. We were both terrified, so terrified that Ludo managed to knock over a freshly filled glass of water that emptied itself into my crotch. I stood up and explained that although I was nervous I hadn't actually wet myself. No one laughed.

What followed was a gruelling two hours of questioning. What did we intend to do? Who would farm the farm? Would they be local? How would we support local businesses and producers? Why had we blatantly flouted clause 416/7a? At this point I had to concede that I wasn't entirely sure how councils worked and what the clause was they were talking about. 'Neither do we,' quipped someone from the back, and that did get a laugh. Ragged with exhaustion and with no idea of what their reaction was, we emerged and had an agonising two hours to wait until Cabinet sat.

'I too think this is a good idea, that will bring benefits to the community and the county as a whole. I give it my support.'

Tears dragged black lines of mascara down my cheeks. The seventh and final member of the Cabinet had given our idea her approval. Seven out of seven. Ludo and I couldn't look at each other. He squeezed my fingers, whispering, 'They could still object.' Council members have two weeks after a Cabinet meeting to raise an objection.

'I know,' I said, 'but it was unanimous. They all like it. Surely, surely it's going to happen.'

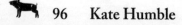

Chapter 8

Sheep But No Farm

I stood on a hillside, buffeted by a stiff wind, surrounded by a landscape both grand and glowering. A thick, low mist hung over the rocky massifs that crowded the horizon in every direction. The grass beneath my feet was springy and wiry and sparse. There were no trees, just rocks and hollows and bogs. The Cumbrian Fells command respect, as do the people that live and farm in this wild, majestic place. Beside me stood a young girl of not much more than ten, chattering away as if we'd known each other for years even though we'd met just an hour or so before.

'Here they come!' she cried, her accent strong and distinct, rooting her to this land of her birth. Over a rise, in a great, white, woolly wave, came the sheep, running towards us, and then slowing, spreading out around us, sides heaving, catching their breath. More came pouring over the hillside, handsome animals with dark curly horns and long, luxuriant tails. The distant hum of quad bike engines grew louder as they approached, driving on the last stragglers.

'Here's Dad and Granddad,' the young girl announced, as the quad bikes crested the hill, each carrying a man and a dog. Andrew, the young girl's dad, pulled up beside us, with Lyn, his faithful, hard-working collie sitting behind him, tongue lolling.

'Have you been looking after Kate, Catherine?'

She nodded, as did I. 'I can't believe that when we got here there was not a single sheep to be seen and now, in less than an hour, you've managed to gather them all to this one place.'

Andrew smiled. 'That's the beauty of the heft,' he said. 'I'll explain it to you later, once we've got these sheep down.' Andrew and his father Donald set off on the quads, guiding the sheep down the slope towards the farm. With Catherine and her mum Rachel who had joined us with six-year-old Abi and the baby Olivia in a pushchair, I walked behind the sheep, keeping them together, although it required little effort on our part. The sheep seemed to know where to go and what to do.

'They're used to it, I suppose,' said Rachel. 'We gather them in twice a year so they know what to expect.' It was three miles back to the farm. There is something magical about walking with a large flock of animals; there is a rhythm and a sense of purpose and an intangible connection with an ancient way of life, long forgotten by most of us in the developed world, but somehow still wrapped up in our DNA.

In between the phone calls to the council, the emails, the endless waiting, the meetings and more waiting I had started filming for a second series of *Lambing Live*. As the farm we hoped would one day become ours still remained wrapped in a tangle of bureaucracy, I was only too delighted to spend the majority of another autumn, winter and spring immersed in farming life, even if it was on someone else's farm. It was a chance, too, to show a different way of farming in a different part of the country with different breeds of sheep. Thanks to the kind-hearted, ever-patient Marston family, we were able to do just that.

Donald and Christine Marston live on the farm that belonged to her parents. They had three children but it was Andrew, the eldest son, who stayed on the farm. He lives next door to his parents with Rachel, who was born and brought up just a few miles away, and their three daughters. The farm, like the Beavans' farm, is a family affair. No one outside the family works there, and although Donald and Andrew do the majority of the day-to-day farming – Rachel and Christine both have other jobs – the whole family pitch in at busy times like lambing. Even Olivia, barely a year old, spends much of her time bundled up in her pushchair and out in the fields.

The farm consists of 250 acres of what is known locally as in-bye land, the land that surrounds the farm in the sheltered valley where it sits, but they also have rights to graze the fell land above the farm. This is common land, largely unfenced, and all the local farms have the right to graze their livestock up there.

'So how,' I said to Andrew, as we stood back in the

farmyard with his sheep now contained in a series of pens, 'can you possibly go up on to the fell which stretches for miles in every direction, find your sheep, identify them from someone else's sheep, round them up without inadvertently taking a few hundred that aren't yours, and persuade them to walk three miles to your farm?'

Andrew explained that all his Swaledales were 'hefted' to what is locally acknowledged and accepted as the Marstons' bit of the fell. The 'heft', as it is known, is simply a small area where the sheep are regularly fed and where they will come if they are looking for food. Each generation of new lambs learns where the heft is from their mothers. The knowledge and understanding of how flock animals like sheep behave has allowed farmers like the Marstons to make the most of the vast swathes of land that would otherwise be seen as unproductive. There's a symbiosis between sheep and fell, but it's not an easy way to farm and there are fewer sheep out on the fells than there once were. Both Andrew and Donald worry about the future of this land, which is as intrinsic to them as their sheep are to it.

Andrew and Donald are well liked and well respected. They are hard working, scrupulously honest and excellent stockmen. They live a simple life with the family and the farm right at its heart. There are few frills and fripperies, but they do have one rather surprising aesthetic outlet, in which they take huge pride – something that I would never have imagined two Cumbrian farmers, as tough and resilient as their livestock, would ever have considered. How wrong I was.

One morning when I arrived on the yard, my first job was to help Andrew load one of his Swaledale rams on to a specially designed stand. The Swaledale is a sheep well adapted for life on the fells. With curly horns and black faces with white muzzles and white hair around the eyes, they are handsome and distinctive. Tough, sure-footed, they have long, off-white fleeces and tails. 'You don't tend to dock sheep like this,' explained Andrew when I asked. 'They need that bit of extra protection. Makes a big difference, if you're standing with your back to the wind, to have your bum covered!' Andrew handed me a bucket of warm, soapy water and said 'you start with the legs'. I have washed some unlikely animals in my time, including an elephant and a rhinoceros, but shampooing a sheep was a first.

I had never been one for 'showing', partly because neither my childhood pony nor I were really showing material. We would arrive at the local village show, my hair and its mane equally untamed and dishevelled, to find our fellow competitors, both human and equine, polished and gleaming, mothers wielding giant tins of hairspray lest the plaits of their daughters, or those of their immaculate steeds, should have one wisp out of place. Showing, I decided, was frivolous and all rather pointless. Yet here was Andrew Marston, the least frivolous person I know, primping and preening a Swaledale ram in preparation for exactly that.

After I washed the ram's legs, the head, with its splendid horns, was also sponged down, dried and brushed. Then Andrew handed me a pair of tweezers. 'Are you serious?' I asked.

He nodded. 'He should have no stray white hairs in the black part of his face and the line between the white and black parts should be as clean and sharp as possible.'

'Sorry fella,' I muttered. 'If this is anything like having your eyebrows plucked, it's going to hurt.'

For the final touch Andrew handed me a sack of thick, brown peat from the fell. 'Rub it into the fleece. It gives it the colour of the fell. The judges like it.' He wasn't joking about that, either.

Peat-dyed and plucked to perfection, still the ram didn't win. I was rather disappointed but Andrew was sanguine. 'There were some much better rams in the class,' he said generously. 'I didn't expect him to win.' But the ram fetched a good price at the auction that afternoon, which, laughed Donald, was almost certainly down to his perfectly plucked face.

As well as sheep, the Marstons breed cattle and a month or so later Andrew selected a young heifer called Juno to show at the prestigious Kirkby Classic. Rachel and I spent hours washing, blow-drying – there really is such a thing as a hairdryer designed for cows – brushing and back-combing, laughing that neither of us had spent anything like this much time on ourselves when we got married. This time, though, it paid off. Juno won not just her class but Supreme Champion. Andrew and Rachel were delighted. And suddenly I got it. This was an animal that they had bred with careful consideration and together, with years of experience and a lot of hard work, they had produced a champion. It was a great validation of their skill as farmers and breeders of livestock. Maybe one day, I thought secretly to myself, I will breed an animal worthy of taking into the ring.

It was another hard winter. The first snow fell in November, more in December. The Marstons' hardy Swaledales tucked themselves behind rocks and into hollows up on the fell, scraped at the snow to get to the grass underneath. Every morning Andrew would brave the bitter cold and take the quad bike laden with feed over the treacherous ground to the heft. The sheep would never be far away, and would crowd around the bike as he – or I, if it was a day I was with him – would lift off the heavy sacks and shake out the sheep nuts on to the ground in a long line. We'd leave hay too, and return in the afternoon to bring more. The ewes were all pregnant. This food was as much for the unborn lambs as it was for them.

Our paddocks at home were knee deep in snow. The pigs barely left their shelter, spending the majority of the day lying head to toe in their bed of thick straw and only bothering to rouse themselves when I appeared with a bucket of food. The donkeys, too, were unimpressed by the snow, and although during the day I would leave their stable door open so they could wander onto the yard and into the adjoining paddock, they too, preferred to stay inside, munching hay and waiting for spring. Both had grown thick coats and looked more like bears than donkeys, so I was surprised one morning when Bertie, the larger, more affectionate of the two, seemed a little shivery and, although he ate a bit of his food, didn't finish it.

'Bert,' I said, rubbing his face, as he looked at me with a slightly pathetic expression, 'what's up? You can't be cold, you're covered in three inches of hair and have a nice warm stable.' As a donkey famed for his greed, not eating was a bad sign. I looked at him closely. His stomach looked a bit tucked up and uncomfortable and when I bent down to put my ear against his soft, hairy belly, instead of hearing the usual reassuring rumbles and gurgles it was oddly quiet. 'Colic,' I said, and phoned the vet.

Colic in horses or donkeys is a broad term to describe

abdominal pain that can be caused by any number of reasons, from a minor gas build-up in the digestive tract – mild and easily treatable – to more serious impaction in the gut that can require emergency surgery. Whatever sort of colic it turns out to be, a horse has a better chance of recovery the quicker treatment starts.

The vet braved the snow and the steep rutted track to our house and confirmed that Bertie did appear to have the early stages of colic. He gave him a couple of injections – a gut relaxant and a painkiller – and advised he be kept on warm, sloppy food for the next day or so. It wasn't the first time my ever-gluttonous donkey had shown the early signs of colic, but after the injection, he usually recovered quickly, wolfed down his food and bullied Lawrence, his smaller but belligerent stable-mate, to give him his. Lawrence, stubborn and unyielding, would just turn his tail on Bertie and threaten to kick until Bertie gave up and sulked.

As expected, Bertie brightened up pretty quickly after the injection, but although apparently happy and eating again, he didn't seem to make the complete recovery that he had made the last time. Twenty-four hours later, on Christmas Eve, he was much worse. I found him in the stable first thing in the morning looking very sorry for himself indeed. His head was hanging, his ears down and he was trembling as if he was hypothermic. He wouldn't eat anything at all. 'I have a horrible feeling this might be grass sickness,' said the vet, looking grave.

I grew up with horses. I spent my entire childhood until I left home covered in horsehair and shit and wondering why I never had a boyfriend. I had seen, I thought, most things that could happen to a horse, but I had never heard of grass sickness. What's more, the ground had been covered in snow for two weeks. They hadn't had any grass. 'It's a strange disease, that, I have to be honest, we don't really understand and can't even make a firm diagnosis until post mortem.'

I looked at him. Did I understand him right? Was this the end for Bertie?

'If that is what it is, then I'm afraid so. I've never known a horse recover from it. It is the shaking in his hindquarters that makes me think that's what it is, but I could be wrong. We'll give him another gut relaxant and I'll leave you with painkillers to give him over the next few days. Let's see how he gets on.'

'Is it contagious?' I asked.

'Doesn't seem to be,' said the vet. 'I've been on a yard with twenty horses and only one will have grass sickness.'

It was with much trepidation that I approached the stable on Christmas morning, dreading the sight that might await me. As I walked across the field I called them. Two heads appeared over the door. Bertie looked completely normal, his eyes bright, no trembling – and he did his usual trick of trying to shove past me to get into the shed and raid the feed bin. It was a beautiful day, cold and crisp, the sky clear blue. I hung their hay net on a tree in the paddock by the stable and they both cantered out into the snow, prancing and snorting.

'He's going to be all right,' I said to Ludo delightedly, but my delight was short-lived. On Boxing Day morning I found him lying on his side in the stable, covered in sweat, eyes wide, his pain and panic palpable. His stomach was horribly distended and I knew there was nothing that could be done to save him. I held his head in my lap, tears running down my face, as the vet injected him with a lethal dose of antibiotic and in moments his suffering was over.

Bertie's body was taken away by the kindly gentleman Jim and Kate Beavan call the Dead Stock Man. There's a saying that goes 'where's there's livestock, there's dead stock,' and since the catastrophes of foot and mouth and BSE, farmers are no longer allowed to dispose of their dead stock on the farm. In the old days, dead lambs would be left in the fields to be scavenged by raptors and ravens, but lowland farms are not allowed to do this any more. Lambing time is a busy one for the dead stock man. This Christmas had been too. 'Seen a lot of grass sickness this year,' he said. 'Taken several horses away just this week.'

I can't imagine a time ever being unaffected by losing an animal. The demise of anything in your care is hard to bear, even if, like Roger, our ancient cockerel, it is old and its time has come. It didn't matter that there was nothing I could have done to prevent Bertie getting grass sickness and nothing more I could have done to save him. I felt responsible for the death of an animal that should have lived for many more years and my tears continued to fall as the dead stock man drove away with the body of my dear, funny donkey hidden under a tarpaulin.

And losing Bertie also meant losing Lawrence. Lawrence, who had remained apparently unmoved by the morning's proceedings, was now on his own. Donkeys need company, preferably of other donkeys, and so we loaded him into the trailer and drove him down the hill back to the rescue centre. 'We've got a waiting list of people wanting donkeys,' we were told. 'He'll soon find another home.'

Some months later I was in the local farm supplies shop when a woman approached me. 'Are you Kate?' she asked.

I confessed I was.

'I think I've got your donkey!'

'Lawrence?' I asked, delightedly.

'Yes,' she said. 'Isn't he adorable? We love him.'

'I'm so pleased he's found a good home. Does he sidle up and rest the weight of his head on your shoulder when he wants something?'

She nodded. 'He does. And he can be horribly grumpy at times, but he'll do anything for a ginger biscuit.'

With no donkeys we suddenly had grazing and a shed that needed new occupants. 'I think,' said Ludo, tactfully, 'we should think about getting something a bit more practical than donkeys.'

I gave him a hurt look.

'I know you loved them,' he said, 'but you've got to admit they were a lot more high maintenance than we thought. We've got enough land for a few sheep and if we ever get the farm we can think about having more.'

Thanks to two series of *Lambing Live* I not only felt more confident about keeping and breeding sheep, I also knew I had a big decision to make: choosing us the right breed of sheep.

'Swaledales!' said Andrew Marston. 'That's what you need.'

His father disagreed. 'You want some lovely Beltex,' he said. 'Fine sheep. You'll not regret it.'

Much as I liked and admired the Swaledale it was a sheep of the fells; it would seem entirely inappropriate to bring them to the relative lowlands of the Wye Valley and keep them cooped up in just a few acres. And much as I like and admire Donald, his fixation with Beltex sheep is a mystery. They are horrid-looking little things, with great square heads, bodies like barrels with a leg at each corner and a habit of grunting like a pig. In fact, I said to Andrew one day when we had gone out to catch the Beltex ram, they look more like pigs than sheep. Andrew agreed. 'Can't see the appeal of them myself, but Dad's got a soft spot for them.'

They may look ungainly, with a gait like an over-large woman with too many shopping bags, but even lame, as this ram was, they are almost impossible to catch. It was Rachel who finally brought him down, with a rugby tackle that would have floored a Welsh International, but it took both her and Andrew to hold him, snorting and grunting in outrage, as I trimmed his foot and injected him for foot rot. And, as I was to discover when it came to lambing time, the lambs made things difficult for their mothers even before they were born. It was the single lambs that caused the biggest problems, and I sincerely hoped I would not be called on to deliver one on my own. Single lambs are, under-standably, often born bigger than twins. A Beltex is quite a small sheep, but it is solidly put together and the lambs emerge like little Tonka toys – that is, if you can get them out at all. The twins are easier because they are smaller, but even Rachel with her small hands and years of experience would struggle and often fail to lamb a single Beltex.

'It's the shoulders,' she said, breathlessly, one after-noon when I had had to call her into the lambing shed for help. We were both sitting in the straw; I was at the head of the increasingly stressed ewe, trying to keep her calm and still, while Rachel was struggling at the back end doing everything she could think of to get her lamb out. It wouldn't budge and the stress to both ewe and lamb could cause either or both to die.

'We'll have to take her to the vet,' said Rachel, resignedly. She was one of eight Beltex ewes that had Caesareans while I was there. At £40 a time I just couldn't see how it made economic sense, but, pointed out Donald, the lambs make a good weight very quickly. In just a few months they would be worth double that and more. But I wouldn't have him or Andrew or Rachel on hand to help if I had a Beltex lamb that had got wedged, Winnie-the-Pooh style, on my land and so, I told Donald, regretfully, Beltexes were just not for me.

Jim Beavan suggested I have Welsh mules, like his. 'Hardy, good lambers, will lamb perfectly well outdoors if that's what you want to do, easy to look after.'

'Yes,' I said to Jim, 'if you're built like a Polynesian warrior. Your ewes weigh more than me. You must remember the shearing.' Jim let out his great, guffawing belly laugh at the memory of trying to teach me to shear.

Watching someone like Jim shear a sheep is a joy. It is an art, a dance as fluid and intimate as a waltz. Jim has sheared tens of thousands of sheep in his lifetime and can transform something akin to a woolly mammoth into a sleek, close-cut beauty in less than a minute. It took me more time than that to get the sheep into the right position to start shearing. Sheep have a reputation for being a bit dim but they always know when there is someone with little or no experience attempting to persuade them to do something they don't want to. It is all too easy for an eighty-kilogram ewe to take one look at a sixty-kilogram woman, dig her toes in, and think, 'Now try and turn me on my back, kiddo.' Even when I did manage to get her there and drag her, apparently resigned, out on to the shearing board, tucking one of her front legs between my legs, as Jim showed me, and clamping her head between my knees, she would wait until the clippers were whirring and I was just beginning to feel a bit more confident before she did a little wriggle, a swift kick, and she was away, half bald, fleece trailing, back to her friends. I could almost hear them laughing.

No, I needed something smaller, but not too small. Our neighbours have Shetland sheep and the lambs take at least eighteen months to reach slaughter weight. My plan was to buy a few ewes that I would breed. I would keep any ewe lambs to build up the flock and we would eat or sell the ram lambs. I didn't want to have to feed a lot of lambs over the winter, so I needed something bigger than a Shetland, but ideally a Welsh breed that wouldn't give me a hernia every time I tried to trim its feet. And, I confess, I wanted nice-looking sheep; not a heavy-set, square-jawed Texel or a rather pink, bald-looking Charollais, however good they are for meat. I needed to be practical but because I wasn't buying sheep in order to make a living, I didn't need to be commercial. The Balwen is a lovely looking Welsh sheep with a black fleece, a striking white face and white socks, but it is small. Then there is the Kerry Hill, another Welsh breed originating in nearby Powys. Again it is striking looking – white-fleeced with black circles around its eyes and a black muzzle, but a bit bigger than I wanted. So we went to see a local breeder who was slowly building up various flocks of sheep that he thought would be appealing to smallholders and it was there I found my perfect sheep.

The Badger Face Welsh Mountain Sheep is a hardy upland breed and an excellent lamber, often producing twins and sometimes triplets. The rams don't grow to be much bigger than a very manageable fifty-five kilo-grams, and the ewes tend to weigh about ten kilos less. The lambs will reach slaughter weight before the end of the year and both meat and wool are good. And they are undeniably good looking. There are two subspecies – the Torddu, which translates as 'black bellied', and the Torwen, 'white bellied'. It was the Torddu I liked, with their creamy fleeces, the black stripe running down the throat to the belly, black legs and wonderful Frida Kahlo eyebrows. 'I haven't really got any to sell yet,' said the breeder. 'Maybe next year?'

But I was impatient, as ever. After two series of *Lambing Live* I was keen to put to use all that experience, all the lessons I'd been taught, maybe even lamb my own ewes the following spring. The breeder was very understanding. 'Phone the breed society,' he suggested. 'They might be able to help you.'

The Secretary of the Badger Face Welsh Mountain Sheep Society, Peter Weale, and his wife Sheila, live on a small, pretty farm just beyond the Royal Welsh Showground. 'Of course, I'm biased,' he said on the phone, when I explained why I thought these sheep were a good choice for me, 'but I think you are right. They are a very good sheep for someone like you. They won't need too much looking after and they're a good, manageable size. I'm very happy to ask any of our members if they've got any young ewes they'd like to sell and in the meantime why don't you and Ludo come and see our sheep and learn a bit about them?'

Peter's career was not in farming but in the diplo-matic service. Sheep came with retirement and finally being able to settle in one place after a professional life that had him permanently on the move. He, too, fell for the Torddu, he told us. We followed him from the house into his rather beautiful yard, with barns on three sides, enclosing a courtyard where May, Peter's pretty collie, lay, head on her paws, waiting to be given a job to do. She was up in one lithe movement, almost before Peter called her, and trotted ahead of us, full of purpose and self-importance.

'I started with just a few, exactly as you plan to do. Now I've got about 200,' he laughed. 'Beware!'

The sheep were skittish; 'they're all youngsters,' said Peter, 'haven't been handled much.' But they were no match for May, who quietly, gently, separated off a few from the rest of the flock and drove them through the gate and into the yard. Peter showed me what to look for, how to check their feet and their teeth. A sheep can be aged simply by looking at its teeth. Like a child a lamb will develop milk teeth at a few months old. They have a neat row of eight at the front of their bottom jaw and no teeth at all on the top, which is a hard pad which works with the bottom teeth to allow them to pluck the grass and then grind it up with their back molars. Once they are a year old, two of the milk teeth will be replaced by two larger adult teeth. In the their second year the same thing will happen and so on until they become what is known as 'full-mouthed' at four years old. After that they start to lose their teeth, becoming 'broken-mouthed' or 'brokers'. At that stage it is less easy to age them exactly but you will know they are older than four and in the latter years of their lives.

We thanked Peter profusely for his time. 'I'll phone you when I've tracked some down,' he said, waving us off. A week or so later he did as he promised, 'but,' he said, 'I just can't find anyone who wants to sell any youngsters at the moment. I'm really sorry. The only thing I can suggest is if you want to buy some of mine.'

'I can't do that,' I said. 'I don't want to take sheep off you if you don't want to sell. Please don't feel you have to do that. I can wait.'

'I'm happy to sell you half a dozen,' said Peter. 'I just didn't want you to think the Secretary of the Society was pushing you to buy his sheep without seeing if there were other members with stock to sell first. And I'll ask one of our members to come along when you choose. He has kept Badger Face sheep for years and is also a very well-respected judge of the breed, so he'll be able to give you some unbiased advice on which ones to pick.'

A few days later, I was back at Peter's farm. Reversing a trailer is not something you want to do in front of anyone, least of all the owner of the sheep you are about to load into that trailer. I now had six ewes, hand-picked and approved, waiting to be driven to their new home, if only I could get the trailer somewhere near the gate of their pen without jack-knifing it for the umpteenth time. Peter, unfailingly polite as ever, made no comment, nor would he have dreamt of asking if I would like him to reverse it for me. Female pride is a terrible thing. Getting redder and redder and more and more flustered and still no closer to the gate I finally conceded that reversing trailers was beyond me and unless we all wanted to stand there for the rest of the day, I should take Peter up on his unspoken offer to put me out of my misery. He reversed it with enviable speed and accuracy, we dropped the ramp, the ewes skipped in and I closed up the back and shook Peter by the hand. 'Let me know how you get on!' he called and waved me off as I drove my precious cargo down the drive.

Chapter 9

ˈTwo Farmers And A Phone Callˈ

It had seemed, a year ago, to be a relatively tame ambition – to have a few sheep and a bit more land, and we had in that time been partly successful. We now had sheep at home; the six Badger Face ewes had survived the journey and without the pressure of an audience I had managed, with only a couple of botched attempts, to reverse the trailer up to the gateway of the field and let down the ramp so they could walk out straight into their new home. The field I put them in slopes gently down to a bigger, much steeper field, edged by large, mature trees that overhang the fence, providing plenty of shade and shelter. It has a magnificent view, out over the forests of the Wye Valley to the patchwork of fields below the sharp ridge of Offa's Dyke. Not that the ewes seemed remotely impressed. As soon as they were back on the grass, they put their heads down and started to munch.

Of course, once they were out in the field with several acres to scamper about in, I did worry that I might never get near them again. Badger and Bella may be good at playing Frisbee and, in Bella's case, chasing – but never catching – squirrels, but neither of them was going to be the slightest use when it came to rounding up sheep. Badger is scared of most things and when the sheep arrived he quickly added them to his ever-increasing list of Things To Be Avoided. Bella, in common with many small animals, and people for that matter, is all bravado, but, when challenged, is almost as much of a wimp as Badger. Despite this, one of her most endearing traits is she thinks everything is a potential playmate. She disappeared one day and eventually I tracked her down to one of our sheds. She was standing, tail wagging furiously, letting out little squeaks and barks of excitement, her eyes fixed on a cat that had come over from the farm to have a quiet sleep on a pile of old boxes. The cat, unfazed and unimpressed, didn't move, merely glared balefully, with the occasional hiss of annoyance at this irritating intruder that had had the audacity to wake her up. Bella didn't move. She didn't chase or threaten the cat, she just stood, and wagged, and yelped and hoped, in vain, that the cat might change its mind, unfurl itself from its cardboard hammock and play.

She thought sheep could be fun too. Out-of-control dogs are the bane of farmers' lives and living where we do, surrounded by other people's livestock, it was vital that any dog we owned knew how to behave around animals. Badger was no problem at all, terrified of any potential encounter and sticking close to our heels. Bella, the first time she saw sheep, was off, tail up, bounding across the field towards them, only to increase her speed when they scattered in fright. I yelled at her. 'COME HERE NOW!' and she stopped in her tracks and turned to look at me. 'COME HERE!' Dogs know when they've done something wrong. Bella slunk back, tail between her legs, and settled at my feet, eyes wide, brown and sorrowful, which of course made me want to laugh. 'NEVER DO THAT AGAIN!' I said, loudly and firmly. She looked even more abashed, cowering in the grass. And she never did.

Sometime later we were walking the dogs with a friend through a field of his sheep when one of that year's lambs, now several months old and weaned, caught sight of us and charged towards us, bleating at the top of its lungs. 'It was bottle fed,' explained our friend, 'so whenever it sees people, it assumes it's going to be fed.' The lamb skidded to a halt at our feet, still bleating. Badger tucked himself swiftly behind Ludo's legs; Bella too, was rather shocked by this sudden, noisy arrival and ran off. The lamb took one look at her, and perhaps thinking that she was the one with the food, set off in hot pursuit. The sight of a small brown terrier being chased across a field by a large, bleating lamb was too much. We laughed until we cried, but poor Bella never got over it. Like Badger, she now views sheep with deep suspicion and sticks to squirrels. Any fantasies I may have had about re-enacting *One Man and his Dog* with six ewes and a couple of mongrels have long since been quashed.

One day I would love to try and train a working sheep dog but for the time being I am making do with the next best thing – a bucket and some sheep nuts. Peter Weale, who had sold me the ewes, had suggested that although there was no need to feed them, if I got them in the habit of coming up for a bit of feed every morning, it would make my daily task of checking them over much easier. He was right. It took barely a week for them to come running across the field in answer to my call and the rattle of the bucket while Badger and Bella sat at a safe distance on the other side of the fence.

But we still didn't have the farm. Once our triumphant hearing by the council committee in July was over, we had telephoned Andrew, our lawyer, to tell him that the council had agreed that we could buy the farm as a whole, and that it wouldn't go to auction.

'That's great news,' he said. 'Yes, there can be objections, but as support was unanimous you should be OK. Anyone who does want to object has to do so within two weeks. At the moment there is nothing more you can do. Go and have a holiday and we'll talk when you're back.'

Oddly, we didn't celebrate the council's decision. In part, the whole thing had taken much longer than we expected and we didn't leave the council building until after seven in the evening. We had to race home, throw our bags and the dogs in the camper van and tear down to Poole to try and get into the campsite we'd booked before it closed its gates for the night. The next morning, we were up at five to get the first ferry over to Cherbourg and then had an eight-hour drive to get to where we were staying, something neither of us relished doing with a hangover.

Two weeks in rural France with the dogs and almost no way of making contact with the outside world was exactly what we needed. We walked miles, swam in rivers, shopped in markets, read books, and tried, not terribly successfully, to avoid thinking about the farm. I found myself unable to shake a pervading feeling of anxiety that while we were sitting outside our cabin in the woods, eating bread and cheese and indulging in a fair amount of daytime drinking, a plot was being hatched in a Monmouthshire corridor that would bring an end to the whole madcap scheme.

'Would it be the end of the world?' asked Ludo. 'No one can say we didn't try, that we didn't do everything to save that farm. If it doesn't work, if there are objections and it does go to auction, it doesn't mean we have to ditch the whole idea. We can try and find another farm, somewhere smaller, perhaps, and less controversial. Imagine, never having to deal with the council again . . .'

It was a beguiling thought, but we both knew Ludo was being disingenuous. Finding another farm, the right farm in the right area, would not be easy and it wasn't as if we hadn't already considered that option time and time again. There had been so many incidences when we had been at screaming point with frustration, when the inefficiencies and inconsistencies of dealing with local government made us lose the will to write another email or make another attempt to track down the right person on the phone. We had announced 'If this doesn't work, I give up!' with boring regularity and we had looked for other places, trawled the internet and the farming press, but knowing that our hearts weren't really in it because, inexplicably, our hearts were already lost to this farm; this farm that was quietly disintegrating as the negotiations proceeded with grinding slowness and that even now could be snatched from us at any time. Any celebration would have seemed premature.

The moment the camper van rolled off the ferry and back onto British soil, I turned my phone on and dialled Andrew's number. 'No one has lodged any objections. We are free to proceed with the sale. And all the complicated stuff has been done, the heads of terms have been agreed, so there is no reason for it to take very long. It's August now, and lots of people are on holiday, but even so, there is no conceivable reason I can think of that won't allow the sale to go through by September.'

As we drove back towards home we did a rough calculation. Our business plan, that wonderful, hypothetical document, had imagined that we would start running our first courses in the spring of 2012, an idea that had seemed ever more absurd as time went on. But now that Andrew had said the sale would be complete by September, perhaps we really did have a chance. We had, back in April, in a flurry of optimism, engaged the services of a local architect. He had already done surveys of the house and the barn, produced some proposed plans for the house and was working on ideas for the barn. If we could agree everything, we could apply for planning permission as soon as the sale went through and maybe even start work before Christmas. As we didn't intend to do anything extensive to either building, we imagined the work might take a couple of months – three at most – and we could, quite possibly, be ready for business in, say April.

'I'll phone the architect and see if we can set up a meeting as soon as possible,' I said, as drove over the border into Wiltshire, 'and I'll call Jim and Kate Beavan and see if they know anyone who might want to be our tenants.'

Paul, who looks after our house and animals when we are away, was at the kitchen door to meet us. 'You're all over the local press!' he said, grinning. 'Front page and everything!'

'What?' I said, dumping a box of wine on the table. 'Why?'

'You've caused a right old hoo-haa about the farm. I've kept the papers for you.'

A chill ran through me. I don't usually have much call to be in the papers, being rather dull and not spending my time falling drunk out of nightclubs or snogging footballers married to someone else. If I'm in the papers at all, it is usually to tell people about the plight of something teetering on the brink of extinction or give advice on what to feed garden birds in the grip of a hard winter. The front page article, together with a rather cheesy photograph of me looking characteristically unbrushed, was innocuous enough – a straight account, without comment, of the council proceedings culminating in the decision to allow the sale of the farm to us to proceed. The letters page was a different story, with people accusing us of skulduggery, cheating the council out of money, using my 'status' to unfair advantage and planning to bring in hordes of visitors that would destroy the tranquillity of the village.

'It'll blow over,' everyone told us. 'It's just jealousy, or suspicion that some dodgy deal has gone on because "you're that woman off the telly". They don't know you've been talking to the council about this for months. For them it's come out of the blue. Perhaps you should hold a public meeting, so that people can hear your version of events and what your plans are for the farm.'

It was a good idea. The farm is on the outskirts of a village with a large, well-appointed village hall. We decided to set a date for mid October. By then the farm would be ours and we would be able to give anyone who turned up a true and accurate picture of our intentions. In the meantime two things were becoming increasingly urgent – we had to find tenants and the grass was in desperate need of a cut.

For the past few weeks, during any spell of sustained dry weather, every tractor in the county was out in the fields towing a mower or a baler. The lanes were full of slow-moving vehicles hauling trailers piled high with new bales and the air was full of the intoxicating summer smell of drying grass. Both hay and silage – cut grass wrapped in plastic before it is fully dry and allowed to ferment – are valuable crops. If a farm has livestock, it will be the hay and silage they produce that will feed the animals through the winter. Any surplus can be sold for good money.

At the farm there was 100 acres of land that hadn't been grazed for at least eight months. The whole place looked like the Serengeti after the rains – every field a sea of rippling waist-high grass. The problem was if it wasn't cut in time, it would get wet and sodden, cover the ground in an impenetrable rotten blanket and destroy the grazing for the following year. Not only that, but cut and baled that grass was worth thousands of pounds, income surely the council didn't want to see go to waste. But no one seemed willing to do anything about it. We phoned, we emailed, we begged, we pleaded, we offered to arrange someone to cut it on the council's behalf, we pointed out that although it was obviously in our interest that the land not be in a state of ruin when we took on the farm, the council had far more to gain by cutting the grass and selling it than they did by doing nothing at all.

While all this was going on Kate Beavan sent me a

text. 'Jim and I think we've got the perfect people for you.'

I phoned her immediately. 'Do you think they would really consider it,' I asked Kate, 'given all the negative stuff that's been in the press?'

'Well,' said Kate, 'they rent land close to you now, so they know all about it, and we've obviously told them all about you' – 'and what a nightmare you are!' shouted Jim from the background – 'and they're still interested. Do you want to ring them?'

There are some occasions when you meet new people for the first time and you immediately feel you've known each other your whole lives. That was how it was when we met Tim and Sarah Stephens. Sarah had been born and brought up in mid Wales, Tim in the valleys that had once been the mining heartland of the country. They had met at the local agricultural college, where they had been at the same time as Jim's brother Huw. Tim was training to be a dairyman, with the idea that he would then go and work on his uncle's dairy farm; Sarah was training to be a farm secretary. They got together at college, but not until the very end of their four years because, as Tim said, he was too busy playing rugby and too shy to ask Sarah out.

By the time they left college the milk quota had been introduced, restricting the amount of milk any single farm could produce, and dairy farms had to cut back on staff. Tim no longer had a job at his uncle's farm and had to take odd jobs labouring, fencing or shearing on local farms to make ends meet. Sarah stayed on at the college to work in their office. They got married, put themselves on the waiting list for a council farm and started to save in the hope they could eventually buy some livestock of their own.

They never got a council farm, but after two decades of hard work and hard saving they had a flock of 200 Welsh ewes and a small herd of Hereford cattle. They rented 150 acres of land from a farmer just a few miles from the farm we were still yet to own, but as there was no house, they had to find one to rent as close to the land as possible. They found somewhere, but it was a good five miles away. Not far, but not ideal, particularly at lambing time, when more often than not they would sleep in their Land Rover. Sarah was still working part time at a local veterinary surgery and Tim was still doing contracting work and the land was rented on what is known as a grazing licence, renewed on an annual basis, offering them no long-term security or ability to apply for grants. To be sure of any kind of future in farming, they needed to find a farm where they could live and be guaranteed enough time there to make it worth investing in the infrastructure. We could offer them that . . . if they didn't mind the fact that we proposed to be there most days, that the farm would be open to the public on the days we run courses, that the house over the months that it had been unoccupied had become uninhabitable, that most of the fencing and many of the gates needed replacing, that the farmyard was a mass of weeds, that the old sheep race had completely disintegrated and there was the small matter that we still didn't technically own it.

They came to see it. 'Grass needs cutting,' said Tim, as he waded across the field behind the house. I recounted our still as-yet-unresolved battle with the council to get it done.

'I'll do it,' said Tim. 'Won't take long. They can pay me and sell the hay, or I'll do it and keep the hay as payment.'

'I'll suggest it,' I said. 'But what do you think, would this farm work for you?'

Amazingly, joyfully, they said it was just what they had dreamt of, that they'd given up on ever getting a council farm and farms the size they could afford rarely became available for rent. Their current grazing licence ran out in November. They could move in, livestock and all, at the beginning of December.

'Hopefully,' I said, 'work will have started on the house, but it might not quite be ready by early December. Is that a problem?'

'Not at all,' said Sarah. 'Some friends of ours have a static caravan they lived in while their house was being done. They've moved out of it now, so we could borrow that.'

'At last,' I said to Ludo with a heavy sigh, 'something that has gone right.'

Ludo nodded thankfully. Meeting Tim and Sarah and them agreeing to be our tenants was the best thing that had happened during this whole sorry saga. And sorry saga it continued to be. Andrew the lawyer was coming up against all sorts of unfathomable delays and 'paperwork issues' which meant our oh-so-simple sale was proving to be a lot more drawn-out and worrisome than he had anticipated. And the grass still remained uncut, despite the fact I had relayed Tim's offer to go and do it for them. It was explained to me that as we didn't own the farm yet, we weren't allowed to cut the grass unless we had a grazing licence that would allow us to rent the farm until we bought it. Fine, I said, issue us a licence and we will pay you rent until the sale goes through. A licence was issued, we signed it, it was sent back and the next day we had a call. It transpired the council was not allowed to just issue us with a grazing licence. It had to go out to tender and be pitched for. I covered up the phone and let out a short, sharp scream. Recovering my composure only barely, I reiterated that for many, many weeks we had been asking them to get the grass cut **FOR THEIR OWN BENEFIT**, that we had found someone to do it for them, offered to do it ourselves, considered, increasingly seriously, breaking onto the farm in the middle of the night with a mower and just doing it. Anything to get it done. 'The forecast is good for the next week,' I said, having become as obsessed with checking the weather as any farmer, 'you must get that grass cut NOW.'

No one likes to be a nag, but as I always say to Ludo when he gives me that 'don't nag me!' look, nagging wouldn't be necessary if things got done on first asking. The grass at the farm was finally cut, the bales stacked in the barns and out in the field. Tim didn't do it. The council got a contractor to do it at vast expense, but by then I didn't care. The grazing would not be ruined; there'd be grass for Tim and Sarah's livestock.

By October we had had several more meetings with the architect and plans for the barn were taking shape. One end would be a teaching room, the other a kitchen and dining room. We would repair the old barn across the courtyard and in it would house pet lambs, or farrowing pigs or any animals that we wanted people to be able to get close to during the courses. Worryingly there was talk of things like copper cladding, and rather more extensive additions to the barn than we had anticipated, all of which sounded expensive and not entirely necessary, but assuming the whole thing would be costed before we gave the go-ahead, we decided to let the plans take shape and rein them in if we needed to.

Our other concerns were rather more pressing, namely the swift approach of the public meeting in the village hall with still no progress on the sale. We wondered whether we should cancel the meeting altogether, but decided, on balance, that wouldn't be a good idea.

'It's not our fault the sale hasn't gone through,' said Ludo. 'We'll have to be honest with whoever turns up and say this is the situation but our actual plans remain the same and this is what they are.'

'Perhaps no one will turn up,' I said, hopefully. 'The letter writers seem to have stopped and there's been nothing in the press. Maybe it's all been forgotten about and people would rather stay in on a wet October night with bottle of wine and *Coronation Street*.'

There was standing-room only. Every seat was taken and people stood crowded at the back, spilling out into the corridor. I have never felt quite so uneasy about anything. Unsure what on earth we were supposed to do, we had found ourselves at the door of the hall, shaking hands with people as they came in, feeling like low-grade politicians or parents of the bride. Most people introduced themselves as they came in, appeared friendly; some didn't. One man arrived, in contrast to everyone else wrapped up in their winter woollies, in a rather sharp suit with a snake-like sheen and no tie. He was carrying a clipboard. It was leather-ette, I noted, with the same cheap shine as his suit. His eyes didn't meet mine. 'Trouble,' I thought. And he was. The moment we had introduced ourselves, explained that the sale hadn't gone through but was expected to in the next week or two, outlined our plans and asked for comments or questions he took the floor. Many of his questions concerned the proce-dure we had gone through or not gone through to allow what he saw as a flagrant flouting of the rules, resulting in cheating the council out of hundreds of thousands of pounds.

Unfortunately these were questions we were simply not in a position to answer. It needed to be done by someone from the council who was not only aware of correct procedure but fully briefed on our case. Needless to say, no one from the council, even the local councillor who lived practically next door, had deigned to show up. Neither had the local MP or member of the Welsh Assembly Government, both of whom we had been to visit and who had given their enthusiastic support. We kept telling him that his questions were a matter for the council and not us until he changed tack. He accused us of trying to set up something akin to a theme park; that we had claimed to the council that our enterprise might bring in as many as 30,000 visitors a year. Out came the clipboard with a flourish. He'd done some calculations and told the room how many coaches that equated to, how many cars per minute would use the lane, how much traffic that would bring into the village, the disruption, the chaos, the high potential for there to be more accidents. On and on he went. I had a fleeting vision of marching up to him, seizing his clipboard, smacking him across the face with it and walking out, but instead I stood there listening to him twist our plans, pick apart our ideas, accuse us of misleading and cheating until the clock struck eight. Our time was up.

'Well,' I said with a weak smile to the silent crowd, 'thanks for coming.'

At that point a woman right at the back stood up. 'Oh God,' I thought. 'Not more.'

'I'd just like to say that some of us think what you're

doing is great and we'd like to welcome you to the village.' I bit the inside of my cheek hard to stop the tears that were dangerously close to falling.

'Thank you,' I said, barely audible over the scrape of chairs being moved back and the room beginning to empty. A few people came up to us quietly to confess that they liked the idea too. A few were acutely embarrassed by the antics of the clipboard man. 'He's not from the village,' they said, earnestly, 'we don't know who he is.'

The local paper the following week reported overwhelming support for 'TV star's farm project' at village meeting. 'Christ,' I said to Ludo, 'what the hell do they do if they object to something?'

'Just forget about it,' said Ludo, slightly irritably. 'I know it was a pretty horrible evening, but actually the paper is right. Most people do support the idea; it's always the ones that have something negative to say that speak out. Forget about that bloody man with a clipboard. We've got other things to worry about.'

Like the sale. Which still hadn't gone through. I dialled the by now all-too-familiar number and the woman who was in charge of handling the sale answered the phone. 'I just wondered,' I said, as neutrally as I could, 'how things were progressing? It is getting close to the end of October and I'm slightly concerned that if things don't get a move on, our tenants and all their livestock will end up homeless.'

'Urgh, well,' she stuttered, 'the sale won't go through until you've got planning permission.'

'What?' I said, trying to keep calm.

She repeated herself.

'WHAT?' I shouted, all semblance of calm gone,

'WHAT THE HELL DO YOU MEAN IT WON'T GO THROUGH UNTIL WE'VE GOT PLANNING PERMISSION? WHEN WAS THAT DECIDED?'

'Um, well, we, err, sort of assumed you wouldn't want to go ahead with the sale until you knew you had permission to do what you want to the buildings.'

I was dumbfounded, speechless, my brain a scramble of confusion. Had we ever said anything about buying the farm only when we had planning permission? Had that been what Andrew advised? Was I going mad? 'We have never, NEVER said that we would only buy the farm once planning consent had been given,' I managed to say, my throat dry with shock. 'Why the hell would we have said to Tim and Sarah that they could hand in their notice and move in in December if that was the case?'

'Well,' the embarrassment evident in her voice, 'I'm afraid that is the only way the sale is going to go through now.' I hung up and broke down. A year of meetings, negotiations and plans. Of dreams and hopes. Of endless time and not an insignificant amount of money spent on architects and legal fees and accountants. All wasted. All for nothing. And worse, what would happen to Tim and Sarah? We'd promised them so much and now we were going to let them down in the most devastating way possible. They had already handed in their notice and as far as we knew someone else was lined up to take on the grazing licence. It was nearly winter. Where the hell would they go?

'Andrew?' I said, trying, and failing, to sound normal.

'What the hell's happened?'

I managed, between sobs, to tell him.

'Right,' he said, firmly, in that utterly capable this-is-why-lawyers-matter voice, 'this is ridiculous. Nothing has been said about this before; it has come completely out of the blue. Leave it to me.'

'I give up, Andrew, I really do. It's bad enough for us, but Tim and Sarah . . .' I trailed off.

'Don't give up yet,' he said. 'Phone everyone you've been dealing with at the council and I'll phone their lawyers. We need a meeting with everyone present and we need it urgently.'

I phoned and left increasingly manic messages with everyone. I texted, I emailed and then I did it all again until I'd heard back from them all and a date was set for the meeting. Ludo came home and we sat in a state of disbelief. 'This is just . . .' Words failed him. 'But we must tell Tim and Sarah, it's not fair to keep them in the dark.'

We sat in a beige office in the council building with Andrew waiting to be called through into the meeting room. We had made the unequivocal decision that if the sale was unable to go through without further delay we would pull out. We had sat down with Tim and Sarah and told them everything. They had been incredibly understanding. There had been no histrionics, no dramas; they would have a word with their landlord and see if they could keep the licence if the sale did fall through. They would make a plan, create a safety net. It would be OK. By the time we were led into the office for the meeting I felt that satisfying sense of calm that only comes with a modicum of control. If they wanted us to buy the farm it would have to be on our terms and if, for whatever reason, that wasn't possible, we would simply walk away.

We never got to the bottom of the council's unexplained, unannounced ruling that the sale could only go through once planning permission had been granted.

Perhaps someone, somewhere was trying to save face or buy time or ensure re-election, who knows? Andrew was brilliant, calmly and methodically working through everything so that not only did the planning consent issue disappear, but we also emerged with a clear plan and a fixed date for completion.

Three weeks later, over a year since our very first meeting with the council and since Ros and Arthur had left the farm, we were sitting on the sofa waiting for the phone to ring. Badger lay between us, head resting on his paws, watchful and aware something was up. Bella had climbed up onto a cushion on the other sofa, and was now lying upside-down, legs akimbo, her eyes firmly closed and a look of untroubled bliss on her face. We, by contrast, were anything but relaxed. Outside, November rain fell against the windows, driven into the glass by a blustery autumn wind. It was a cold, dank afternoon, but we hadn't lit a fire, or turned on any of the lights. We just sat, in a state of almost suspended animation, not talking, not looking at each other, hardly breathing. Waiting. Waiting. The ring of the telephone made us both jump. Ludo picked it up and passed it to me in one, quick, urgent movement as if it was red hot. 'You answer it.'

I pressed the button. My throat was dry. 'Hello?'

'It's happened,' said Andrew's voice. 'The sale is complete. The farm is yours.'

'Is it too late to change our minds?' I asked. There was a pause as Andrew tried to work out whether I was serious or not. I didn't know myself.

'Yes,' he said, in his no-nonsense-or-it-will-cost-you-a-fortune voice. 'It is too late. Go and have a drink.'

Chapter 10

Work Starts At Last

Our quest for a 'few more acres' had now been realised but as we stood somewhat shell-shocked in the
gateway of what was now 'our' farm, it did strike us
that we had rather more land than we had bargained
for. Almost exactly four years earlier I had walked out
of my study, shut the door and taken the three steps
it required to cross the entire expanse of what then
constituted the sum total of land we could claim as
ours. It was, however, the start of a journey that would
take me through the kitchen where I paused to pick

up a bag and out of the front door of our London terraced house for the last time. Did I have the slightest inkling then that this journey, a move from city to countryside, would be any more than a geographical shift which gave us more space, cleaner air and further to drive to the nearest shop? Of course not. Ludo was going to continue working as a television producer. I would carry on presenting. We might have a dog and a few chickens, we would be able to go for long, beautiful walks straight from our back door; life would be enhanced but fundamentally not that different.

Thanks to time, fate and a strange kind of love affair, not so much with the farm but the *principle* of the farm – its history, its place in rural society – the latter part of those few short years had seen our lives change exponentially. Ludo had given up his career; we had plundered our savings, re-mortgaged and tied our futures to 117 acres of Monmouthshire countryside and some dilapidated buildings. We were beyond the brink of a time that people might describe as 'life-changing', already on the scree slope that would see us scrabbling and slipping towards who knows what. 'Thank God,' I said to Ludo, as we leant on 'our' gate, looking out across 'our' fields, 'we're not doing this alone.'

When we were able to present Tim and Sarah Stephens with the tenancy agreement drawn up by Andrew and they signed it, it felt almost more pivotal than when Andrew phoned to say the sale had finally gone through and we were the new owners of the farm. Their knowledge and experience felt a bit like a security blanket; they gave us confidence that we couldn't entirely mess things up, because their future was as wrapped up in this farm as ours was. But having the keys and the bit of paper that said the farm is ours, and having Tim and Sarah signed up as tenants, did not mean that overnight life suddenly became simple.

If all the farm needed to thrive in the modern rural world was for us to get up at five o'clock in the morning, stick on a pair of boots and a waterproof coat with baler twine and a penknife in the pocket, carry some heavy sacks and drive a piece of machinery with satis-fyingly big tyres and a throaty diesel engine, its future would be assured. But life, whether on the land or not, is never that straightforward.

The restoration of the main stone barn and the repairs to the house were a priority, particularly as Tim and Sarah would be moving to the farm in December. They had bought their friend's static caravan, so they had somewhere to live on site while work was being done on the house, but if the winter was to turn out to be anything like the last two, with a month or more of heavy snow and temperatures of minus ten and less, Ludo and I wanted to be sure that the caravan was a very short, temporary solution.

Earlier in the year, the architect we had commis-sioned to survey and draw up plans for both house and barn had made a good start. All the measurements had been done and he'd come up with a solution for the house, which as it stood, would win no prizes for beauty or architectural imagination. Probably once a small, stone cottage, typical of the region, with a dairy and a few small outbuildings around it, over the years bits had been joined up or added on, so in its present state it was quite a big house, covered in thick concrete render, painted white, with dark brown PVC window frames and doors and an internal layout that defied reason. The front room that had been Ros and Arthur's kitchen had a staircase that led to the room above, but you could get no further than that. The rest of the house was cut off, reached from another door from the kitchen and another staircase. The old dairy had, at some stage, been incorporated into the main house to become a sort of pantry, behind the kitchen, but it was windowless, low ceilinged, damp and dark.

'It would make much more sense', said the architect, 'to make this two houses. It would split quite naturally with two bedrooms on one side and three on the other. You could rent one side out for holiday lets or something, which would bring in a bit more income. You'll need planning permission to do it, but it would come under change of use, so it shouldn't be too complicated.'

It was a great idea; he showed us some preliminary drawings and we approved them at once. That left the barn.

'Whatever we do,' we said, as we sat in his basement office, 'we don't want the barn to lose its agricultural integrity. We don't want a barn conversion. We don't want to convert it at all. It needs to be waterproof and warm, but the people using it will be coming to do courses on a farm. They'll be wearing wellies. They'll get muddy and rained on. It doesn't need to be sleek, or smart. It needs to be adapted so we can have a classroom, a kitchen and an eating area, but we want to change its appearance as little as possible.'

As time went on and we seemed no closer to owning the farm, our intention to start our first courses the following spring, as it said so confidently in our business plan, seemed ever-more unrealistic. Once the designs were agreed, not only would we need full planning permission, which could take months, particularly if any of the local letter writers chose to object, but also we would have to commission a bat survey before we even applied. Bat surveys require a team of licensed and expert ecologists to survey the buildings, check for any evidence of bat activity, carry out a number of further surveys at dawn and dusk over a period of weeks in the summer and, based on the data they collect, write a lengthy and detailed report, copied to the local planning authority, which not only tells you what species of bat might be using your property, but how many, what they are using it for and what you can, and mostly can't do, if bats are found. Not only does the whole process take several months, but if bats are found in your belfry or anywhere else, it won't only dictate the type of work you are allowed to do – once the requisite licence has been acquired (and more weeks have passed) – but what time of year you are allowed to do it.

It may seem ridiculous that we were forcing the pace and we didn't just accept that things weren't going to happen when we hoped they would, but everything had already taken so much longer than we'd anticipated, it had all been so horribly stressful, that we were afraid that if we weren't able to get going and start generating some sort of income, however small, we'd run out of money, if not enthusiasm for the whole idea. In addition, it began to be apparent that some differences of opinion between ourselves and our architect were beginning to emerge.

I think before engaging an architect people should be required to go on some sort of course. Before a long filming trip to a slightly unpredictable region of the Middle East I had to go on a hostile environments course. I learned all sorts of things like the importance of taking a doorstop with me to shove under my hotel room door to prevent someone undesirable bursting in the night. (Though I couldn't help but feel that although it might stop a wayward drunk, it was unlikely that a £1.99 doorstop from the local hardware shop was going to make a huge difference to someone armed with a bazooka and a couple of hand grenades.) I also discovered that the clever use of a crisp packet and some Sellotape can save the life of a person with a punctured lung (do they have Sellotape in the Yemen?) and that hiding behind a car door when someone is shooting an AK-47 at you might work in the movies but in real life you would be reduced to lifeless pulp in seconds.

I'm not for a moment suggesting that architects are on a par with gun-toting lunatics who will shove a bag on your head and lock you in the boot of a car for the sake of some cash, but in my albeit limited experience, they do have a tendency to turn tricky, even a little volatile, if the idea they have laid out with a flourish in front of their hapless client isn't greeted with rapturous applause.

Things get even more awkward if a client admits to something acutely embarrassing like 'it's a bit beyond my budget', and any sort of working harmony is lost altogether if the idea, that would look so fine on the pages of an industry magazine, is not at all what the client is looking for and the client has the temerity to say so.

In a final, desperate attempt to try and stay on schedule, we suggested to the architect that perhaps we look at a cheap – but still attractive – way to adapt one of the existing tin-roofed barns into a temporary eating and teaching space. He rose to the challenge but after producing drawings told us it would be 'somewhere in the region of £30,000'. We gulped. 'Not really in our budget,' we mumbled.

Once the sale of the farm was complete, we phoned him to say the planning application for the house could go in. 'We haven't done the planning application,' he said. The first drawings were done, but the application would need more detail, as well as the completion of a lengthy questionnaire. It would take a good two or three weeks to do it, and they hadn't done it because we'd said the barn was the priority.

'Yes,' I said wearily, 'but only because we thought you'd done all the work on the house.'

Thoroughly dispirited, we trooped down to his office, checked the plans for the house once again and agreed that completing the application was now the main priority, and designs for the barn would have to be set aside.

'I have got the latest drawings here. You might as well look at them and we can continue to work on them as soon as the application for the house has gone in,' he suggested.

It looked fine, not much changed, exactly as we'd requested, but there was something missing, something that didn't seem quite right. 'Where's the lean-to?' I asked.

Tacked on to one end of the long stone building is a sort of shack made of corrugated iron. It was, no doubt, a cheap, quick-fix solution to store something at some stage during Arthur's time on the farm which had, like all storage space, clearly proved invaluable, and because it hadn't fallen down it had never been replaced by something more permanent. It was a good size and would provide us with useful space. If we replaced it with something the exact same size and in the exact same position, it would not need to be included in the planning application. But the drawings we were looking at missed it off altogether.

'It spoils the elevation,' said the architect, a little petulantly. 'It looks so much better without it.'

'But it is really useful space,' I argued. 'We'll probably have our office in there and even if we don't, it is the perfect place to store extra furniture and all that sort of stuff.'

'Why don't you store it in one of the other barns? There are plenty of them.'

I gritted my teeth. Why was I having to do this, to justify why we wanted something we were utterly within our rights to have? 'We can't store stuff in the other barns', I said, 'because, under the tenancy agreement, those barns are for use by Tim and Sarah. We've got a perfectly practical space available to us already, if you just reinstate it on the plans.'

He wouldn't do it. 'It would ruin it. That's the side of the barn people are going to see first. Why don't you take the plans away, have a good look at them, and think about it.'

We walked away from the office, feeling, as I did with increasingly regularity after these meetings, miserable and compromised. I was cross about the house. I felt let down that he hadn't done the work and annoyed with myself that I hadn't checked, or perhaps made it clear, that we wanted the application to be ready when the sale went through. And I felt awful for Tim and Sarah, whose winter would now unavoidably be spent in a static caravan. But the issue of the lean-to was the final straw.

'I can't work like this any more,' I said to Ludo in the car. 'It's got to the point where I dread having to phone him and I dread these meetings more, and we haven't even started the building work yet.'

'Well,' said Ludo, thoughtfully, 'we've paid him for

the first tranche of work. If you think it is not going to work out, and I have to say I think you're right, now's the time to make the decision.'

I sighed. 'It will take us right back to square one,' I said, miserably. 'We'll have wasted months of time and a huge amount of money. I can't bear it.' But I realised that I also couldn't bear to go and sit in that office again and have another argument over what was best to do with our buildings to make them work for our business. Ludo agreed. Two days after we took ownership of the farm, we sent a letter formally relieving him of the work. Finding another architect went to the top of Ludo's to-do list, together with rejigging the business plan.

We did actually know another architect, who on the face of it would be ideal. Not only an architect, he is a farmer too, so has an intrinsic understanding of how farm buildings work, and what farmers like. His own farm, where he raises sheep and handsome, if errant, Gascon cattle, is barely two miles from ours. He couldn't be more local. But he was, we knew, already pretty stretched. He had not one, but two farms to run, seventy miles apart; he was working on several other architectural projects all of which were at the stage where they demanded more time than he had, and there was the small matter of his much-adored one-year-old daughter. But he also happened to be our friend, Stafford. We had met him and his long-suffering partner Beatrice, known by everyone as Bert (which occasionally leads to a misunderstanding and a raised eyebrow in the more conservative living rooms of Monmouthshire), not long after they moved to the area. Clever, funny and great company, we liked them both immediately. The thought of adding even more to his already impossible workload, and maybe souring the friendship as a result, had been the reason we hadn't asked Stafford to be our architect in the first place.

Ludo and I agonised about asking him now, but we were desperate for work to be able to start on the house. In a couple of weeks, Tim and Sarah would be moving onto the farm.

'I'd love to do it,' said Stafford, with characteristic enthusiasm.

'You don't have to take it all on,' I gabbled. 'I know how busy you are. It's just the house that is urgent. And promise me, if you start to get even a little bit annoyed when I phone you, or Bert thinks you've taken too much on and starts to resent us for it, promise me you'll tell us and we'll make another plan.'

'I promise,' he said. 'Now, shall I see you up at the farm in ten minutes?'

The autumn, which had begun golden and mellow and sun-drenched, had turned. The landscape was no longer ablaze with rich colour, but grey, windblown and just drenched. Winter had come, stripping the leaves, chilling the air and uprooting, on one particularly wild night, one of the old ash trees that stood in the field in front of the house. It lay like a fallen giant, forlorn and broken. 'Well, at least you won't be short of firewood,' remarked Stafford, as we met at the kitchen door.

We walked around. An empty house that hasn't been lived in, even for a few weeks, starts to feel dead. This house had stood empty for over a year. Without people, without their life and warmth, with no windows open to the spring air or fire in the grate on a cold day, it had become as stale and lifeless as a tomb. Many of the walls were stained and mouldy. Stafford looked grave. 'You've got a serious damp problem in here. I'll get on with some measuring and drawings, you see what can be done to get it dried out a bit.'

I googled 'giant de-humidifiers' and unearthed a company with the reassuring name of Dri-Eaz. The upshot of my conversation with a man called Paul, who listened sympathetically to my descriptions of walls oozing moisture like a fat man on a hot day, was the arrival of a lorry, just a couple of days later, full of squat, efficient-looking machines. We plugged them in, trailing their long plastic tubes into any nearby sink or bathtub, and switched them on. Immediately they started whirring and humming; water gathered in the tubes, a few droplets at first but soon it was trickling in a steady stream into the various sinks and tubs. 'See what I mean,' said Stafford. 'A serious damp problem.' And he went back to his drawing board.

If we hadn't realised before the enormity of the project we had taken on, it was all too eye-poppingly apparent now. Day after day Ludo and I walked around the farm, noting the crumbling stone walls, sagging fences and gates hanging off their hinges. Where before we had seen beauty and possibilities, now we saw myriad problems, an insurmountable amount of work and a fast-depleting bank account. We had been so fired up by our righteous mission to 'save the farm' whatever it took, so convinced that running courses would require little in the way of infrastructure and would quite quickly start to bring in a bit of income, that we had overlooked the fact that the farm we had first seen over eighteen months before was very different now. The house didn't just need a lick of paint and a new kitchen. The barns needed serious structural work, not a simple bit of titivation. The hedges were wild, overgrown and full of brambles, the drive full of potholes and mud, drainage ditches blocked, trees falling down.

Before Tim and Sarah could move their livestock onto the farm Tim came and inspected the fences. 'They're in pretty bad shape,' he said, confirming what we already knew. 'There are a couple of fields that will be OK to start off with, but we'll probably have to re-fence the whole of the perimeter just for starters.'

Tim is an expert fencer. In that year's All Wales Ploughing match, a surprisingly compelling day out even for those not obsessed with tractors, Tim had come third in the fencing competition. He and Paul, his long-standing fencing partner, had to erect twenty-five metres of stock fencing against the clock. They were the fastest, only losing out on the winning spot because of some technicality with staples, or strainers, or something. Anyway, he seemed undaunted by the task that now faced him, even when the total he reached by adding up the outside perimeter of the various fields was 4,000 metres.

'Bloody hell,' I gasped, 'that's going to take years.'

Tim just smiled. 'Noooo,' he said in the long drawn-out way he has when he wants to emphasise the nega-tive. 'It's pretty quick once you get started.'

And with that, the static caravan arrived and was installed in one of the barns for a bit of extra protec-tion. Tim and Sarah's furniture was stored in a lockable room in the old stone barn, their washing machine rigged up in another bit. A garden shed was erected in the barn next to the caravan as a temporary kennel for four of their eight dogs. The working dogs were given another kennel in an adjoining barn. Beetroot the cat took up position on the back of the sofa in the caravan and made it home. The tractor arrived, and the old pick-up, the quad bike with the dodgy starter motor and the faithful Land Rover. But the greatest day of all was when we turned up one rather grey December morning to find four Saddleback pigs asleep in the Dutch barn; Rags and Champ, Sarah's horses, housed in a makeshift stable made from straw bales and hurdles; and out grazing in the fields behind the house, 200 Welsh ewes and a dozen cattle. December may traditionally signal the end of the year but for us, this particular December was heralding, not the end, but a new beginning. This land, our land, had come to life once more.

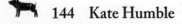

Chapter 11

Going Green

Nearly all our Badger Face Welsh Mountain sheep at home had bright green bums. Contrary to what you might think, this was something to celebrate, rather than something to panic about. A green bum may not sound very healthy, and indeed if my own bum were green I would probably call a doctor, but in this case, no doctor was needed because it could only mean one thing. For the first time in their short lives, my ewes had had sex.

Sheep do not make good pets. They were domesticated

by humans for their milk, their meat, their hides and later their wool. Over the millennia (the first sheep are thought to have been domesticated over 10,000 years ago) the once wild animal that originated in Central Asia in what was known as the fertile crescent, has since been imported and exported, bred and crossbred to produce hundreds of different domesticated breeds to suit the varied climate and conditions of the vast array of the world's countries that now have sheep. Some farms have sheep purely for the wool they produce; others will have different breeds more suitable for producing meat. There are farmers who make money from their sheep by breeding ewes and rams to sell on as breeding stock. I hoped that by breeding our little band of ewes we'd get a bit of everything – some animals to keep, some to sell and some to eat. Peter Weale, from whom we bought our ewes, had phoned in the summer and told us he had a few more young ewes he was willing to sell, so Ludo and I were now the proud owners of a flock of ten. To transform them from woolly grass-eating machines into something more useful we needed a ram.

There is little point in owning a ram with only a small number of ewes and a small amount of land. Back in October, while we were still jumping through the council's hoops with the farm, Tim and Sarah suggested we do what many smallholders do and borrow one instead.

'Our friend Russ, who runs a community farm near Pontypool, has Badgers,' said Tim. 'I'll give him a ring and see if he's got a ram he could lend you.'

Russ's farm is perched on a steep slope just outside an old mining village. We walked around admiring the careful layout of beautifully fenced paddocks housing chickens, sheep and a basking Tamworth sow with her noisily boisterous litter of young piglets.

'Do you think our farm will ever look like this?' I whispered to Ludo.

'Maybe,' he said doubtfully, 'but it will take a while.'

Russ's two rams were in the yard. 'He's the oldest one,' said Russ, pointing to a magnificent animal with a fine set of curled black horns, a luxuriant fleece and a haughty glare. 'I've had some lovely lambs off him,' he said, 'and I always get a good number of twins. He's been running with some of my ewes, but you are very welcome to borrow him for yours. Or you can borrow the youngster, who's his son. He was born this year, so he's never been with the ewes before, but I don't think he'll have too much difficulty! When are you planning to lamb?'

There is a saying that goes: 'If you put your ram in with the ewes on Fireworks Night, you'll have lambs on April Fools Day.' Some farmers will try and lamb much earlier than that, putting the ram in in September in the hope of getting lambs in January. That way they will have lambs ready to sell early in the year and for a better price than when the majority of lambs are ready. For someone like me, who doesn't have those commercial concerns, it is, as Jim Beavan pointed out, easier to lamb later when there is a chance the weather will be better and the spring grass has started to come through. 'In any case,' said Jim, with his characteristic twinkle, 'if you plan to lamb in late March or early April, all mine will have lambed by then so you'll have had plenty of practice before having to lamb your own!'

'It's mid October now,' said Russ, 'so I suggest you take whichever ram you want away today, put him in with your ewes and they should come into season in the next week or ten days. All being well, you'll have lambs about the time you want them.'

I looked both rams over. There was little to choose between them; both looked in the peak of condition, with good strong markings, and, as Jim would say, 'a fine pair of balls'. More importantly they were both quiet and nice natured, which not all rams are. Mindful that our ewes had never been to the ram before, I was in a quandary whether to go for old and experienced, or a youngster who was also a first timer. 'It won't make any difference,' assured Russ, so we chose the youngster and helped Russ load him into the trailer. 'Good luck!' called Russ, as he waved us off. 'Let me know how he gets on.'

Before we introduced the young ram to his virgin queens, Tim suggested we raddle him so that we could see exactly what ewes had been covered and when. We smeared the thick, bright green oily paint into the thick fleece between his front legs and then opened the gate and let him out into the field. A couple of the ewes looked up from their grazing, gave him a brief once over and went back to eating; the rest ignored him altogether. We burst out laughing. 'You wait,' said Tim, 'they'll notice him soon enough.'

Every morning I gave Ludo a progress report. 'Two more green bums!' I'd announce as I came into the kitchen for breakfast, 'and he's getting very frisky with number 78.' Three weeks after we saw the first ewe with a green bum, we changed the colour of the raddle, smearing the ram this time with lurid orange paint. A ewe will ovulate every three weeks, and a ram will only mate with a ewe that is not pregnant, so this was a simple way to discover whether he had done his job well. Any ewes that had orange bums we would know had not got pregnant first time around.

It was exciting. It felt like our first foray into real 'farming'. Our chickens and geese were giving us eggs; we had raised and eaten our own table birds and made sausages from Duffy and Delilah's piglets. But as long as the poultry and Duffy and Delilah were fed, watered and checked every day they continued to live on happily without any more involved or complicated intervention from us. With our sheep we were looking ahead to the future for the first time, taking an active role in breeding both in order to provide food but also to purposely increase the size of our flock. Instead of our rather haphazard animal management thus far, we were now doing things consciously. We had chosen the male and decided when he should be put in with the females based on the knowledge of what time of year the lambs would be born. The raddle told us that two of the ewes got pregnant second time around, so we knew they would lamb last, and that two of our ewes had not been mated at all.

'It's not that unusual for young ewes to fail to come into season the first year,' said Tim. 'But', he added, ever the practical farmer, 'you should make a note of it and if they don't come into season next year, you'll know you won't be able to breed from them and you should think about eating them instead.'

While we were busy match-making sheep, Stafford had revealed himself to be something of a perfectionist, working and reworking the drawings for the planning application, returning time and time again to the house to measure and ponder and suck his pencil and measure again. He worked far into the night and started at some unspeakable hour in the morning. I get up early but there would always be an email from Stafford sent even earlier. That he was working was undeniable, but days became weeks, Christmas got closer and I worried that if the application didn't get put in soon, it would simply become mired in the Christmas backlog, never to be processed at all. I phoned, emailed, sent texts begging him just to SEND IT! and finally threatened to break into his house, steal his computer and send it myself. But he didn't make me want to cry, or hit him, and he claimed that he hadn't reached the point – yet – of wanting to wring my neck, so as far as working relationships go, we were doing OK.

The bat survey had been done and the report, when it was emailed through to us, revealed we had a small number of pipistrelles in the roof of the house and brown long-eared bats in the barn. The proposed work on the house didn't involve anything to do with the roof, which mercifully was sound.

'I have to submit this bat report with the application,' said Stafford, 'and I expect the council ecologist will come and have a look and advise on what we need to do, but as we are not doing any works that will cause a disturbance we should be fine. The barn's going to be more complicated. I suspect we'll need a licence because that roof has definitely got to come off.'

'Does that mean we can't do anything to it at all?' I said, despair settling like a familiar blanket around my shoulders.

'Kate,' said Stafford kindly, 'it is nearly Christmas. With the best will in the world, even if you didn't need a licence, that barn is not going to be ready by the spring. But I've got another idea which won't take very long to do, won't be too expensive and will give you somewhere dry and weatherproof in which to hold courses until we can start work on the barn.'

But that idea would have to wait – we had more

urgent issues to attend to. In contrast to the previous two Christmasses, when the countryside had been blanketed in snow and every garden had a resident snowman that lasted well into the New Year, Christmas 2011 was wet. Instead of snow, there was mud, everywhere.

'We should be thinking about trees,' said Ludo. 'Isn't this the time of year to plant them?' It seems curious that later autumn and winter should be the best time to plant trees, but Ludo was right, it is. As everything shuts down and stops growing in the winter, the roots of trees and hedge plants are inert and dormant. They can be dug up, packed in bags, sent in the post, and as long as the roots aren't allowed to completely dry out by exposing them to the air, the young trees can last for weeks before they are planted. If they go into the cold winter ground, they are ready and waiting for the first spring warmth, which will start to heat the soil and trigger the roots to wake up again. Spring rain will help them establish and start to thrive – it is simply working with nature.

Monmouthshire has a long tradition of cider and perry orchards. Every farm would have had one and cider making would have been as much part of the farming calendar as lambing or harvesting. Indeed farm labourers were paid, in part, or in some cases entirely, in cider. Given the potency of some of the local stuff I've tried, it is amazing they were ever in a fit state to do any labouring at all. There is a local cider called Black Rat. Jim Beavan introduced me to it when we were having a drink in his local one evening. Jim is a proper drinker; he can down a pint of beer effortlessly in one, as if it were water, and happily polish off ten or more pints in an evening. But even he is floored by Black Rat. 'Four's about all I can manage,' he said, almost ashamed. I couldn't even finish a half before the room started to de-focus and the idea of curling up in a ball on the floor in a quiet corner somewhere suddenly became very appealing.

Perry can be lethal too. I had never heard of perry until we moved to Wales. It is a cider but made from pears. Perry pears, like cider apples, are basically inedible. Small and hard, it is astonishing they produce any juice at all, but they do. Full of sugar, once fermented the juice turns into a delicious, dry, refreshing drink, which is a lot more potent than it tastes. There has been more than one occasion when half a pint of perry on a Sunday lunchtime at the Clytha Arms has gone down all too easily and been followed, swiftly, by a second, and not being much of a drinker anyway, I've needed a steadying arm to lean on when I leave.

We had long harboured plans to plant a cider and perry orchard at the farm – not, you understand, so we could spend our days in a state of almost permanent inebriation, but because orchards are dying out. Cider and perry fell out of favour as lager grew in popularity, and orchards were abandoned or forgotten, their crop lying in rotting drifts under the trees. The art of cider making, once as much a part of rural life as making cheese or butter, became another quaint, near-forgotten skill, kept alive by a few old boys who had no one to pass their cider-making secrets on to. Presses and scratters, the machines that chop the apples into a pulp before pressing, rotted and fell apart in barns and sheds all over the county. The beautiful thick slabs of stone – known as teardrops because of their shape – which are the intrinsic part of the traditional Monmouth press – are often to be found being used as garden ornaments or just abandoned somewhere. We found one, in almost perfect condition, under a hedge in front of the farm-house. It must weigh half a tonne, so for the time being it's staying there.

More recently orchards are being cut down, cleared to make space for another crop or something more valuable than just a few old apple and pear trees. But with every orchard that is lost goes another little bit of our heritage, another ancient local variety of tree that will never grow again.

I've never been one for pickling the past – things will always change, adapt, evolve. In fact we've been having an ongoing row on that subject with the listed buildings officer at the council. Our house is Grade II listed, although only after it was restored by the rather clever, artistic people we bought it from. Before that it had been allowed to rot, and no one gave a damn. It is an undeniably lovely house that may date – in parts – from the seventeenth century, but that doesn't mean it shouldn't be able to function in a modern way in a modern world. The roof, for example, is not tiled with old local slate; when the previous owners bought the house most of the roof had already collapsed and they replaced it with concrete tiles because slate was prohibitively expensive. There is nothing seventeenth century about a concrete tile, but inexplicably a bank of PV (photovoltaic) solar panels on part of the roof no one can see is not acceptable to the listed buildings man who clearly puts more store by a concrete tile than the health of the environment. I love old buildings, and they absolutely should be protected, but not in a way that makes them obsolete in the modern world, because in the end that sort of protection won't save them. All it will lead to is decay and dereliction.

Luckily for our orchards, the modern world has

suddenly woken up to the fact that an orchard and its fruit are things to be treasured. A resurgence in popularity of cider, and with it a renewed interest in cider making, has given them a place, a purpose and a value. And with a growing market in 'artisan' products, made in a less mass-produced commercial way, there is a place for old varieties once more.

The Gwent Wildlife Trust, which has its headquarters just a few miles down the road from the farm, has done much to champion the restoration and replanting of orchards in the area. It even employs an orchard specialist called Alice who arrived on the farm one morning in fog so thick it was impossible to see more than a few feet in front of our faces.

'Orchards were commonly planted quite close to the house,' she said, standing in the field directly behind the farmhouse staring helplessly out at the impenetrable grey blanket of cloud, 'but I can't tell how exposed this area is. Are there many trees and hedges around this field?'

'No,' I said, 'and the prevailing wind comes straight off the mountains, but there is a corner of a field in front of the house that is bordered by hedges on two sides and big ash trees on the other. I'll show you.'

We made our way gingerly through the murk, passing the ghostly outlines of some of Tim's sheep, and made our way to the corner of the field that borders the lane and the entrance to the farm. Although this strange triangular bit of land is now part of the large field directly in front of the house, the line of large, ancient ash trees that bisects it looks like an old field boundary and if we were to reinstate it, we could, said Alice, have an area of about an acre that would be well protected from the wind and provide enough space to plant about fifty trees.

'You could even keep grazing sheep in here,' she said, 'as long as you put good guards around the trees.' Naturally we wanted to grow old varieties if at all possible but knowing nothing at all about cider and perry trees we were at a loss where to start. It would be more than tempting to choose trees by the name alone – a bit like the way I choose which horse to back in the Grand National – after all, who wouldn't want a Handsome Norman, or a Slack me Girdle? But as Alice patiently pointed out, a good name didn't necessarily make them the right trees for us. 'I'll put you in touch with someone who knows more about old local varieties than anyone,' said Alice. 'He'll give you some pointers.'

Paul Davis is an astonishing character. He spent many years travelling around Africa in his vintage Land Rover, which never gave him any trouble, he said, because anything that did go wrong could usually be fixed with a bit of twig, or an elastic band, or something. He drove the Land Rover back to the UK and with his wife decided to settle just outside Brecon in mid Wales and start a small plant nursery. Sometime later someone asked him if he could graft some apple trees for them. 'I'd never done it before,' said Paul, cheerfully, 'but I got some books and it didn't look that hard so I had a go.' Now he and his wife graft nearly 2,000 fruit trees a year, many rare and old varieties, which he delivers in his same old Land Rover.

'I'll put you together a nice mix and try and make them as local as possible,' he said. 'You're a bit late ordering, so I probably won't have all fifty you need, but I can probably do you about thirty and let you have the rest next autumn. I can get them to you in early March. Does that sound OK?'

There had, in the meantime, been a lot of head scratching and sucking of teeth in the house. The planning application was in and Stafford had started asking local builders to come and tender for the work. Walls had been poked, floors dug into, slabs lifted, all accompanied by much muttering and creasing of brows. I heard quite a lot of words I didn't recognise, often preceded by not terribly polite ones I did, and it became ever more evident that getting the house into a state that was actually habitable without the need for a wetsuit and the permanent whirring of industrial de-humidifiers was going to be a challenge.

Stafford and I sloshed across the yard, past the main stone barn to the other old barn that spans the opposite side of what I, in the manner of an estate agent, referred to as a courtyard, but was actually a waterlogged patch of mud and weeds between the two barns, with a tumbledown wall on the third side separating it from Tim's yard and another decrepit wall on the fourth side with a rusty gate leading into a field. The barn had clearly once housed animals, but had almost certainly not been used much, if at all, when the modern sheds were built. It had a hugely high wall at the back, which was bowing alarmingly, and, said Stafford, at least half of it was on the brink of collapse. The roof sloped steeply down from the back wall to meet a much lower front wall and the dark, mud-floored interior was broken up by the roof girders that sat almost exactly at nose height. Even Stafford, who is a bit shorter than me, had to stoop.

'What do you want to use this barn for?' he asked, looking at the crumbling walls.

'Well, we thought it would be a somewhere we could put animals so that people on courses could get a good look at them and handle them somewhere that is controlled and under cover. For example, if we were doing a sheep course, we could have some sheep in here so people could get close to them without having to chase them around a field, and be able to have a clear view for demonstrations of things like feet trimming and teeth checking, and then have a go themselves. Also, our smallholding animals are going to be kept largely separate from Tim's so we're going to need some inside space of our own for lambing, or when pigs are farrowing, that kind of thing.'

'It would be a good roof for solar panels,' mused Stafford. 'South facing, no shade, perfect. Are you still considering biomass?'

I nodded. After our failure to get permission to put solar panels on the roof at home, I was determined to try and make the farm as environmentally friendly as possible. I had spent hours scouring the internet trying to work out what system or combination of systems would work. The technology is constantly improving, and the choice bewildering. Ground source or air source? Biomass or PV? Sheeps' wool or fibreglass? Can we effectively store rainwater and use it for the water troughs? Is there anything clever we can do with cow poo? If we even think of a wind turbine will we get a flood of solicitors' letters?

Stafford has installed a biomass boiler at his house. Around us is a lot of Forestry Commission land and they have finally got wise to the fact that there is a burgeoning market for well-seasoned logs. As long as there is room to store the sixteen or so tonnes of wood needed to run the boiler for a year, the wood is available and much, much cheaper than using any sort of fossil fuel. The biomass boiler Stafford has, and had suggested I investigate, is of German origin and is as Teutonic in its efficiency as it is in its design.

On Stafford's suggestion I phoned a bloke called Ben, who runs a green energy company nearby. He gave me an estimate of what it would cost to buy and install a biomass boiler that would run on logs. I nearly fainted. 'I know,' he said, ruefully, 'you have to be rich to be green. But there are grants available and you'll be eligible for them because it is for a business. These systems are super-efficient, far better than ground source or air source, and you know there is a good, reliable source of wood around here. It will pay for itself pretty quickly and then every year will save you money.' So biomass it would be, and PV panels too, if Stafford could fix up the barn in time before the government dropped the current amount they would pay for the electricity generated, which was what they were threatening to do.

Stafford was scribbling in his notebook. 'This bit of the wall is going to have to come down,' he said, pointing at the bulging section that looked as if it would only take the lightest of nudges to reduce it to a pile of rubble. 'Once it is down, there is no point rebuilding it again. It would simply cost too much and actually, you could make this building much more useful by doing this.' And he drew a sketch that left the stronger part of the existing barn as it was, with a lean-to wood store behind that would give enough space for a year's supply of wood. The other end would become a double-width barn, still with its stone frontage and wooden doors, but with a steel frame and Yorkshire boarding that would create a big, light airy space, perfect for lambing or demonstrations.

'I'll need to fiddle with the roof a bit to make it

work, but it should be all right. When did the government say it was going to drop the feed-in tariff?'

'Beginning of March, I think.'

'Right,' said Stafford, 'nothing like a deadline. This barn will be done by the end of February so you can get your panels up on time and start making some cash.'

'We'll just have to give it all to you,' I laughed.

'All the more reason to make sure it's done in time,' he replied, with a grin.

We had spent so much of the last year in a state of limbo, heads full of plans and ideas, but always with the nagging fear that the farm would never be ours. Now, finally, Tim and Sarah could settle in and Tim's part of the farm was already beginning to look renewed and lived in. One barn was full of bales of sweet-smelling hay that would feed his animals through the winter. The gates to the cattle-sheds had been checked and oiled and a thick bed of straw laid down in preparation for the cattle coming in. The saddleback pigs had made themselves thoroughly at home in the old Dutch barn, the horses were happy in their make-shift stable and the dogs cosy and content in their converted garden shed. The sheep had found all the holes in the fences and the cows were making the most of the last of the grass.

We, too, could stop dreaming and start doing. Ludo and I could at last see a time when the farmhouse would cease to be a cold, empty shell and Tim, Sarah and Beetroot the cat would be able to move out of the caravan. Crumbling barns would be made solid and secure. We'd have the technology to make the farm both environmentally friendly and low cost to run. And we'd have an orchard, which would provide us all with delicious heritage cider, once the trees have matured – which will take about seven years. But then, as we had discovered in the many, many months it had taken for us to get to this point, the wait makes the end result that much more special.

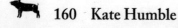

Chapter 12

A Glimpse Of Things To Come

The New Year dawned but it didn't herald a change in the weather. It was still wet. Water lay in pools around the farm and the fields were sodden. Tim had brought his cattle in. Most farmers will bring their cattle into sheds in the winter. Even a small number like Tim's herd would churn up the ground, reducing it to a quagmire and damaging the grazing. At this time of year there is nothing for them to eat anyway. What grass there is has no goodness in it and both cattle and sheep were being fed hay and what is known as 'cake', a grain mix that bears more resemblance to pulped cardboard dried in slim cylindrical rolls than a Victoria sponge. Unappetising as it looks, both sheep and cattle love it.

At home our sheep were being fed too, but the constant rain was taking its toll. If sheep could cope with anything, I thought, surely it would be rain, but apparently not. On one particularly grim, grey day, I went out as usual to feed and check on all the animals before driving Ludo to the local hospital. He was having a long-awaited exploratory operation on his ankle, which, without any warning, would suddenly and painfully give way, leaving him hopping and wincing and cursing. Scans and x-rays had show up nothing so the surgeon decided he should operate in case there was some tendon damage. If that proved to be the case, it would put Ludo in plaster, unable to drive or get around for a minimum of six weeks. I didn't even want to think about how we'd manage if that were the case.

Ludo wasn't the only one ailing that morning. Four of my so-called hardy Badger Face ewes were limping. Not only that, one of our neighbour's four Shetland ewes that were staying with us was hanging back from the others – a sign that something was amiss. As she turned her head I caught sight of her left eye. It was blue and cloudy and her other eye didn't look very healthy either.

I put her in a pen and then checked the others. All the Shetlands had various stages of eye infection and every single sheep needed its feet seeing to. I stood in the drizzle, head in hands, trying to pull myself back from the brink of despair. The owners of the Shetlands were on holiday, so I couldn't ask them whether this eye affliction was something they recognised and what I should do it about. I felt particularly bad because this had happened while they were in my care and I still didn't know enough about sheep to know whether it was something I had done wrong that had caused it.

I called the vet. 'Conjunctivitis,' he said, as he injected the Shetlands' eyelids. 'Probably not helped by this very windy weather. Keep them apart from the others, because it's very contagious.'

'What about their feet?' I asked, terrified I'd done something to inadvertently cripple them all.

'It's the mud,' said the vet. 'Terrible for foot rot. Cut away any over-grown or flaking bits, and spray any sores between the toes with iodine.'

I dropped Ludo at the hospital and rushed back home. Two back-breaking hours later the sheep had all had pedicures and the Shetlands were tucking into hay in their own private paddock. The dogs came to meet me as I walked back to the house to dry out and have a cup of tea. Bella had somehow, in the hours I'd spent with the sheep, mysteriously developed a limp and one of Badger's eyes was weepy and sore. I stood looking at them both staring up at me with slightly pathetic expressions and felt utterly defeated. My sheep, my dogs and my husband were all either crippled or half blind. 'Maybe I'll just run away,' I thought, as I waited for the kettle to boil. But instead I went and ordered fence posts.

Tim had suggested that this might be a good time to start the fencing. 'At least the ground's soft. It's a lot harder if the ground's frozen. Do you need a list of what to order?' We had come up with an arrangement. Usually a tenant farmer is responsible for the upkeep of fences and gates, but it seemed hardly fair that Tim should foot the bill for repairs at the outset. Instead we agreed that Ludo and I would buy all the materials and Tim would do the work, with Ludo, ankle allowing, as his apprentice. I looked at the list. It was unfathomable. I called Jambo.

There are many things to love about living where we do: the beauty of the countryside, the glorious walks, having one of the best kayaking rivers in the country on our doorstep and friendly pubs down the road, but best of all are the people. In the short time we have been here we have met and become friends with farmers and lawyers, builders and yoga teachers, cooks and writers, IT experts, documentary makers, artists, mothers, grandmothers, dog walkers and whippet owners. And Jambo, who'd been amongst the very first people we met, and who knows more than anyone else I know about a great deal of things, including fencing.

'We need four kilometres of the stuff, Jambo,' I said. 'No one's going to believe me.'

'That's nothing,' said Jambo, 'we've just fenced a section of the M5 three times longer than that. Talk to Dave who supplies wire fencing to us. He'll help you.'

As Jambo predicted, Dave was unfazed by the amount of wire I needed and Tim had helpfully specified the type of stock fencing he wanted to use and told us that he would be putting a strand of barbed wire above and below it. All was going beautifully, as if I did this sort of thing all the time, until Dave asked, 'Do you want your stock fencing in 50-, 100-, 200- or 300-metre lengths?'

'Ummm, any difference in price?' I asked.

'Nope.'

'Err, I'll get back to you.'

Steve at the timber yard had even more questions. What diameter of fence post did I require? What about the strainers? Tanalised or non-tanalised? Machine finished or natural?

'I'll ask Tim,' I said, faintly, 'but I'll need a thousand of them. Can you deliver?'

I went back to the hospital. Ludo was lying on a bed, sleepily watching *Countdown*, his ankle bandaged but not in plaster, a surgical boot and a crutch at the end of the bed.

'Are you OK?' I asked.

'Yes,' he drawled, still hungover from the anaesthetic. 'No tendon damage, just some chips of bone that were floating around. They got them out. Should be fine in a week. How's your day been?'

'I've taken all the sheep to the abattoir, the dogs have gone back to the RSPCA, I've sold the farm and bought two one-way tickets to South America. There's a place in Chile where it hasn't rained for 300 years. It sounds like heaven.'

'That's nice,' he said, drowsily, and fell asleep over the final conundrum.

Despite the weather and the gloom and lethargy it brought with it, there were small, tentative signs that progress was being made. The council had given us the go-ahead to start work on the house. A local builder had been chosen and could start work in a couple of weeks. In the meantime work began on the dilapidated tin barn. It was this barn that Stafford had identified as being a good temporary place for us to hold the courses that we still hoped to start running at some point in the near future, although I think both Ludo and I had accepted that it wouldn't be the spring. Kelvin the builder arrived on the farm and started digging footings and levelling the earth floor in preparation for the concrete.

'There's nothing that man can't do with a digger and a dumper truck,' said Stafford, 'and he's an incredible water diviner. He'll wander around with a couple of bits of wire and all of a sudden the wire will twitch and cross over and at that point there'll be a drain or water pipe or well. It's amazing.'

'He won't need his divining rods to find water on this farm,' I said, a little ruefully. 'We're at saturation point. It would be more useful if he knew how to build an ark.'

With Kelvin came Andy, a builder specialising in agricultural buildings, who would rebuild the tin barn. 'What colour do you want your sheets?' he asked me one afternoon as he was finishing off the block work that would help keep the new shed watertight. I looked at him blankly, wondering why on earth he had any interest in the colour of my bed linen. He tried again. 'The corrugated sheets for the walls of the barn?'

'Oh!' I said. 'Of course. Umm.' What colour are barns, generally? Aren't they just, sort of, barn-coloured? Did farmers really spend hours worrying about the colour of their barns and whether they clashed with the paintwork on their tractors?

Andy helped me out. 'How about Goose-wing Grey?'

'Hell,' I thought, 'he's turned into Laurence Llewelyn-Bowen. He must be taking the piss.' He wasn't. At his behest I studied the colour chart on the corrugated sheeting website. Barns, it transpired, can come in all sorts of colours, even 'Mushroom' or, if you really want to stand out from the crowd, 'Poppy Red'.

'I quite like the idea of Meadowland Green,' I said to him the next day.

Andy just looked sceptical. 'You'd better check with Stafford.'

Meadowland Green, it turns out, is not an acceptable colour for a barn. 'Big mistake,' said Stafford, shaking his head and biting into a biscuit. 'And Goose-wing Grey is not one of the standard colours so it is more expensive. I suggest you go with Blue Slate Grey. Is that OK?'

'Fine,' I said, 'as long as the roof can be Sugarplum Pink,' and beat a hasty retreat before he could throw his digestive at me. The truth was there was no time to argue whether the barn should be any particular shade of green or grey because we suddenly had a deadline. In just a couple of weeks we would be receiving members of the public at the farm for the very first time.

The farm sits on a ridge above the River Wye within the Wye Valley Area of Outstanding Natural Beauty. The small, dedicated team that runs the AONB office in Monmouth had been amongst the few people who seemed prepared to openly support our plans for the farm. Sarah Sawyer is the AONB's Community Officer and it was her idea to organise a volunteer day. Although we had ceased to be the main news story in the local paper and most of the negative letter writing had stopped too, there was still, according to Sarah, a lot of rumours floating around about what we were doing or planning to do on the farm.

'We have a great, really active and enthusiastic bunch of volunteers,' said Sarah. 'They are all local, and if you invite them to come and help with something on the farm and give them a bit of a tour too, it might help counter some of the gossip.'

It was a good idea and we certainly had plenty that

needed doing, but, as I said to Sarah, it seemed a little unfair to call on local volunteers to clear drainage ditches or cart rubble to put in gateways. 'Aren't you planning to plant a new hedge?' she suggested. We were. The farm is quite high and exposed and the wind, when it blows, comes straight off the Black Mountains. We thought if we planted a hedge around the back of the house it would not only protect the house from the prevailing weather, it would also join up two existing hedges, making a great wildlife corridor, as well as acting as a windbreak and shelter for livestock.

'Hedge planting is a perfect task for a volunteer day,' said Sarah. 'There's a variety of things that people can do and at the end of the day they can really see the results of the work. How many people would you like?'

'Well,' I said, 'our courses, when we start running them, will be for around twelve people, so if you can rustle up as many as twelve it would be a good trial run for us.'

'I'll see what I can do,' said Sarah. 'In the meantime, there is a lot to organise.'

So added to my ever-growing list of phone calls to planners, getting quotes from builders, ordering concrete, buying vaccines for sheep and somehow fitting in a shower and a shopping expedition to restock the fridge, I had to think about loos, signs, rotavators, plastic guards to protect the trees from deer and car parking.

In amongst all this I had rather rashly offered to go and help the Beavans with their January lambing. Back in September Jim had 'sponged' a hundred ewes. A special sponge impregnated with progesterone is inserted into the ewe's vagina. Progesterone suppresses the oestrus cycle and once the sponge is removed, fourteen days later, it will stimulate the ewe to ovulate

24-36 hours later. When I put a ram in with my ewes, it took some of them several days to come into season so I knew roughly when they would start lambing, but not how long it would go on for. Ewes that have been sponged will generally mate immediately and lamb within a day of two of each other. It means lambing time is more predictable and controllable. But it also means that with a hundred ewes all due within a day or two of each other, Jim and Kate were going to be on duty twenty-four hours a day. 'I'll be there with you for the early shift,' I said to Kate.

At sometime before five that morning, I was sitting at my computer, frantically ordering the fence posts I should have ordered the day before, when a text came through. It was from Kate Beavan. 'Hope you haven't left yet. We've had an emergency!' My heart was in my mouth. What could have happened? A fire in the lambing shed? Had Jim had an accident? Heart pounding, I scrolled down to read the rest of Kate's text. 'We've run out of teabags. Please bring as many as you can!' Relief flooded over me. I grabbed teabags and biscuits, pulled on my overalls and raced out into the dark.

I went in to check the ewes while Kate, who'd already been up for two hours, went and made her longed-for cup of tea. On a frosty morning, there are few places I'd rather be than a lambing shed with its smell of warm lanolin and new lambs. All was quiet, but one ewe was on her own, lying down in the back corner. I watched her as she got up and pawed at the straw, lay down again, licking her lips and bleating quietly – classic signs of labour.

'Go on,' said Kate, revived from her tea, 'you remember what to do.'

After a slightly undignified chase I got the ewe on the ground and rolled up my sleeves. 'All there,' I said, smiling at Kate, as I felt the two front feet and, resting just above them, the nose and the dome of the head. The lamb was in the right position and the birth was progressing well.

'Let's allow her do it on her own,' said Kate, and we stood back. A few minutes later a fine, healthy lamb was born. We cleared the birthing fluid from around its nose, waited for its first gasping breath, then let the mother take over. She started to lick it, nickering gently, establishing that all-important bond.

'I could do this all day,' I said to Kate, beaming.

'You're going to have to,' she quipped. 'There are another two going into labour now.'

When I got home, exhausted and elated, there was a message from Sarah Sawyer. 'Twenty-one volunteers have signed up! Hope that's OK!'

'Help,' I thought. 'I hope to God it warms up a bit before then.' The warm, wet weather that had been with us through most of January had been replaced by plunging temperatures and dramatic frosts. The Monmouthshire countryside was beautiful, sparkling in the pale winter sunlight, but the ground was hard as iron.

'Maybe it will thaw overnight,' I muttered to myself as I stood in the kitchen, list in hand. Thermos flasks? Tick. Plates, bowls, mugs, cutlery? Tick. Tea, coffee, sugar – where's the sugar? Have we got enough milk? Will the barn be finished in time? Ludo was delivering straw bales up to the barn for people to sit on; Tim had borrowed a long trestle table; Kelvin had plumbed in a sink and connected a water heater; and Andy and his team were still frantically working to make the barn weatherproof.

Katherine Marland, friend, neighbour and wonderful cook, had agreed to provide food and she was as nervous as I was. As our plans for the farm progressed and started to crystallise, Ludo and I had both hoped that Katherine, or Kather, as she has been known since childhood, would like to come into partnership with us, not only catering for the courses but also teaching courses herself. She grew up on a farm in Derbyshire, and is as keen as we are to champion seasonal, local produce and connect people back to where food comes from. She also, according to Ludo who is something of a connoisseur, makes the finest bread and butter pudding he has ever eaten. We broached the subject when we got permission to buy the farm and to our delight she agreed.

The volunteer day was going to be a big test for all of us. Would they like and approve of what we were doing at the farm? Would they turn their noses up at a tin barn furnished with straw bales? Would Kather's lunch of thick, home-made vegetable soup and sourdough bread, followed by her irresistible chocolate biscuits and ginger cake make them all swoon with delight and have them clamouring to sign up for courses as soon as she had a kitchen to teach them in? 'This time tomorrow it will all be over,' I muttered, trying to calm the butterflies that danced in my stomach.

I broke off from packing provisions to go outside in the fading light to check and feed our animals. It was wickedly cold. Most of the chickens had already taken themselves into the house and were perched, huddled together, feathers fluffed. The previous week we had acquired some new layers, ex-commercial hens from a farm a few miles beyond Abergavenny. As I went to close the door of their house I noticed one seemed to be bleeding profusely from under her tail.

There is, without question, a big difference between keeping animals as pets and keeping animals from which you make a living. When the health of the beloved family pet is threatened most of us will go to any lengths to make it better again. We once spent £600 on not one, but two operations to remove a grass seed that had got firmly wedged up Badger's nose. The first operation identified where the seed was, but our local veterinary practice didn't have the specialist tool to remove it. Off we went to the veterinary college outside Bristol. They phoned me once the operation was complete. 'We couldn't find anything. He must have sneezed it out. That will be £300.' Would I, in retrospect, have taken the risk and left the seed to work its way out? No. But farmers, whose livelihoods depend on wildly fluctuating and never dependable profit margins, simply don't have that luxury. I thought back to when I was working with Jim Beavan on *Lambing Live* and how I had been surprised at how sad it made him when he had to send an old trusted sheep to the abattoir. Farmers, I thought, had to be unsentimental about their animals; but what I am discovering ever more frequently is that being practical doesn't make you unsentimental.

However, I felt I had a duty to try and save this particular chicken. She, along with twelve others, had come from the farm of David and Sue Lewis. When we went to meet them and pick up the hens, we stood in the field behind their house looking across at the Black Mountains while David told us the history of the farm.

'I was born here. We had a dairy herd that had been started by my grandfather. All our cows had to be shot during the foot and mouth crisis. I couldn't be on the farm when the Ministry men came to do it. I went to the hotel where my daughter worked for the day. Two weeks later I had a heart attack. Losing my cows nearly finished me off.'

The family never went back to dairy farming. Now David and his son Richard raise a few cattle for meat and goats, to supply a growing demand for goat meat.

'I'm really interested in finding out about goats,' I said.

'Come up and talk to Richard anytime. He'll tell you all about them. They can be a challenge, mind you!'

'Exactly,' said Ludo, who thinks that keeping goats will be nothing but trouble. 'We've come for chickens, remember.'

Eggs are now the main business of the farm, and David and Richard produce barn-laid eggs for the biggest egg supplier in Wales. But commercial layers are kept for just a year and then they are slaughtered. 'It seems such a waste,' said David. 'They may not be so productive but they will still go on laying for another three or four years. We always try and find homes for ours. I also can't bear to kill the ones that aren't quite right. You always get a few with a dodgy leg, or a bad eye. Most people will just dispatch them, but we keep them. We've only got thirteen left, and they're not the best, but if you promise to give them a good home, we'd love you to have them.'

But now, after only a week in my care, something very untoward had happened. 'What's happened to you?' I cooed at the bleeding hen, trying to sound calm. I picked her up. Blood dripped down my coat. There was no apparent injury so it was clearly something internal, or, as it turned out on further examination, something internal which wasn't where it should be. She was prolapsing. I had seen prolapse before, but only in sheep. It can be relatively common, when a sheep is in lamb and expecting triplets. I had no idea what to do with a prolapsing chicken.

'How much of the oviduct has come out?' asked Liz Sivewright, lecturer, ex-nurse and chicken expert. Liz runs a local poultry club and was utterly unfazed when I phoned her and told her what I'd found.

'About four centimetres. There's no egg stuck, as far as I can gather.'

'Bring her in to your kitchen,' said Liz, 'clean her up, wrap some ice in a cloth and hold it against the prolapse. It should go back in. Then put some honey and pile cream on it and keep her in a box overnight.'

'Honey?'

'It's a natural antiseptic,' said Liz. 'I've used it before and it's worked a treat.'

The only box I had was full of Thermos flasks. Holding the bemused bird I set about unpacking it. The phone rang. It was Stafford, our architect.

'Can't talk now,' I said. 'I've got a prolapsed chicken bleeding all over me.'

'You know what you need to do, don't you?' said Stafford. Stafford is a farmer as well as an architect so I thought I'd listen.

'What?'

'Put your fingers either side of its neck and pull hard.'

'Bugger off!'

Half an hour later the chicken was tucked up in her box by the range in the kitchen, her insides no longer outside, and I was feeling like the new James Herriot. Ludo returned. 'The barn looks amazing,' he said.

'Andy and his team have nearly finished the doors. The sink's plumbed in and the water heater's working. We're ready for them!'

It didn't thaw overnight. We stood with Sarah looking woefully at the boxes of hedge plants. 'The roots are frozen,' said Sarah. 'If we try and plant these we'll just kill them. And the ground's like concrete.' It was the first week of February and at 8.30 a.m. it was still only minus six degrees. The barn was full of bales, the trestle table set, the Thermos flasks full and I'd found the sugar. 'What are we going to do?' I asked.

'Plan B,' said Sarah brightly. 'You give the volunteers a tour around the farm and I'll go with Tim to look at other jobs we can do.'

I set off across the frosted fields with twenty-one strangers, who, unperturbed by the weather, had all turned up, suitably attired and brimming with enthusiasm. My nerves, which had momentarily calmed, came racing back again. I felt terribly exposed all of a sudden. What if they thought these fields and hedges and trees that made up the farm I loved were not so special after all? As we walked, I outlined our plans, pointing out where the orchard would be, the old pond choked with willow we hoped to clear, the stone walls we'd rebuild.

'You're going to run courses, aren't you?' asked one woman. I gulped, unsure of her tone. Was she being accusatory? Challenging? Or was she simply interested? I realised, as I nodded and started telling them that we were, in the future, when the buildings were restored and the farm in better shape, planning to run courses in smallholding and rural skills, that this was something of a pivotal moment. Up until now, when our business plan had been discussed in public or printed in the local paper, it was to inform people what we intended to do with the farm should we ever take ownership of it. Now that we did own it, what people thought of our ideas mattered so much more, because if they liked them, found them appealing, our business plan might stand a chance. If they didn't, then 'Humble by Nature' (as we had decided to call it after much discussion and indecision) – 'Courses in Animal Husbandry, Cookery & Rural Skills, on a working farm in Monmouthshire's beautiful Wye Valley' – would be no more than a few pages of columns and figures and some pretty pictures on Ludo's computer. Our business would fail before we even got started.

The volunteers seemed to enjoy the walk. They asked lots of questions, made polite noises about the courses and as we returned to the barn, greeted the steaming mugs of coffee with Kather's plates of home-made cake with appreciative murmurs. But I hoped for more than murmurs. I wanted a full-blown, shouted-from-the-rafters assurance that everything was great.

Sarah and Tim had found them the perfect task: not hedge planting, but hedge clearing. On one of the farm boundaries was an ancient hedgerow, much overgrown, the hazel, blackthorn and hawthorn straggly and twiggy, overgrown with ivy and brambles. Armed with saws, clippers and thick gloves, and fortified with coffee and cake, they marched off into the frost – a small, but fearless army, ready to do battle.

A few hours later we stood in the barn, drying up the mugs and eating the last of Kather's biscuits. 'They all really enjoyed themselves,' said Sarah. 'It was a great day.'

'Well they did a fantastic job,' I said. The volunteers had cleared a huge area of hedge, cutting out brambles and dead wood in preparation for Tim to lay it, then returned, rosy-cheeked and victorious, glowing with the satisfaction of a job well done, and tucked into bowls of Kather's soup and chunks of home-made bread. We all looked at each other, not willing to voice what we were hardly daring to think – that the day had been a success. In less than three months since we had taken on the farm we had hosted our first members of the public. We'd fed them hot food in a dry, weatherproof barn that just a few weeks before had been no more than a leaky corrugated roof over an earth floor. I felt absolutely drained, exhausted by the fear that it would be a disaster and weak with relief that it hadn't been. I looked over at Ludo, at Kather, at Tim. They too appeared exhausted, but also elated. We had done it. 'Humble by Nature' had made its first tentative step from being a few lines on a page and a scramble of ideas in Ludo's and my heads, to being something real.

'You could run a hedge-laying course,' said Tim, breaking the silence. 'It's a lovely thing to learn – very hands-on and satisfying – and you really see results at the end of the day. You'd need to do it soon, though, because it needs to be done while the hedge is dormant. Once spring comes it's too late; you'll kill the hedge.'

I hadn't imagined being able to run an actual course so soon, but everyone seemed to agree we should give it a go. 'OK,' I said, 'let's do it in a month's time.' So with one momentous day behind us and another milestone just ahead, we all went home for a well-deserved early night.

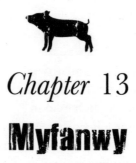

Chapter 13

Myfanwy

Ludo met my parents before I did. He was three years old when they got married and came along to their wedding with his parents, who were old family friends of my father's stepfather. I didn't meet him until I was sixteen. We were both at a family gathering, one of those toe-curlingly dull affairs that are a fate worse than death for teenagers. I still shudder at the memory of handing around bowls of peanuts to cardigan-wearing bores who I surely couldn't possibly be related to and making sullen replies to their chirpy enquiries as to what my favourite subject was at school. Then my eye caught sight of someone across the room who wasn't wearing a cardigan. His blond hair stuck up in rebellious spikes and he was smoking. My teenage heart gave a lurch. I gave my unruly mop of hair a self-conscious flick and willed him to look in my direction. He did. He was so handsome I felt myself blush. I looked at my feet. My heart thudded. Any minute, I thought, I'm going to be rescued from this bowl of peanuts and yet another conversation about my A-levels and whisked away by an impossibly good-looking spiky-haired smoker and my life will never be the same again. I peeped back up through my hair. He had turned his back on me and was deep in another conversation.

'You bloody well ignored me!' I accused him, four years later.

'You were sixteen,' he said defensively. 'I was twenty-four. It was barely legal. Plus, I wasn't entirely sure we weren't related.'

We met again not long after I had returned from a year travelling across Africa on my own. By now I was twenty, we had established that we were not related and he had taken me out to dinner. I'd been so nervous I'd spent the evening rushing to the loo to be sick and suspected that at the end of the night he would politely bid me goodnight and never phone me again.

Remarkably, he did phone, and we were now 'going out', although as neither of us had any money we mostly stayed in. I had discovered that he could speak fluent French, knew how to cook artichokes (which I had never eaten in my life) and was equally obsessed (but for different reasons) by Elvis Costello and Charlotte Rampling. Pleasingly I could almost always beat him at backgammon; less pleasingly he announced one day that he was in a band and they were playing on Saturday night and did I want to come? I had, in the past, spent a fair amount of time in dark, smoky rooms with sticky floors amongst an audience of six drunks waving limp arms in front of the studiously blank faces of musicians ritualistically torturing their instruments. My heart sank. The girlfriend of a band member has to be unquestionably loyal; not only must she attend every gig, but be there early to help carry cables and amps, then stand at the front cheering, clapping, dancing and looking adoring throughout, then sit and listen patiently as the gig is dissected in minute detail by the band afterwards, before finally schlepping the gear back outside and driving her sweaty, stinky musical hero home as he swigs beer and recounts the entire evening chord by chord.

Ludo had been in this particular band since university. 'We're just a party band,' he said to my tentative enquiries. 'We don't play any of our own stuff, just covers. We play for fun because we love it.' Fully prepared to spend the evening cringing with embarrassment, I left the club sweaty and high on endorphins from dancing all night. They were good, really good and one thing became blindingly obvious: Ludo needs music like the rest of us need air. Music is as intrinsic to his life as breathing. When, over the years, as band members got married or moved away and the band broke up, he joined another one, and when we moved to Monmouthshire it didn't take him long to seek out some other kindred spirits to form a local one.

The guitarist is a man called David Wilson. He lives across the border in Gloucestershire, is mildly obsessive about creating the perfect sourdough and manages the Duchy Home Farm for Prince Charles. One night, after a band rehearsal, he stayed for supper. 'Talking about hedge laying,' he said – which we were – 'we've got the Hedge Laying Championships at the farm next weekend. The Boss is passionate about it; he's the patron of the Hedge Laying Society. It's a great day. Why don't you come? Bring Tim and Sarah too. They might enjoy it!'

The February frosts that had thwarted our hedge planting had turned to snow. It was a perfect winter's day; bright blue skies, the sun glinting and winking off a fresh fall of snow. We walked with David through a magical white landscape, dogs chasing ahead, towards a line of cars on a ridge. The air was full of the buzz of chainsaws and the thwack of axes. As we got closer we could make out small knots of people spaced along several lines of neatly spaced young trees, chopping at them with broad-bladed weapons that wouldn't have seemed out of place in a medieval battlefield. What appeared at first glance to be the wilful destruction of perfectly healthy trees, turned out not to be destruction at all. This was the ancient art of hedge laying and we were watching some of the top hedge layers in the country doing what they do best.

Along with Tim and Sarah, we walked along the rows of hedges, Tim explaining the art of pleaching – cutting into the trunk of the hedge plant, but not quite severing it, then bending it to form the mainframe of the hedge. He told us why a hedge should be laid uphill and what a heathering does. It was rather like witnessing a magic trick. Within a matter of a few hours, a line of straggly trees would be chopped, split, and bent, stray twigs and dead wood cast aside, stakes knocked into the ground and the branches twisted between them, flexible hazel heatherings (slim poles about five feet long) woven across the top of the stakes to hold everything firm, untidy ends trimmed away and suddenly there would be the completed hedge, as neat and beautiful as an intricately woven basket.

'Is our hedge going to look like that?' I asked Tim, and he pulled a rueful face. Since the volunteer day, when he had rashly suggested that we could do a hedge-laying course I had been niggling him to agree to teach it. I tried again now.

'Umm, well, I don't know about that.' Tim has the sort of quiet charm and easy-going expertise that makes him both authoritative and approachable and we thought he'd make a brilliant teacher for some of the courses we planned to run. That afternoon, as we walked around the hedges, with him explaining the different techniques and styles he had, unconsciously, proved what we suspected. And we really wanted him to be one of our teachers, not just because we knew he'd be good but also because we wanted both him and Sarah to feel part of the business with which they share the farm.

'Prince Charles is apparently an excellent hedge layer,' I said to Tim, 'but I suspect he might be a bit busy. You are the only other person we know who can do it, so it's got to be you.'

The previous autumn, when the sale of the farm still hadn't gone through, things hadn't gone to plan with the architect and our many detractors were still airing their views in the letters page of the local press, our long-held plan to start running courses in the spring had seemed, at best, foolishly, hopelessly, optimistic. Yet here we were, planning our inaugural course for the first weekend of March. Only once we announced we were going to do it did we realise how utterly unprepared we were. With no proper website yet, our marketing was a little haphazard, relying on emails and friends telling friends. Although our temporary barn was weatherproof we had no furniture, no means of cooking or heating food and no plates or cutlery to eat it with. Time seemed to speed up; days raced past in a frenzy of preparation and ever-increasing to-do lists. At night Ludo and I would both lie, sleepless in the dark, wide-eyed, brains racing, muttering things like 'fire extinguishers!' 'first-aid kits!' and wondering if we should just forget the whole idea, because we'd never be ready. Tim, who had finally, if a little apprehensively, agreed to teach the course, spent hours preparing the site; Ludo spent hours sending out emails and writing course notes. I tracked down billhooks, old chairs, and wooden trestle tables. Kather emptied kitchen warehouses of their stock, returning to the farm again and again with boxes of plates and glasses, mugs and cutlery, as well as somehow finding time to prepare hearty dishes of beef and chorizo pie, vegetable crumble, and her famous chocolate biscuit cake. The evening before the course Ludo and Tim set up a screen and projector, arranged tables and chairs, while I manically, and somewhat pointlessly, drove them both mad by Hoovering around their feet.

The course was full. We had decided, as this was the first course we'd ever run, and it involved people using very sharp tools, to keep numbers to just six. Some of the people coming we knew and lived locally, but there was one man who had driven from the other side of Swansea and another who had come all the way from North Lancashire. They gathered in the barn and I handed out coffee. Conversation was lively. They were excited. I was terrified. I looked at Tim and Ludo.

So were they. But the rain that had been falling determinedly since daybreak had stopped. The sun had come out. It was time to start.

In the afternoon Sarah and I walked across the field, laden with flasks and mugs and cake, towards a scene reminiscent of an old-fashioned village fete. The bell tent we had been lent to provide refuge for the hedgers if the weather turned nasty was full of children bouncing off the straw bales. Someone had brought a Victoria sponge. Wives, children and dogs had all gathered to see how their menfolk had fared. Tim and his pupils were lined up in front of their newly laid hedge, tired, grubby and grinning from ear to ear. Cameras snapped. Husbands proudly showed off the section of hedge they had laid. 'It looks fantastic!' I exclaimed. Tim looked both relieved and rightly pleased. 'Not quite up to royal standards, perhaps,' he said with a grin, as he reached for a chunk of Kather's chocolate biscuit cake, 'but it's a good start.'

That first course felt like something significant; a turning point. We had been so bogged down – literally and metaphorically – by the work going on at the farm, which seemed to create more mud and ever-increasing piles of rubble and little else, that it was hard for either Ludo or I to believe we'd made any progress at all. Now that the thaw had come and spring was around the corner, Sarah Sawyer was back with her trusty troop of AONB volunteers, keen to get the hedge in before it was too late in the season.

'There's been huge progress,' she countered, 'even just in the last couple of weeks! That barn was just half a wall and some pillars last time. Now it's got a proper frame and rafters. The house is beginning to take shape and the weather's fantastic today. No frost or snow to contend with. We'll get the hedge in in no time. Did you say you had some trees as well?'

I showed her the assorted sacks of ash, birch, oak and maple saplings that had been given to us by various friends. To mark this year of the Diamond Jubilee the Woodland Trust was hoping to see a million new trees planted throughout Britain. With advice from one of their experts, we had ambitious plans to plant 2,000 native trees on the farm, cleverly grouped and laid out so they wouldn't impact on the grazing Tim and Sarah needed for their animals. We had applied for a grant and couldn't start planting until that came through, but in the meantime we had gratefully accepted any offer of trees that came our way.

'You've got deer guards,' Sarah noted with approval, nodding towards the stack of plastic tubes in the shed. 'Where shall we put the trees?'

'We thought we'd put them in the field in front of the house and restore Winnie's Park.'

Ros and Arthur had been the first people to tell me about Winnie. She was born on what is now our farm ninety-one years ago and still lives in the area. 'Give me a ring in the New Year,' said Ros before Christmas, 'and I'll put you in touch.' But once building work started and we were overwhelmed by the scale of what we were doing, by the amount of questions that needed answering and the materials that needed ordering, Ros's kind offer of an introduction to Winnie was never taken up.

During a mad dash to the supermarket to buy milk and spirit-lifting packets of biscuits for the workforce I bumped into Anne, who lives down the road from the farm. 'I was thinking, the other day,' she said, 'that you must meet my next-door neighbour. Her name is

Winnie. She was born on your farm. Give me a ring and I'll get you both round for a cup of coffee.'

Anne's number, carefully written into my notebook, remained uncalled. In the end, fate intervened during another supermarket run. 'Are you Kate?' asked a sprightly woman with a mop of grey hair, pushing her trolley down the biscuit aisle, where I had, inevitably, ended up.

'I am,' I confessed.

She gave me a broad smile. 'I'm Winnie!'

Winnie was born on 1 June 1921. Her father was the tenant on the farm at the time. He'd taken on the tenancy from his father, Winnie's grandfather, and he was to pass it on to Winnie's brother when he retired. They, like Tim and Sarah four generations later, also had sheep and cattle on the farm, but her father kept a few pigs in the pigsty that was once next to the house and they had a house cow for milk. The room that was Arthur and Ros's pantry was the dairy.

'Mother would separate the cream and make butter and cheese in there,' said Winnie as we sat nursing cups of tea by the fire in her living room with Laddie, her beloved collie, at her feet. 'She taught me how to do it – we all learned those things in those days. I hated making butter. It was terribly boring, churning and churning until your arm ached, but making cheese was fun.' Fridays were the highlight of the week. Early in the morning they would pile their produce into a horse and cart and drive down the hill to Monmouth to sell it. 'There were stalls on both sides at the top of the high street where the horses would be kept for the day and we would go with Mother to see all the traders.'

Winnie left the farm when she married Cyril ('I met him at a dance. He was a wonderful dancer!') and

'The ugly pig' – a Middle White piglet, one of our first Pig Club pigs.

Opposite page: The farm comes back to life.

This page, clockwise from the top left: Tractor driving is not just for boys!; Tim's flock; the first of two thousand new trees; Ben and Marina Fogle visit Old Man Oak; the new barn; laughing with Liz Knight while we make honeysuckle sorbet.

This page, clockwise from the top left: Biscuit and Honey; happy as a pig in…; Honey and Biscuit (you can never have enough goats).

Opposite page: The new sheep race being put to use.

This page: Mucking out – my favourite job!

Opposite page, clockwise from the top left: A very happy Badger; with Liz Shankland after winning at the Smallholding Show; happy pigs; the farmhouse and the Piggery transformed; the Wassail!

With my beloved mongrels.

moved north of Monmouth to the farm where he worked. Her old home is much changed since then; the pigsties and dairy gone, modern cattle sheds alongside the old stone buildings, but the field that still remains in front of the house was one she had particular memories off. 'We called that field 'the park'. It was full of trees. There was a pond in there too. I fell in it once. Mother was furious!'

Winnie's Park has become less park-like in the intervening years. Some of the trees remain; a couple of grand old oaks and a handful of ash, gnarled and twisted with age, but many have gone, including one that had been blown down in a gale the previous autumn, leaving mainly open pasture. It was time for a new generation of trees. I had walked around the previous day with a bundle of bamboo canes, sticking them into the ground throughout the field in what I hoped might be an approximate imitation of a Capability Brown planting plan. 'No problem at all,' said Sarah, 'you leave us to it and we'll see you later.' Tim and I hitched up the livestock trailer and waved to the small army of volunteers, armed with shovels and saplings, as we drove out of the farm gate. Myfanwy was waiting for us.

As well as teaching rural skills like hedge laying, a big part of our planned curriculum was to teach practical, hands-on animal husbandry to people who were interested in keeping a small number of animals for their own use. The courses would be aimed very much at people like me and Ludo, who have a bit of land and want to make it productive. We couldn't possibly make a living from what we do at home. We sell surplus eggs, the occasional chicken and sausages, but the main reason we do it is the enormous satisfaction that comes with looking after livestock and growing things, and being rewarded with meat, or tomatoes or honey that taste so very much more delicious because we played an intrinsic part in their production. To be able to teach these courses we obviously needed some animals.

'We mustn't rush into it,' Ludo had warned, sensibly, 'we're not ready to take on any livestock yet. And we should talk to our course experts about breeds and numbers.'

'Absolutely,' I agreed, not for a moment suspecting that any sort of future arrangement that would benefit our fledgling business would hinge on our ability to give a new home to a large, much-loved pig. Exchanging goods and services is as much part of the rural economy now as it was in the days when farm labourers worked for cider and shearers were paid in wool. We've traded eggs at the local farm shop for vegetables, and at the micro-brewery down the hill for beer. Our neighbours Rhys and Judith took a couple of chickens in return for a huge joint of beef, and a goose egg for a jar of Judith's very fine runner-bean chutney. Ludo even swapped two of our own, home-raised chickens, plucked and oven-ready, for a yoga lesson. So, I had reasoned to myself in the offices of Sawdays, an independent publisher outside Bristol, why not accept Nicola's offer?

Sawdays publish guides to quirky and unusual places to stay; anything from small independent hotels and bed and breakfasts, to a hay barn in France, a converted horsebox in Scotland and a gypsy caravan in Herefordshire. I had been commissioned by a newspaper to write about staying in a log cabin in the Lake District and had gone in to the office to finalise arrangements. I was also keen to ask advice about marketing the holiday cottage and activities on the farm, hoping they might agree to put us on their books.

'Happily,' said Nicola, who looks after the self-catering properties. 'Once the cottage is ready I'll come and see it and if it's suitable we'll help you market it. In return, I've got a favour to ask.'

'Go on,' I said.

'I have a pig – a Berkshire sow,' said Nicola. 'At the moment she is living at the community farm down the road, but they can't keep her any longer. Can you give her a home? She's gorgeous and she's called Myfanwy.'

Ludo had sighed and looked resigned. 'You can't just adopt every blinkin' thing that's offered just because it's got a Welsh name. If someone comes along with a three-legged llama called Dyffed, will you take that too?'

'No,' I said, defensively. 'But we will one day be running courses on how to look after pigs. At the moment we've got Duffy and Delilah, who, as we know, are not the most practical examples for would-be pig keepers unless they are looking for a smallish pig that will roll over when you tickle its tummy. And Blackberry is about to be on her own.'

Tim and Sarah had come to the farm with two rather bolshy Saddleback sows called Blackberry and Apple, and Apple's two offspring, now fully grown and ready for the abattoir. They didn't intend to keep any of them, but Bob had suggested otherwise. Bob Stevenson, now retired, was once a vet at the practice Sarah works at in Usk. He was also President of the UK Pig Veterinary Society and remains a consultant for the British Pig Association. In short, he's a man who knows his pigs. Hugely energetic and enthusiastic, on first meeting both Ludo and I knew this was the man who we wanted to teach our pig courses, but didn't for a moment think he'd have either the time or the desire.

'I'd love to!' he replied to my tentative invitation when he came up to inspect the Saddlebacks, 'and I think it might be worth keeping Blackberry. I know she didn't get in pig last time, but that might have been the boar's fault, and she's a nice example of her breed. It's worth tracking down another boar and giving her a second chance before she goes for sausages.'

So thanks to Bob, Blackberry had a stay of execution, but with the others booked in to go, she would be the only pig on the farm, and pigs, as I reminded Ludo, don't like to be alone. 'Myfanwy will keep her company and she is also a Berkshire, one of Bob's favourite breeds, and one he'd love to feature on his courses.'

Ludo sighed again. 'Well, don't agree to anything until Bob has had a look at her.'

A couple of days later Bob and I drove down to the community farm to meet Nicola and be introduced to Myfanwy. It was a cold, raw day and Myfanwy's paddock, which she shared with another two sows, was knee-deep in liquid mud. Nicola called her and she came out of her ark, lumbering towards us and the encouraging rustle of a bag of apples. Bob, unperturbed by the mud – which was of the particularly sticky, boot-sucking kind – climbed over the electric fence and walked towards her making pig-friendly noises. Myfanwy stood obligingly as Bob inspected her. I had never seen a Berkshire sow in the flesh before and hadn't realised what striking-looking pigs they are, with their white markings against a predominantly black body and wonderfully scooped faces and upturned snouts.

'She's very nice,' Bob announced. 'We'll need to keep

an eye on that back leg – her toe turns in just a bit, but that's easy enough to deal with. And she's too fat! Has she had a litter?'

Nicola confirmed she had, but two years ago. Bob nodded. 'That's the problem with pigs. Once they've had piglets, you need to keep breeding them, otherwise they get a little bit too fat and comfortable and it can be very hard to get them in pig again, but I think she'll be an asset on your farm. We'll slim her down a bit and I know a nice handsome boar not too far away if you want to get her in pig. So you'll have a Saddleback, a Berkshire and as a third breed I'd suggest a Welsh White. That'll be a good diverse mix then for your courses.' With that, the deal was struck and a date arranged to pick her up and bring her to her new home.

Myfanwy's imminent arrival put the pressure on. She and Blackberry would need to be kept apart for at least a week to minimise the risk of spreading any sort of disease, so she would need her own paddock and her own shelter. I did hope that she might be able to go into the newly restored stone barn, but work had been held up by any number of things from bad weather to delayed concrete deliveries and challenges with the roof design, and my increasing frustration had to give way to the realisation that it was not going to be ready in time and there was nothing I could do about it.

In the meantime we had been talking to Tim about the design of what we were calling the 'Smallholder Field'. The lease we'd had drawn up for Tim and Sarah gave them exclusive use of all the farm's land apart from fifteen acres. We would turn one corner of a field into a garden and orchard for the holiday cottage; we had earmarked the sheltered triangular field at the entrance to the farm for the cider and perry orchard and then there was the area we wanted to turn into a model smallholding, a sort of outdoor classroom, where our animals – less commercial breeds that were suitable for smallholders – would live. Over mugs of tea and a slab of Dairy Milk, we sat in Tim and Sarah's caravan sketching out the layout.

'Let's start with the animals you are planning to have,' said Tim, pencil poised over his notebook.

'Sheep,' I said, 'probably a couple of breeds. If all goes well with lambing, we should have some of our Badger Faces to bring up, and maybe we'll get a few Jacobs, because they are very popular with smallholders. We'll have chickens, of course, the two or three sows which we'll plan to breed from. Goats, possibly.'

'We're NOT having goats,' growled Ludo, 'or alpacas, or guinea fowl. I think what is important is to give people an idea of what a particular area of land looks like and what you can realistically keep on it. Perhaps we need to split up the land into, say, an area of a quarter of an acre, another of half an acre, an acre, that sort of thing, so we have a selection of sample smallholdings.'

Tim started to draw out a plan, creating four fields ranging from a quarter of an acre to two acres, a specially fenced area for poultry and a 'pig paradise'. This, he proposed, would be a long, wide strip of land with plenty of shade running along an existing field boundary. The strip could be turned into multiple paddocks using electric fencing, which would give maximum flexibility and allow areas that had been well and truly dug up by eager snouts to recover.

'It looks perfect,' I said admiringly, 'but a lot of work.'

Tim drained his tea. 'I'll go and pace it out to see if everything fits and then start with fencing in a bit of pig paradise so Myfanwy's got somewhere to go.'

A few days later, Ludo held open the gate as Tim backed the trailer slowly into the paddock. I let down the back of the trailer and Myf stood at the top, snout aloft, sniffing the air, then with the slow dignity of the very large, made her way down the ramp.

'Bloody hell,' said Ludo, incredulous, 'she's enormous.'

Badger, who was standing beside Ludo looking on, shrunk behind his legs in terror. Bella took a few bold steps towards her and then thought better of it. Myf ignored them both, and made her stately way across the grass. She sniffed at the water trough, peered into her new straw-filled ark then wandered back into the middle of the field, stuck her snout into the ground and dug a great furrow. With a contented grunt she lay down on the newly cleared earth, closed her eyes and basked in the last rays of the sun. While Tim and I had been driving back down the motorway with a giant pig in tow, Sarah Sawyer had texted to say she and the volunteers had had a good day and got everything done. Leaving Myf to settle in, we went to inspect the newly planted hedge and walked through the field that was now dotted with sapling trees encased in deer guards.

'Progress,' said Ludo taking my hand. 'We seem to be making progress.'

Chapter 14

New Trees And
Old Traditions

Emboldened by the success of the hedge-laying course, and with the farm animals settling in and work on the house well under way, we decided the time was right to branch out and do a couple more courses. One of the joys of having a farm that is suitable really only for livestock rather than growing crops is the fact that many of the field boundaries are hedges. Many arable farms, particularly in places like Norfolk and Lincolnshire, removed hedgerows to maximise the area they could grow crops, much to the detriment of the countryside. Hedges are invaluable for wildlife; they also provide shelter from the weather, both for crops and animals. On wet, windy days, many of our fields will appear to be empty until you spot the sheep huddled up against the protective barrier of the hedge.

There are also some magnificent trees on the farm, including one that Ros and Arthur called Old Man Oak. An ancient giant, squat and gnarled, it takes six adults with their hands joined to span his trunk. According to Paula from the local branch of the Woodland Trust, who had come to visit the farm with their forestry expert Phil, the tree's size and appearance would make it between six and eight hundred years old.

'Imagine the things that tree has witnessed over the years,' she said, gazing up into the broad canopy of still-leafless branches. I remember when I first discovered the tree. It stands at the edge of a very wet, boggy field, surrounded by smaller trees and shrubs, all hiding what we think must be an old green lane. The lane, now made almost impassable by overgrown hollies and blackthorn, runs along the tumbledown stone wall that marks the boundary with our neighbours. This rather wild, untamed strip of land, with its giant oak sentinel, is my favourite part of the farm and, on the many occasions it looked like the sale was not going to go through, I had announced to Ludo several times my intention to chain myself to Old Man Oak to ensure that at least he and his domain survived.

One thing the farm lacks is any woodland. There are a couple of copses, like the one that Old Man Oak stands in, and the northern boundary is Forestry

Commission land, dominated by rather dark and brooding conifers, and of course we had plans for the new orchard, but I had sought the advice of the Woodland Trust to see if there was a way of increasing the number of trees on the farm without taking away too much grazing from Tim and Sarah.

'What do you want your trees for?' asked Phil, the man from the Trust, as we walked across the fields.

'Our plan is to be able to run the whole farm on a biomass boiler,' I said. 'We'll also use wood-burners, so it would be nice if we can coppice some for firewood to be able to supply at least some of our own. The wind can be brutal up here, so we are hoping more trees will help act as windbreaks, and we want the farm to be as wildlife friendly as possible, so the more trees the better.'

'I think', said Phil, 'we can come up with a planting plan that will enable you to do all those things. Leave it with me.'

The weather was glorious: dry, sunny and warm, particularly for March. Spring was knocking at the door. If we were going to plant any trees at all we needed to get a move on. Phil's planting plan was ingenious. By planting small areas of trees in the corners of fields, alongside existing copses and as shelter breaks along field boundaries, the farm could have another 2,000 trees without losing any significant areas of grazing. All the trees we would plant would be native broadleaf varieties like oak, ash, cherry and birch, as well as smaller shrubby bushes of hawthorn, blackthorn and hazel.

'Would you consider teaching a course?' I asked Phil, whose knowledge of trees and how to identify them without the benefit of leaves had entranced me. 'We could do a sort of tree safari around the farm, showing people how to identify trees and then some planting. What do you think?'

A group of ten people gathered in the barn. Some were friends, who we had asked to come along to give us constructive feedback on the course, but some were complete strangers, including a young woman who had joined our fledgling mailing list, signed up and travelled all the way from Manchester.

'I love trees,' she said, in answer to my slightly incredulous enquiry as to why she had come so far, just for the day. 'I just don't know much about them and there are no courses closer to home that offer this sort of thing. I just liked the idea of coming here, learning how to identify some trees and then planting some. I haven't got a garden, so I can't plant any at home, but it will be a good feeling to know that there are trees growing here that I put in the ground.'

'God,' I thought, nervously, as I handed her a fresh cup of coffee and introduced her to some of the others, 'this had better be good.' Everyone was wandering, slightly apprehensively, between the tables covered in bundles of twigs and branches, which Phil had carefully laid out and numbered. When Phil explained what they were about to learn, our trainee tree planters let out a collective gasp.

'Really?' said one, incredulously. 'We can really look at a bundle of sticks and tell you what trees they came from?'

'It takes a bit of practice,' said Phil, 'but once you know what to look for, it's easy. The colour or type of bark, the way the buds are forming and the pattern they make are all clues. And it is important to be able to identify them, because you always plant trees in the winter when they won't have leaves to help you. If you want to plant a nice mix of trees, like we're going to today, and you want big trees like oak at the back of a shelter break and smaller shrubs at the front, you need to know you've got the right one. They won't always have labels, and labels have a habit of getting lost.'

Phil's plan was to plant the first of our shelter breaks across the top of a field, joining an area of copse on one side and a hedge on the other, creating a wildlife corridor.

'We'll plant the trees fairly close together – I've marked the spots with canes and each one has a colour corresponding to the species of tree to be planted there. This is where your identification skills come into play!'

At first we were painfully slow. The dry weather had made the already stony ground harder still; we had to keep checking that the bare, twiggy sapling we were about to plant really was the species Phil had stipulated for a particular spot; we couldn't get the hang of the post-rammers, knocking in the supporting stakes at hopelessly wonky angles and putting the tree guards on upside down. But as the afternoon wore on we got better; we developed a system, discovered that we didn't have to dig an enormous hole for each tree, just a neat triplet of slits in the soil with a spade.

'This is the last one!' said Phil triumphantly, and we all stepped back to admire our handiwork. We'd planted almost 100 trees in just a couple of hours. We celebrated in the spring sunshine with tea and cake, Badger and Bella looking hopefully on, in case someone had enough energy left to throw a Frisbee for them.

'I really enjoyed the day,' said the girl from Manchester.

'Well,' I said, 'you are very welcome to come back. We're planning to plant 2,000 trees in all, so if you ever feel the need to dig, you know where to come!'

Our first orchard trees were ready for planting too. True to his word, Paul Davis had put together a mix of cider apple and perry pear trees, many of them old Monmouthshire varieties. He delivered them in his faithful old Land Rover, along with stakes and guards and a promise to see us at the end of the year with the rest of them. In the meantime I had been doing a bit of research into cider making and its traditions, which, needless to say, involved a certain amount of drinking. Mike Johnson is a local cider maker who holds regular open days and cider tastings on his farm down the road. He produces single variety ciders as well as blends, and his cider tastings are a revelation.

'Each variety of cider has its own characteristics and taste,' he said, handing me and Ludo a small plastic glass of straw-coloured liquid. 'Some are sweet, some are sour, some a combination of the two. Blending different varieties can often give you a better, rounder flavour than a single variety can.' We spent a happy hour sipping and pouring, sipping again, mixing a sour to go with a sweet, discovering a wealth of combinations and possibilities.

'We've got to do this as part of an orchard course,' I said to Ludo. 'It's fascinating.'

'As long as you don't take part in it,' he said, firmly. 'You're slurring your words already.'

He had a point. The orchard course, which progressed smoothly and informatively all morning, became somewhat more giggly and sleepy after lunch and Mike's cider tasting.

'I told you,' hissed Ludo, as he carried out extra

strong pots of coffee from the kitchen. 'They'll all be asleep in the field.'

'Don't worry,' I said. 'The wassail will wake them up!'

Ludo's eyes went to the ceiling. 'At this rate we won't have any trees planted to do the wassail for.'

Wassailing is an ancient pagan ritual that I had been entirely ignorant of until we moved to Monmouthshire. Traditionally it happens on Twelfth Night and its purpose is to wake the apple trees and scare away any lurking evil spirits to ensure a good harvest the following autumn. The ceremony is led by a 'butler' and involves, like all the finest pagan festivities, a lot of drinking, singing and noise. While learning the art of cider tasting at Mike Johnson's farm, we met John. Small, wiry, with a face like a character from a Hardy novel and floor-length pale brown dreadlocks, John has tended Mike's orchards for many years and is something of a cider connoisseur. He also regularly performs wassails in orchards throughout the county.

'Can you do a wassail for a new orchard?' I asked John.

'I don't see why not,' he said. 'I've never come across a good reason not to hold a wassail!'

While Ludo was encouraging our mildly tipsy course-goers to dig holes and plant the trees so they stood at less of a drunken angle, John arrived at the barn and I helped him unload his kit. Intrinsic to any wassail is the wassail itself – the drink that is served and drunk from a communal bowl. John handed me a flagon of mulled cider to heat up and pour into a maple-wood bowl, while he filled a tray with nuts and fruits and, curiously, pieces of toast. Then he began his transformation, blacking his face with soot from a burnt cork and donning a long black tailcoat and top hat decorated with sprigs of yew. Kather's husband and children had joined us and John handed them saucepan lids and sticks.

'What are these for?' asked Kather's son Benjy.

'Those are your drums,' said John. 'You need to bash them as hard as you can to make lots of noise to frighten the spirits away.'

Benjy, who is six, needed no further encouragement. John led the way, resplendent and not a little menacing in his butler's garb, dreadlocks swinging jauntily as he marched. We followed behind – a gleeful, tuneless band with our tambourines, drums and saucepan lids – and made our way across the farmyard and out into the field. We bashed and crashed our way towards our totally unsuspecting course-goers, who, at the sound of this unholy racket, stopped digging and watched our approach with bemused expressions.

'Join us!' called John, and they did, our noisy procession snaking around the edge of the newly planted cider trees. John led the singing of the traditional wassail song as we circled the trees and then passed around the wassail cup of warm mulled cider, with shouts of 'Wassail!' after each sip. The slices of toast were then dipped in the bowl and hung in the branches of one of the trees as an offering to the tree spirits and cider was poured onto the roots.

'Here's to thee, old apple tree, that blooms well, bears well. Hats full, caps full, three bushel bags full. Hurrah! Hurrah!'

'I know we're not going to be able to harvest any fruit from these trees for seven years,' I said to Ludo as we finished the washing up, 'but I don't think there's any harm in having an annual wassail anyway, just to keep the trees happy.'

Ludo gave me a less-than-enthusiastic look as he dried up the last of the mugs.

'Fine,' he said. 'But if we're going to do it as part of an orchard course, let's not do the cider tasting as well. Bashing saucepan lids with a hangover is not going to encourage anyone to go away and plant an orchard of their own.'

I nodded in agreement. We had tried to pack too much in to one day, but then we were learning. Perhaps others would have started a new business like this in a more methodical way, carefully drawing up a list of courses, timetables, planning and scheduling months ahead. We hadn't really expected to run any courses at all at this early stage, just four months after taking ownership of the farm. We had simply invited people to come and take part in seasonal tasks that we were doing anyway, based on the simple, but hardly business-like, philosophy that if we found laying hedges and planting trees fun and interesting, others might too. And although we had paid far more for the food and our experts' time than we had come close to making back, it was, I said to Ludo, trying to sound as if I knew what I was talking about, 'a good investment'. We were getting feedback – most of it positive – under-standing what worked and what didn't, honing things. 'Or to put it another way,' observed Ludo wryly, 'keeping everything crossed, making it up as we go along and hoping for the best.'

Chapter 15

Going It Alone

The sky was clear, studded with a thousand stars. Ludo and I stood with Tim and Sarah in the farmyard. It was half past midnight.

'We've had two sets of twins in the last fifteen minutes,' said Tim softly, 'and there's another ewe thinking about lambing now.'

'Cup of tea?' asked Sarah.

We nodded and went with Tim to inspect the sheds. In the first all was quiet, the ewes that had already given birth tucked up with their sleeping lambs in individual pens, the others standing, ruminating, or lying in the straw, resting the bulk of their swollen bellies. Tim had put hurdles up between the hay shed, the Dutch barn and the yard between the two to make one giant maternity ward. With about 200 ewes all due to lamb in the next few weeks, space was at a premium. Our torches picked out one ewe standing apart from the others, tail slightly raised, pawing at the straw – the early signs of labour.

'Let's go and have our tea and then check her again,' suggested Tim.

Back at home some of my Badger Face Welsh Mountain ewes were beginning to resemble coffee tables; their udders were starting to swell. The time was fast approaching when I would be lambing my very own sheep for the very first time. Tim had given me a shopping list of things to get – lambing bottles, colostrum mix, iodine. There were also the things I hoped I didn't have to use – needles, syringes, penicillin and a stomach tube. It was not a little daunting. Which was why we wanted to do a night shift at the farm – not just to give Tim and Sarah a break, but also to know that if we were faced with an emergency, they would be there. This was a final crash-course before I had to go it alone.

Sarah went to bed and Tim came with us to check on the ewe. The first of her twins was just beginning to show – the tips of its feet just visible beneath her tail.

'Catch her up, then,' said Tim and I caught her and tipped her gently on her side. The lamb was perfectly presented – front feet first, head just behind, a textbook delivery. The second was similarly straightforward. But there was problem. The ewe didn't appear to have any milk.

'It'll probably come,' said Tim, 'but I'll go and mix some colostrum. We'll need to feed them until it does.'

Once they were fed and settled, Tim went to bed. 'You'd better get some sleep too,' he said. 'Check them all again in a couple of hours.'

It was gone two o'clock. We climbed into our camper van and passed out. It seemed just moments later our sleep was shattered by the alarm.

'I love overalls,' I muttered, as I pulled them straight over the clothes I'd been sleeping in. 'Will you feed the twins while I check the sheds?'

The beam of my torch picked up a ewe well into labour, but as soon as I approached her she was off. Trying to run, holding a torch, not losing sight of one ewe amongst a hundred and catching it without dropping the torch was nigh on impossible. Finally, I got her. The head of a lamb had come completely out. The little face appeared lifeless.

'Oh God!' I plunged my hand in – I needed to find the feet, try and push the head back in and bring it out feet first so it wouldn't get stuck. I felt around desperately. No feet. The press was full of stories about a midge-born virus that seemed to have originated in a German town called Schmallenberg. It caused, amongst other things, birth defects in lambs and newspapers were strewn with graphic photographs of lambs with their limbs fused together or otherwise horribly deformed. The farms affected had mostly been in the east of the country, and there had been no reported cases in Wales, yet, but could this be the first? 'Ludo!' I yelled. 'You need to wake Tim!'

'Sorry,' I said to him, as he appeared bleary-eyed in the shed. 'I've tried everything, but I can't seem to find the legs and I'm not sure if the lamb is even alive any more.'

The head of the lamb was still sticking out. I'd cleared the bag away from its mouth and nose so it wouldn't suffocate, but it looked completely lifeless, eyes closed, and the tip of its tongue that was poking out of its mouth was an unhealthy shade of blue.

Tim, calm and unflappable as ever, knelt down and put his hand into the ewe. 'I see what you mean,' he said. 'There's no room in there at all.'

For an agonising ten minutes he gently tried to manipulate the lamb into a position where he could deliver it. 'I've found the shoulder,' he said, 'but I just can't get the legs out. They are tucked right underneath and my hand is too big. You try.'

Gently, gently I slipped my arm in, feeling the body of the lamb, trying to work out the contours, feeling the shoulder, finding the top of the front leg, trying to ease it forward, terrified that I might break its bones if I pulled too hard, or that I might damage the ewe. Slowly, slowly, the leg started to come. I managed to ease it to the front and get the foot out. I felt a tiny bit of resistance, a slight tug back. The lamb was still alive.

'Hold on, little one,' I whispered, 'we're going to get you out of there.' I found the other leg, managed to straighten it and then, hooking my fingers around both the front feet, I gently pulled the lamb free. It plopped into the straw and we rubbed it vigorously to get the heart pumping. Tim stuck a bit of straw up its nose, which sounds like a cruel trick to play on a small creature that has already had a pretty traumatic start in life, but the straw triggers a reflex that makes the lamb sneeze and start to breathe. The lamb did indeed sneeze and snort and we watched delightedly as its little chest took its first breath of air.

'He'll be fine,' said Tim, as we moved him under

his mum's nose and she immediately started to lick him. He had a twin, which was delivered much more easily, and within a matter of minutes the ewe was on her feet and both lambs were suckling.

'Teamwork,' said Tim, smiling. It was true. But small hands can't beat years of experience. Would I really be ready to do this on my own?

All I could do now was wait and enjoy the spring sunshine. Buds started to appear on our new trees and in the early morning, as I ran through the sleeping countryside with the dogs, the birds, which had been largely silent throughout the winter, started to sing again. Back in January, I had decided that along with addressing all the usual New Year's resolutions, imposing some sort of running timetable on my life would help keep me sane. It would give me a part of each day when my head could dwell, not on the enormity of the project we had taken on, the expense, the respon-sibility, the criticism, but on something as simple and uncomplicated as putting one foot in front of the other and breathing at the same time.

Our house is just a few miles south of the farm, on the same ridge, looking over at the steep wooded slopes of Offa's Dyke. We are bordered by farmland on one side, woodland on the other and hills in every direction. This is not the terrain for sleek white running shoes and designer Lycra. I invested in some good off-road trainers, bundled myself into thermals, a woolly hat and gloves, and prepared to get muddy.

It is astonishing the variety of reasons you can come up with not to go running in the morning, and how persuasive and reasonable they become the longer you lie, warm under the duvet, watching the uninviting grey chill of a winter's dawn creep under the curtains. The only way I found to avoid sense prevailing was to get up as soon as my eyes opened, before my head really knew what was going on, and be outside in the gloom, trainers on, braced to take on the day.

I ran in winter sunshine, snow, rain and once, memorably, an ice storm which encased every blade of grass in a glass-like shell that cracked and snapped beneath my feet. I became super-conscious of the weather, how the landscape responded to it, and the plants, and the few hardy birds and animals that hadn't flown south or gone to sleep for the winter. I had a distant encounter with a fox, a brief view of a retreating badger; I startled squirrels squirrelling and blackbirds lurking in the hedges. I counted buzzards fishing for worms, once six of them in just one of our neighbour's fields.

Once the frost of frigid February had thawed, the mornings lightened, and the sun got warmer, I shed a layer of thermals. Throughout March the dawn chorus got louder, the great spotted woodpeckers started drumming and then came the joyful day when lapwings were swirling and whooping in the field next to the house and not far off the heart-lifting call of a curlew. Snowdrops, primroses, celandines, violets all followed and, at the end of March, earlier than I've ever seen them before, the first bluebells. We had day after day of sunshine. The farm transformed from mud bath to an almost clichéd picture of rural idyll, its bleak monochrome winterscape suddenly awash with colour. The trees came into leaf, the hedgerows were full of nesting birds, and new lambs raced and frolicked as their mothers greedily gorged on the fresh spring grass, joined by the cattle, newly released from their winter sheds.

But the papers were full of dire warnings of drought.

Much of the east of the country had had an unseasonably dry winter, and there were pictures on the front pages of half-full reservoirs and rivers in Yorkshire running dry. A hosepipe ban was imposed on large swathes of the country. Our newly planted trees and hedges started to wilt and had to be watered, but such was my relief not to be doing daily battle with the weather, I didn't care. Neither did the builders working on the farmhouse who could finally ditch their woolly hats and multiple layers of hoodies and show off their tattoos.

'Hopefully,' I said to Tim and Sarah, 'it'll only be a few more weeks before you can move out of the caravan and into the house.'

'It's fine for the moment,' said Tim. 'Having the caravan right next to the lambing shed means I can hear what's going on without having to get out of bed!'

It did cross my mind to take my sleeping bag into the shed at home. The first lambs were on their way and I was as nervous and jumpy as if I was about to give birth myself. Last thing before going to bed I would go out to the shed, half of me hoping I would hear the contented nickering of a happy ewe talking to her newly born lamb and part of me dreading that one might be in labour and in need of help. For the first few nights I was greeted by withering 'what do you want?' looks, and I would go away, set my alarm for 3 a.m., lie awake waiting for the alarm to go off, get up, go out again, to be greeted with 'what are you doing now?' looks, go back to bed, reset the alarm for 6 a.m., fall asleep at around 5.30, be rudely awakened half an hour later, stumble out to the shed to find no lambs and wonder how on earth I was going to get through the day and the next night and the next . . . And we had just ten ewes. Tim and Sarah with their 200 ewes, and the Beavans with 900, do this for months.

'I'll go and check them,' I said to Ludo after the ten o'clock news, 'and see you in a bit.' I swung the beam of my torch around the yard. A few of the ewes were lying down, munching, others stood at the hayrack, but I could hear bleating, the call of a ewe who has lost her lamb. Then I saw her. She'd been in the shed and was coming back into the yard, looking distracted and a little frantic. She turned again and went back into the shed. There was no sign she had given birth, no blood or discharge around her tail, but I went to check anyway. She had tucked herself into one of the pens I had set up ready in the shed. As I suspected, there was no lamb, but she was clearly in the early stages of labour and as this was her first time, was obviously feeling very confused. When a ewe is getting closer to lambing she will tend to get quieter, find a dark corner away from the others, paw at the straw and lie down. A clear discharge will appear under her tail, then she might get a bit more restless, before finally lying down and going into the last straining moments of labour. This ewe was an hour or so away from that, so I decided to leave her in peace and come back at midnight.

It was another reason to be grateful for a warm, dry March. Cold, wet weather can kill lambs all too quickly and it is also miserable for the shepherd. Walking out across the fields under a cloudless sky full of stars was no hardship at all. The ewe still hadn't given birth, but she was certainly closer and mercifully a lot calmer. I decided not to interfere and to spy on her from the feed shed next door. I sat on a bale of hay listening to her next pawing at the ground, lying down, getting up again – all the classic labour signs – for over half an hour.

'Maybe I should just go and check,' I muttered to myself. I tipped her gently on her side and whispering what I hoped was a lot of soothing nonsense, slid my hand under her tail. The tips of two feet were just there, exactly where they should be.

'Oh God,' I said to myself, 'that's not a nose.' In an ideal birth a lamb should come out front feet first, followed by the head. I should have been able to feel the end of the nose resting on the front legs and the dome of the head behind. I was just feeling fluff. It was the tail. 'Oh hell, I've never dealt with a breach birth before.'

I managed to ease the lamb out backwards. She was beautiful and now she was lying next to her mum, being licked and fussed over and I was looking on, feeling a little bit tearful, like a proud granny. Over the next couple of days we had a set of ram lamb twins and another couple of single lambs, all born on their own without help or incident. Our little flock was growing.

Then late one night I had a difficult delivery. The lamb was in the right position but it was big and the ewe was really struggling. I felt hopelessly inadequate as I fumbled and tugged and by the time the lamb was out both the ewe and I were exhausted. The lamb was fine, but the following day the ewe, although eating, seemed a bit off colour. I went to check on her last thing and another ewe had gone into labour and clearly needed help.

It was pitch dark. Ludo arrived just as I was trying to catch her. He dived for her as she ran past. He missed. I heard a groan, but was too intent on catching the ewe and pinning her down to notice what had happened. She was wriggling, desperate to get away. I could feel the lamb.

'I need you to hold her. QUICKLY!'

Ludo stumbled over, holding the ewe's head as I delivered another huge lamb.

'I'll finish off here now,' I said, as ewe and lamb lay contentedly together. 'You go to bed.'

I found Ludo fast asleep with a tea towel over his face. In it was a bag of ice. I lifted it gingerly to reveal a huge gash over the bridge of his nose and under his left eye. 'Missed the ewe,' he mumbled, 'hit the fence post.'

The next morning I felt completely out of my depth and utterly exhausted. I came into the kitchen to find Ludo looking like the boxer who'd lost. We were both supposed to be going to London to have a meeting with the people who were designing the website we desperately needed to advertise the courses.

'We can't both go to London,' I said. I couldn't get hold of Tim and was now frantically dialling Stafford's number. 'We've got a sick ewe and one that is literally about to pop. I'm working so I've got to go but could you stay here if I postpone that meeting?'

Ludo nodded wearily.

'Staff!' I yelled into the phone over the noise of his tractor. 'I've got a ewe that won't stand up. Penicillin? How much? Where do I stick the needle?'

I went to London and Ludo stayed behind on midwife duty. I'd injected the sickly ewe and both Tim and Staff were on stand-by if Ludo needed help.

'All quiet,' said the text last thing that night. Next morning at 6.30 my phone pinged.

'Twins just born. Sick ewe on feet & eating fine. Easy this lambing lark.'

Chapter 16

The Harsh Hand Of Mother Nature

'And now to the weather,' said John Humphries, at three minutes to seven on another lovely morning. 'Is it ever going to rain again? You'd better be careful what you wish for, I suppose . . .'

And so began a spring and summer so wet, 2012 will be remembered almost more for the sheer awfulness of the weather than Britain's triumphant hosting of the Olympic Games. 'Wettest Summer in 100 Years!'

screamed the headlines, as day after day there were reports of floods and landslides and forecasters warning of a month's worth of rain falling in just a matter of hours. To add to the country's woes, the financial crisis wasn't getting any less critical, the recession was still biting and no one dared to spend any money. Not a good time, pointed out Ludo, in something of an understatement, to be starting a new business largely dependent on being outside.

Not only was it a wet April, but cold too, with a howling north-easterly wind. The early spring grass became a slick expanse of mud which, in the case of the pigs' field, swiftly became a quagmire from which Myfanwy and Blackberry had to be rescued. The sheep were struggling too. Rain and wind can be a lethal combination, particularly for young lambs. I saw first hand the value of hedges, which provided welcome refuge and shelter for Tim and Sarah's sheep, but still it wasn't uncommon for Tim, on his daily rounds, to find a lamb, cold and shivery with laboured breathing.

'Pneumonia,' he said one morning, when we found a ewe standing over a very weak-looking lamb. We took them into one of the sheds and gave the lamb a shot of antibiotics. 'If you get them in time, they can recover,' said Tim, 'but this is the worst sort of weather for lambs. Even quite big, robust ones can go downhill so quickly.'

My ewes and lambs at home still had access to the shed where we had lambed and I kept it bedded down with straw, but nevertheless I noticed one lamb was starting to look a bit off colour. The lambs – we'd had a grand total of eleven – had all reached the age when they felt brave enough to leave their mothers grazing while they formed a mob and chased around the field like children let loose in a playground. But this lamb started lagging behind, unable to keep up, and although all the lambs would be breathing hard after their exertions, her breathing remained laboured. I called Tim for advice.

'Put her in a pen with the ewe and see how she is in the morning. If there is no change, bring her up here and we'll take a look at her. You don't need to bring the ewe. They'll be OK apart for an hour or so.'

I hoped a quiet night in a warm shed might do the trick, but it didn't. The next morning the lamb showed no improvement, so I picked her up and put her on the back seat of the truck. She lay down, her legs tucked neatly beneath her and her nose against the window, looking out at the passing countryside as if she did this all the time. Tim and Sarah both agreed it looked like a classic case of pneumonia and gave her antibiotics and anti-inflammatories.

'What do I do now?' I asked.

'There's nothing more you can do,' said Tim. 'The drugs will either work or they won't.'

Over the next twenty-four hours the lamb's condition didn't improve, but neither did it get any worse. Tim and Sarah came over for lunch and came out with me to see her.

'I just wonder,' I said as we looked at her standing beside her mum, sides heaving even though she had done nothing more exhausting than get to her feet, 'whether it could be something else, something physical that antibiotics can't cure.'

'If I were you,' said Sarah, 'I'd take her to see Hilary. It would be a shame to lose a nice ewe lamb like that.'

Hilary is a vet who works at the same practice as Sarah. She is married to a farmer and is a smallholder herself, so she not only knows her livestock, she is also particularly understanding of the emotions of somebody like me who only has a small number of animals and feels the loss of any of them is a huge personal failure. I carried the lamb into her consulting room.

'She's a good size,' remarked Hilary, 'and she's certainly grown well, but I can see what you mean about her breathing.'

'She's become much more lethargic, too,' I said, as Hilary placed her stethoscope against the lamb's chest.

'Here,' she said, after a few moments. 'Listen to that.' I put the stethoscope in my ears and heard a strange whooshing noise, like a propeller through water.

'Is that her lungs?' I asked.

'No,' said Hilary. 'It's her heart. That sound indicates it has a hole in it. It's very unusual and I'm really surprised she hasn't shown any signs until now. How old is she?'

'About a month,' I said, miserably. Hilary took her stethoscope off. 'She would have been born with the hole, but it only became apparent when she got too big for her heart to be able to support her. There's nothing we can do, I'm afraid. She won't survive. I'll need to put her down.'

I laid the little body on the back seat of the truck and drove home. Hilary advised that I took it back to the ewe, so she would understand her lamb was dead. There has been much debate on whether animals understand death or mourn loss in the way that humans do. Elephants, giraffes and chimpanzees have all been witnessed going through an apparent 'mourning' process. I carried the lamb through the driving rain and gently placed it at the feet of her mother. She called, that soft mother-to-lamb nicker. When the lamb didn't respond, she started to nuzzle it, seeming to try and encourage it to its feet. Whether I was witnessing a ewe 'mourning' the loss of her lamb, I don't know, but it was nonetheless heartbreaking to watch.

I spent the rest of the morning slithering and slipping through the mud, catching and treating limping lambs, all struck down with scald, a type of foot rot, caused by the never-ending wet weather. As the last one scampered away to find its mum, I succumbed to the wave of gloom that had been threatening to lay me low all morning. I stood in the pouring rain, muddy and soaked, face in my filthy hands, hot, stupid tears oozing through my fingers.

Helga Haraldsdottir put my plight into sharp perspective. For once I wasn't sorry to leave the farm, particularly as I was heading for Iceland, a country of which I am particularly fond, to film a television series on volcanoes. Helga lives on a small farm in southern Iceland. It sits, tucked beneath snow-capped mountains, facing the sea. On the day I visited, the sky was blue, the air crisp, the sun bright.

'I've got farm envy!' I said to her, as we stood admiring her Icelandic sheep and the first of that year's lambs, still wobbly on their spindly, day-old legs.

'It didn't look like this two years ago,' said Helga. 'You wouldn't have envied me then.'

The brooding ice-covered peak behind her farm is not a mountain but a volcano, with the unforgettable if unpronounceable name of Eyjafjallajökull. In 2010, after 200 years of biding its time, it erupted, filling the sky with ash that shut down much of northern Europe's airspace, and transformed Helga's farm and those of her neighbours, into places that must have seemed like hell on earth. 'For days we couldn't see our hands in front of our faces,' remembered Helga. 'It was as dark as night all day. I had managed to get all my animals inside, but we had no idea how long it would last and what we would feed them.' There was only a little hay left after the winter and all the fields were buried in ash that lay ten centimetres thick.

Remarkably all her animals survived. Friends came to the rescue, finding space on their unaffected farms for Helga's sheep and horses. I asked her if she had tried somehow to clear the ash off her land. 'We couldn't even begin. We just had to hope the grass would grow back through it.' Miraculously it did. 'Living in a country like Iceland, nature is in charge,' said Helga, smiling. 'We accept it; we have no choice.'

I remembered her wise words when I came back a week later to more rain and another sick lamb. But this time I didn't despair. The leaves were out on the trees, the hedgerows were full of wildflowers, the grass was growing and Offa's Dyke wasn't going to erupt any time soon.

The lamb was only one of what transpired to be several hundred deaths on my smallholding that year. Although I could comfort myself that I was blameless as far as the lamb was concerned, sadly the loss of an entire hive of bees was largely my fault. Not long after moving to the Wye Valley I was asked to make a film for *Springwatch* about the plight of the honey bee. The wild honey bee population in Britain had become all but extinct. Not only that, there were worrying and increasing reports of both domestic and commercial hives suffering what was being called Colony Collapse Disorder, when entire populations would die without any obvious cause.

We made the film with a local beekeeper called

Gareth Baker. His enthusiasm and passion for beekeeping was infectious, and my first glimpse of bee society – the endlessly fascinating and complex behaviour – was so compelling, I went away at the end of the day determined that I too would learn to keep bees. I did a beekeeping course and with the help of our local beekeeping association, found someone with a small 'starter' colony of bees they were willing to sell. I set up a hive in a quiet corner of the garden, with the entrance pointing towards Rhys's fields and the bees thrived.

After the particularly long, cold, snow-bound winter that started at the end of 2010 and stretched well into the New Year, my neighbour Adam had come up to our house on the first warm day of spring to help me check on them. The bees were alive, but, Adam said, not looking very strong.

'Give them some extra food and leave them in peace,' he said. So I did as he advised. Despite being taught to check the hive weekly, to take out the frames and look for eggs and brood which would tell me the queen was laying; to look for signs of the killer mite varroa or diseases like chalk brood; to watch out for queen cells which might indicate the bees were threatening to swarm, I did none of those things. I confess I missed my weekly contact with the bees, that exhilarating moment of taking off the roof, levering up the crown board with my hive tool and with a gentle puff of smoke from my smoker, being allowed access to their busy, bustling world. But the bees didn't miss me and my slightly fumbling attempts to 'keep' them. They got on with being bees. The queen laid, the workers worked, the brood hatched, the colony grew. When I did open the hive in mid-August, the time when many beekeepers would be harvesting their honey, I hoped to find a restored, healthy colony, with enough honey stored to get them through the winter. The colony was certainly restored and every space in the hive was filled with wax comb and honey. I called Adam.

'They have done well,' he laughed. 'I didn't think you'd get any honey this year, but why not take half and leave them the rest. Their stores and some extra sugar syrup should see them through until the spring.'

Bees don't hibernate exactly, but during the winter the colony reduces and shuts down. The drones are kicked out and just a core of worker bees remains to look after the queen. The queen won't lay during the winter and the bees will tend to huddle together in the middle of the hive keeping warm, staying put, and living off their stores. Only when the weather starts to warm up will they start to leave the hive and forage for food again. As I'd been taught, I hadn't opened the hive at all during the winter for fear of letting a blast of cold air into the carefully regulated temperature of the chamber and killing the bees. However, what I should have done, particularly in January when the weather that started 2012 had been so mild, was to 'heft' the hive; literally lift it partly off the ground to feel its weight and ascertain whether it has enough stored food to keep the bees alive. Frames full of honey are remarkably heavy and a well-stocked hive will take some effort to heft. Mine, when I did finally heft it, probably two months too late, was almost no weight at all. I opened it to reveal my worst fears. There was no reassuring hum, just the scurry and scuttle of a mouse making good its escape from the nest it had made in the bottom of the brood box, amidst a drift of dead bees.

Along with Nicola Bradmeare from local charity Bees For Development, I gazed mournfully into the guts of the hive. 'I did wonder whether it was varroa,' I said. The varroa mite attacks honey bees. It was thought to have been introduced sometime in the early nineties and has been responsible for decimating honey-bee populations throughout the country ever since. Small, purple and voracious, it lays its eggs on the larvae of developing bees. A hive infested with varroa will have bees with barely formed wings. Unable to fly, they are unable to survive and as varroa takes hold the colony will collapse. But my bees, apart from being dead, looked perfectly healthy. There were no signs of deformity. Nicola picked one of the dead bees up and turned it over. 'Starvation,' she said. She showed me that the bee's tongue was sticking out, a sign that it had died looking for food. I felt absolutely devastated.

'That was the problem last winter,' said Nicola. 'It was wet, but so mild that on any dry days the bees were probably far more active than they've been the previous two winters. It was warm enough in January for them to leave the hive and waste energy looking for food, but of course there would have been nothing for them to feed on, so they would have been even more dependent on stores within the hive, and there just wasn't enough.'

The rapid and alarming decline of the honey bee that I first learnt about when doing the film for *Springwatch* has continued to be been well documented and publicised. I myself have quoted more than once Einstein's theory that the human race won't survive longer than four years without honey bees. The response has been remarkable. The honey bee has become something of a cause célèbre and beekeeping, once seen as a pastime that kept old men occupied and out of their wives' way, has been taken up by Hollywood celebrities, pop stars and journalists. Keeping bees is a simple and effective way of making sure the world has bees in the future and I was hoping that, despite my wilful neglect of my colony, Nicola would advise us on setting up an apiary at the farm, not only to make our own contribution to the conservation of the honey bee, but to offer courses to others who want to do the same. But keeping bees in the traditional way is more time consuming and complicated than many suspect. Bees For Development advocate a more hands-off approach to keeping bees, using top-bar hives that mimic a wild bee space and don't use frames like the standard National hives do.

'They are a great solution for people who want to help bees, but don't want to have to "keep" them in the usual way,' said Nicola. 'It isn't really possible to collect the honey from a top-bar hive, but put one in an orchard or near a vegetable patch and they will repay you by pollinating all your fruit trees and plants.'

On Nicola's advice, I called Tony Davies, a biology teacher at a local school. His uncle had kept bees all his life, but when he was in his eighties, decided the time had come for him to give up and pass on his bees and his knowledge to another member of the family. Tony took them on as a hobby, but soon began to devote more and more of his spare time to his bees. He invited me to go and see one of several apiaries he has set up around Monmouthshire.

There is something rather magical about watching someone like Tony going through a hive. There is calm methodology to the process, a routine and a rhythm. Done properly, the bees hardly react at all. I've seen experienced beekeepers open hives and take out frames without gloves or even a bee-suit. Tony showed me a top-bar hive he'd made. It bore an alarming resemblance to a small coffin, but when he opened it he showed me why it is shaped like it is, with slightly sloping sides so the bottom is narrower than the top.

'The only thing we put in the hive are the bars – there are no frames or wax foundation. The bees do all the work themselves, as they would if they were building a nest in a hollow tree. They use the frame as an anchor point for the comb they gradually build and as you'll see,' he said as he gently lifted one of the bars clear from the hive, 'when they are allowed to build a comb without the restrictions of a frame, it is shaped like an inverted tear-drop, wider at the top and narrower at the bottom, which is why the hive is the shape it is.'

Tony agreed to make me two top-bar hives and a National hive and provide the nucleus colonies to go in them. 'We'll have to hope the weather gets better,' he said. 'None of the colonies are flourishing yet and I'm still having to feed them, which is ridiculous this late in the year. But I'll keep in touch and let you know when I've got some for you.'

Ludo agreed that it was also time to start thinking about other livestock for our proposed smallholding courses, and someone to teach them. Tim, emboldened by his experience teaching hedge laying, had agreed to teach the sheep courses and Bob Stevenson was still keen to teach the pig courses. We had a couple of local poultry experts lined up, but for the smallholder course we needed someone who had a good general knowledge of all those animals, as well as plenty of practical experience running their own smallholding.

The ideal solution presented itself when the publisher Haynes, famous for its manuals on everything from car maintenance to plumbing, asked me to write a foreword for one of their latest publications. It was a manual on smallholding, written by Liz Shankland, broadcaster, writer, smallholder and breeder of champion Tamworth pigs. Liz lives not far from the farm and I had long wanted to get in touch, but hadn't quite plucked up the courage. Now I had the perfect excuse.

Liz came to the farm and we stood with Tim in the field that he had transformed into our model small-holding, with the different-size paddocks, each with their own water troughs, and a specially fenced, fox-proof area for poultry. Liz nodded with approval.

'People have real difficulty picturing how big an acre is and imagining how the land could be arranged or divided to make it work best. What livestock are you thinking about getting?'

Ludo and I had agreed that we needed a range, not just of animals, but breeds that might serve different purposes. We would certainly have chickens, both layers and table birds and already James and another Liz, who would be teaching the poultry courses, were tracking down everything from Wyandottes to Welsummers. We had some Black Orpington eggs that had been given to us by some friends of Ludo's mum, and were in the incubator at home, and Jo and Emily, our neighbours from across the road, had bequeathed us a handsome gander and three geese which were already happily ensconced in the new orchard. Although Tim had plenty of sheep, which would prove invaluable for the courses, we also wanted to showcase some rare or more unusual breeds that would have different appeal for smallholders. We planned to bring some of our Badger

Face Welsh Mountain sheep to the farm and our friend Janey had agreed to sell us some of her Jacobs, beautiful horned creatures with spotty fleeces that people love to spin. We were considering a third breed, possibly Horned Dorsets because, unlike most sheep, they will breed at any time of year.

'Pigs?' asked Liz.

'We've got a Berkshire sow and a Saddleback, and we're hoping to get a Welsh White.'

'What about your KuneKunes? Will you bring them to the farm?'

'Really?' I said. 'I'd have thought you'd be massively disapproving of KuneKunes.'

'Not at all,' said Liz, laughing. 'They're not great meat pigs as you know, but they are small and nice-natured and although they root up the ground a bit, it is nothing compared to what a big pig like a Tamworth or a Berkshire will do. They are ideal for someone who likes the idea of having a couple of pigs more as pets than to end up on a plate with apple sauce. You should definitely bring them up to the farm. What about goats?'

I looked at her, delighted. I love goats. They are destructive, will eat everything and are a nightmare to keep in, but the meat is delicious, and the milk fantastic for cheese. Ludo has consistently resisted my pleas over the years, but how could he refuse a published small-holding expert who had just agreed to teach our courses?

'I hate them too,' Liz reassured him, 'but people will be interested in them and it would be good to be able to demonstrate the challenges of keeping them before they go off and get a herd of the little buggers.'

Before Ludo had a chance to change his mind I phoned Adam Henson. Adam had been my co-presenter on both series of *Lambing Live* and it is down to him that almost everywhere I go I get asked 'How's Humble the lamb?' The very first lamb I delivered at the Beavans' farm was the little black one that Kate Beavan had named Humble in my honour. That, I thought, would be that. Humble went out into the fields with her twin sister and her mum to get on with the business of growing up. Except she didn't do it very well. One morning Adam and I went out with Jim on his usual rounds to check the sheep and Adam noticed that Humble, distinctive because she was the only black lamb in the flock, was a bit unsteady on her legs and walking awkwardly. She was noticeably smaller than her twin, too, and was obviously not getting as much food. Both Jim and Adam agreed that she should be brought in and bottle-fed, although Jim was sceptical about her chances of survival. All this was caught on film and the nation, naturally, took this funny little runty lamb to their hearts. It became clear very quickly that she was never going to grow properly and for Jim, as a commercial sheep farmer, she was useless.

'You'd better take her back to your farm!' I joked to Adam, live on air, and that did it: he was committed. The morning after the last programme, Adam drove away from the Beavans' farm with a little black lamb in the back of his truck.

'I'll come and visit her!' I said.

'You can come and claim her,' said Adam, ' as soon as you've got some sheep of your own. In the meantime I'll be charging you maintenance costs . . .!'

Humble, it turned out, more than paid her way. Viewers of *Lambing Live* flocked to the Cotswold Farm Park to meet the little wonky lamb that was my name-sake. One man drove all the way from Milton Keynes to be at the gates of the farm park at nine o'clock on the morning after the last programme, hoping to see her. His journey was in vain. The farm park was still closed for the winter and Adam and Humble still hadn't left the Beavans' farm. But once there, she became a firm favourite, not just with the public, but also with the staff. She grew up, got a bit greyer, seemed to prefer the company of goats than other sheep, liked playing football and was always a little bit grumpy. When I did suggest to Adam that I could take her off his hands now that I had my own sheep, the girl who had been looking after her looked so devastated we decided that Humble would remain at the farm park for good.

Tim and Sarah had never been to the Cotswold Farm Park and Adam, who'd come with his family to spend Easter with us, issued us all with an invitation.

'Can I take you up on it,' I said on the phone, 'and while we're there get some advice on goats?'

'Of course!' said Adam. 'And bring your livestock trailer. We might find something you want to take back with you . . .'

I first went to the farm park on a school trip. It has changed a good deal since then with its shop and café, children's tractor rides and shearing and milking demonstrations, but it is the animals, all rare breeds, which remain the biggest draw. Humble was there, a rather large, matronly ewe these days.

'She doesn't look remotely pleased to see me!' I said to Adam.

He laughed. 'She is a funny sheep, that one. Most sheep that have been hand reared remain quite affectionate, but she just isn't. People still ask to see her, though.'

We walked around the paddocks, marvelling at the

sheer number and variety of breeds. There are primitive breeds like the Soay sheep from St Kilda. Small, scruffy, wily and fleet of foot, they are descended from Viking stock. With them are the Highland Cattle, that look like they could be descended from woolly mammoths, and further on there are pigs and piglets of all shapes, colours and sizes. There are miniature donkeys, spotted ponies, geese, chickens, bantams and, of course, goats. I didn't dare to admit to Adam that it was on a school trip I discovered, to my delight, that goats would obligingly eat everything, including the long list of typed-out questions given us by our teacher that we were supposed to complete and hand in at the end of the day.

A smallholder is going to be interested in goats either to milk or for the meat. To have an animal that needs milking is a big commitment and not one any of us felt able to take on. But goat meat is growing in popularity in the UK and it was breeds that are good for meat that I wanted to find out about. Adam showed us his small herd of Boer goats, which are the ones traditionally raised for meat. They are not very big animals, but chunky. 'The meat is very good,' confirmed Adam.

'They are a perfect animal for smallholders,' I said to my still less-than-enthusiastic husband. 'Good breeding stock will always sell and so will the meat.'

Ludo looked sceptical.

'Come on,' said Adam, 'I believe I've got an ideal solution.'

Waving from the car windows a couple of hours later, we swung out of the gateway and turned homewards. In the trailer were Biscuit and Honey, Boer-cross goats that Adam and his children had hand-reared.

Friendly and easy to handle, they would make ideal demonstration animals for our courses and if we found a good Billy, the start of a breeding herd.

'You can bring them back if you don't like them,' called Adam, 'but they shouldn't give you any trouble . . .'

Chapter 17

A Foray Into Foraging

In December 2011 Ludo and I had gone along to the Abergavenny Christmas Food Festival – the smaller, festive version of the main festival that is held in September and draws foodies from all over the country. There we didn't meet Liz Knight, who just three days before had given birth to her third daughter, but we did discover her wonderful herb and spice mixes, her elderberry vinegar and wickedly delicious mincemeat made from wild fruits and cobnuts.

'She lives locally,' said her friend who was running

the stall. 'You should get her to take you foraging. Where you and I see fields, she sees a larder full of wild flavours and endless possibilities.'

It struck me that someone who had just had a baby wouldn't relish a call from a complete stranger suggesting they abandon their new-born to teach foraging courses at an establishment that was yet to be, in any way, established. So I waited until the spring and on one of April's rare dry days, Liz came to the farm, baby in a sling on her chest, to walk the fields and talk about potential courses.

'Look at this!' exclaimed Liz, as if she'd found gold.

'It's ground elder,' I said, unimpressed.

'I know. Everyone hates it, but it's wonderful. It was brought over by the Romans as a herb. Put it in stews, chop it up for omelettes. And dock leaves! I cooked smoked trout wrapped in dock leaves the other day. It was delicious!'

In our culinary wander around the farm I discovered the gently perfumed taste of new bramble leaves ('infuse in hot water for a lovely tea'), the sharp lemony flavour of wood sorrel and the rich honey of its flower ('try the two together! Amazing!') and the complex peppery sweetness of the cuckoo flower which made our eyes widen in wonder that something so small and delicate could pack such a flavourful punch.

We had used the word 'hub' a lot in our early meetings with the council; we had the hope that that was what the farm one day could become – a sort of focal point for local people to exchange ideas and show off their talents. 'Rural skills' has a broad enough remit to allow for all sorts of things from hedge laying to animal husbandry and, of course, finding, growing, producing and cooking food. I knew the moment I met Liz that she was exactly the sort of person we wanted to work with and I knew too that if we put her together with Kather the two of them would draw huge inspiration from each other. They both have a similar philosophy when it comes to food: relishing the seasonal, the wild, caring about the provenance. They are both adventurous and experimental, but their food, their recipes and their methods are accessible and don't overwhelm. I loved the idea of them running a course together and almost as soon as I suggested it to them both emails were flying back and forth full of ideas, recipes and menus. We had not done a food-based course before and it was Kather who raised the spectre of Environmental Health.

When we walked around the farm for the very first time, long before we had even had our first meeting with the council, it was the old stone barn that lies at right angles to the farmhouse that made our brains race. Although dilapidated, with some alarmingly big cracks in the stone work and a couple of walls that seemed on the verge of collapse, it looked to us to be the perfect place to hold the courses. The barn is in three sections; one, we had envisaged, would make a perfect classroom, a smaller, narrower bit could be an entrance hall with an office above and the biggest section, with its magnificent, cobweb-strewn roof beams, would be the kitchen and eating area, designed to allow it to also be a space for teaching food and cookery courses. But work on the house had had to take priority and nothing had, as yet, been done to the barn. Stafford had drawn up the plans, keeping the agricultural integrity of the building as agreed but finding clever ways of joining all the elements together.

'Before I can submit the planning application,' he

said, 'we are going to need a structural engineer's report. The barn is in a pretty perilous state and we need to know what we are letting ourselves in for before we launch into any work on it.'

The structural engineers sent teams to drill holes, take soil samples and establish that the barn basically sits on clay with almost nothing in the way of foundations.

'It's managed to stand there perfectly happily for a couple of hundred years,' I pointed out to Stafford. 'Why are they making such a song and dance about it now?'

When their recommendations came in, together with an enormous bill, Stafford phoned and suggested we get a second opinion. 'What this lot are proposing would hold up a building the size of something at Canary Wharf,' he said. 'And it will cost more than your entire budget for the barn. I've got a recommendation for another engineer so we'll see what he comes up with.'

While waiting for this second report, we also had something else to consider, something that would dictate not just what we did to the barn, but how, when and even whether we could do anything at all. The bat survey that had been done the previous summer had found that a small number of brown long-eared bats were using the barn as an occasional roost. I was delighted. Bats are fascinating creatures, as well as being invaluable indicators that the world around them is in good shape. The presence of bats proved that the farm had a healthy ecosystem with plenty of foraging sites harbouring plenty of insects – all good things not just for bats, but for a whole range of wild creatures. Bats have suffered a great deal from loss of habitat, the use of pesticides and increased light pollution, all of which have contributed to a severe decline in numbers over recent years and led them to become a species protected under European law. And it is that very protection which, I suspect, will cause more damage to bat populations than anything else.

When a building has bats you have to have a licence to be able to undertake any work that might disturb them, and to get a licence you need an ecologist. I found one, thanks to our local Wildlife Trust, and made a date to meet him at the farm. Stafford and I showed him around the barn, outlining the plans and showing him where we intended to put the bat loft that was stipulated in the survey. He seemed happy with everything and said he would get on with writing the mitigation report we would need to submit along with the planning application. He also suggested we have an on-site meeting with the bat officer from the Countryside Commission for Wales, one of the bodies that would be key to us getting a licence. In the meantime, Stafford, mindful that we were desperate for work to get going on the barn, had done some research.

'Given that most of the work that we are doing is repairs, rather than big structural changes, there is a lot we can do without planning permission. The planning application could take ages, and given the state of the barn and the weather, it is perhaps best we undertake the repair work and put in the planning application later.'

'What about the bats?' I asked.

'We'll still need a licence,' said Stafford, 'but we don't need to wait for the planning to come through before we can apply for it.' It seemed like the perfect solution. Suddenly, after all the setbacks and delays, it felt like we had taken a giant leap forwards. Once we had the mitigation report from the ecologist and the engineer's recommendations we could apply for the licence, which would take about a month, but experience told me not to be too optimistic. I knew to allow for the unexpected, but even so, it might mean work could start in a couple of months. Kather would have her kitchen and we would be able to start running courses, including Kather's cookery ones, in earnest. It was the end of March. I left the country on the filming trip to Iceland, once again feeling buoyed up with excitement and enthusiasm.

I read and re-read Ludo's email. If I understood it correctly someone, who lived in the local village but who wished to remain anonymous, had been watching the building works on the farmhouse from somewhere – we're not sure where – and contacted the local Wildlife Trust. The Trust contacted us to say they had had reports of a new chimney being put on the roof of the farmhouse, and as the bat survey had found there to be a bat roost in the attic and as we had not applied for a licence we were breaking the law and their informers would be reporting us to the police.

'What new chimney?' I emailed back, aghast.

'Exactly,' wrote Ludo, 'there isn't one. They made a mistake, but we still had to submit photographs, plans, reports and all sorts to the Wildlife Trust to get these people, whoever they are, off our backs.'

My little bubble of optimism started to shrink and burst altogether when I got back two weeks later to find that we still hadn't had the engineer's report, despite promising it would be with us for over six weeks, and neither did we have the mitigation letter from the ecologist, which on our last meeting he said was almost complete. Not only that, he had changed his mind about the repair licence and said he was only prepared to put together the application for a full licence once planning permission was granted. Any thoughts that work would start on the barn anytime before the end of the year were banished.

The alternative was to make the tin barn that we had been using for the few courses we had run so far feel a bit more hospitable. The space at the moment was a bit big, echoey and bare, furnished with just a few tables and chairs and a couple of gas heaters. We had the means to boil a kettle and heat up food but, as Kather pointed out, if we wanted to make this our main base for the time being, and certainly if we wanted to run courses that would involve food demonstrations, we would need to comply with environmental health regulations.

'Not something it comes anywhere close to in its present state,' said Malcolm, a helpful contact of Kather's who came to give us advice. 'You really need to build a sort of pod within the barn, that has no way for mice or other vermin getting into it. You need wipe-down walls, a moppable floor. Your gas cooker is not legal unless you have an extractor. You need a dedicated hand-washing basin as well as the sink you've already got. When's the course?'

It was my fault. I'd rushed things. So enthused by Liz Knight's culinary tour of the farm, I'd been desperate to book a date with her to do a foraging course. Kather too had been swept up in all the excitement, and the email that went out to friends, neighbours and the beginnings of our mailing list setting a date for the week after Easter had brought in some bookings. We were committed. We had just eight days to make ourselves legal.

'What happens if we don't do all the work yet?' I asked Kather, afraid that the deadline was just too tight. 'Leave it until after the course?'

'People know about the farm,' said Kather, 'they know we are running courses and they know we are providing food. All of which means it is perfectly possible for the environmental health officer to also know about us and to demand an inspection with almost no notice. If we are seen to be contravening the regulations we'll be shut down, and that will be it.'

So with that, Kather called Shane the plumber who brought along Leigh the plasterer. She found an electric cooker, which didn't need expensive extraction, and someone to put in the floor. Chris and Ryan, the electricians working on the farmhouse, agreed to work late to get the electrics in. Leigh, who turned out to be more master craftsman than plasterer, transformed the plasterboard box housing the kitchen into a work of art using wood scavenged from around the farm. Ludo and I, along with Tim, Sarah and Kieran, a student studying countryside management and getting work experience with Tim, shifted barrow-loads of building detritus, polished, scrubbed and Hoovered. Liz and Kather were frantically picking, baking, stewing and bottling, creating a wild feast that would introduce our guests to the delights of primrose curd and lavender-scented soup, rabbit with wild garlic pesto and wild boar with juniper. But only if we passed the inspection.

The morning before the course was scheduled to happen Kather and I greeted the environmental health officer with slightly manic smiles, clutching a mop and a washing-up brush, the air in the kitchen thick with pine disinfectant. He looked around at the results of what had been a Herculean team effort. He checked the paintwork, noted the extra sink, the recommended flooring, the gleaming new cooker. And he smiled. 'This is fine. You can go ahead with your course. Good luck!'

The rain stopped and a tentative sun peeped from behind the clouds. Liz and Ludo took everyone off to forage for leaves that would be used to make a wild salsa verde and the wild trout roulade Kather was planning to demonstrate when they got back. Kather put the finishing touches to the foraged feast she was serving for lunch, I washed up, set the table and got everything ready for the salsa verde-making. Leigh had made chopping boards for everyone from slices of tree trunk and Tim had made a brand from some scrap metal, which he heated up and burnt into the surface of the boards. HbN it said – Humble by Nature. Leigh had made us some cupboards too, from the wood of the old ash tree that had blown down in the autumn with hinges scavenged from the old sheep race. Liz had brought armfuls of wild flowers and leaves that were arranged in jars and pots around the room. There were flowers on the lunch tables too, and pretty tablecloths that Kather had brought from home.

It struck me, as I allowed myself to pause for a moment and take in the transformation of what had been, just a few months ago, a leaky, rusty tin shed with a dirt floor and no walls, that if this project did fail, we had achieved one thing that we had hoped to do, something that was almost more important than anything else: we had found and brought together some truly wonderful people, people with talent, ingenuity and boundless enthusiasm. People who were prepared to devote a huge amount of time, energy and effort to try and make this work. It was all too easy, I realised, to think that everyone and everything was conspiring against us, when yet another promise wasn't kept, another deadline was missed, the house sprang a mystery leak, the rain kept falling, half the farm was underwater and we were threatened with imminent arrest. But the last few days had been an uplifting reminder that along with our detractors we had some tremendous supporters. My reverie was broken by Liz and Ludo's return with their noisy band of followers, bags crammed with leaves and flowers, all brimming with the excitement of discovery. I left them to it and went back to the washing up.

Chapter 18

A Rainy Day Romance

'**A**re you going to the Smallholders' Show?' said a text from Liz Shankland. 'Because if you are, I want to ask you a favour.'

The Smallholders' Show is held at the Royal Welsh Showground every year. There's terrier racing, falconry displays, sheep dogs rounding up Indian Runner ducks, stalls selling everything from bee suits to dog baskets. There are hog roasts and cider stands, displays of every kind of craft you can think of, and, of course, there's the livestock. Some breeders come simply to showcase their animals and perhaps sell some too; others come to show. There's a horse show and a dog show, but there are also classes for everything else and it is not remotely unusual to find someone sitting in a corner giving a chicken a blow-dry or rubbing conditioner onto a pig.

Tim and Sarah were keen to go and between us we knew various people who were going to be there, so we decided to have a bit of a farm outing. It would also be a good opportunity, as Tim pointed out, to have a look at some other breeds that we may not have considered. I was still interested in finding some Horned Dorset sheep. Our friends Joe and Emily Ryder who farm across the road from us, had given us the idea of having Dorsets. They have the polled variety – without horns – and highly recommend them, for their meat, their wool and their docile temperament. The polled Dorset is more widely found than the horned variety, which are now classed a rare breed. They fell out of favour, like many horned sheep, because their horns make them harder to handle in big numbers, making them less commercially viable.

'Yes,' I texted back to Liz, 'we'll be there.'

'Good,' came her reply. 'How do you feel about wearing a white coat?'

Liz was born and brought up in a terraced house in the Welsh town of Merthyr Tydfil. She worked as a journalist and broadcaster and it was only twelve years ago that she and her husband Gerry found a house halfway up a mountain with six acres of land, abandoned city living and became smallholders.

'I had no idea what I was doing,' she said, 'but I started with some chickens and people loved the eggs so I ended up with about fifty. Then we got some ducks, sixty bronze turkeys, an accidental flock of sheep, and goats, which escaped and ate all my fruit trees.'

But it was pigs, and Tamworths in particular, that were to become the mainstay of her smallholding. Tamworths are the oldest of the British native breeds, sometimes known as 'the Ginger Pig' because they are, undeniably, ginger. Liz chose them because they are hardy and can cope with the rain, wind and freezing temperatures that are the everyday challenges of living 800 feet up a mountain. But she also claims they are the pig with the most personality and they have the added bonus of tasting good. She started by buying weaners – pigs of about eight weeks old that had just been weaned – and raising them on until they reached slaughter weight, but then decided to start breeding her own. She showed her first pigs in 2007 and came away with a handful of rosettes and a new ambition – to one day breed a champion of champions. Which she has done, more than once. So I expected to find Liz calm and nonchalant at the Smallholders' Show, safe in the knowledge that she knew exactly what was ahead and that she had nothing to prove.

'Can you help me with the boar?' she asked, thrusting a white coat in my hand. Iestyn had been born just five months before, but was already a splendid-looking animal. Lying in his pen, ginger, sleek and handsome, he seemed utterly unfazed by all the attention. Liz, by contrast, was in a state of barely suppressed panic.

'He needs a brush and then can you give him a bit of a polish with that?' she said, handing me a sponge and a bottle of hair conditioner. 'I've got to get the sow ready. Where's the board? Where's my stick? Oh God, I need a drink!'

I let myself into the pen and brushed the already immaculate Iestyn, who lay, stretched out on his side in the straw, eyes closed, oblivious to the fuss that was going on around him.

'It's almost time,' gasped Liz, still flustered, still desperately on edge. I gave Iestyn a final polish with a conditioner-soaked sponge.

'What do you think?' I said to Liz.

She smiled. 'He looks great. Sorry, I'm always like this at shows. A bag of nerves. I can't tell you how many times I fall out with Gerry before a show. It's a nightmare. Oh! They're calling us. Come on!'

I still had really no idea what I was doing, but Liz handed me a pig board and a thin cane and as we guided Iestyn between the pens towards the ring she told me all I had to do was walk behind him, keeping him straight and away from the other contenders so the judges could get a clear view. She would be at his head. I buttoned my white coat, flicked a bit of straw off Iestyn's rump and we walked into the ring. It was only then that I realised what an incredibly nerve-racking thing I had agreed to do. A sea of faces surrounded us. Ludo, Tim and Sarah were there, giving us encouraging smiles. I was too nervous to smile back. The judges stood in the centre of the ring, immaculate in their ties and tweed, regarding us all with stern faces. I was terrified that I would lose control of the pig, that he would go careering round the ring, knocking judges flying, and was concentrating so hard I didn't even notice that Liz had been handed a red rosette. Iestyn had won!

Liz and I hugged. 'Now we deserve a drink!' she said.

We didn't find any Horned Dorsets but we did find

Adam Henson, who, over celebratory sausage sandwiches, told us that he had found a breeder. 'He's in Wiltshire, so not far. How many do you think you want?'

'Maybe four ewes,' I said, 'depending on the price.'

'I'll give him a ring and let you know. We can go down together.'

Finally, after what seemed like months of non-stop rain and unseasonal cold, came a break in the weather. At the end of May, the sun came out, briefly but fiercely, heating up the well-soaked earth and triggering a spurt of growth so dramatic it was almost audible. I took Badger and Bella out into the fields, where the grass was suddenly thigh-high. The air was full of the low rumble of tractors busy cutting, baling, wrapping, making the most of this early bounty. The dogs sought respite from the heat by jumping into water troughs where they would stand, tongues lolling, bellies submerged in the blissfully cool water.

There was no such easy respite for my ewes who lay in the shade, panting in their thick fleeces. 'This is the danger time,' said Tim. 'We need to keep a close eye out for fly-strike. The easiest thing to do is to shear them. I'd say yours are ready.'

Fly-strike is a horrible affliction. As the weather gets warmer, blowflies, drawn particularly by the inevitable muck that collects around a sheep's tail, lay their eggs on the sheep. When the eggs hatch, the maggots burrow beneath the fleece to feed on the living flesh of their host. It can be hard to spot, particularly if it happens before the sheep are ready to shear. Unchecked, it will kill. I had been keeping a nervous eye out, watching for any sheep that looked particularly twitchy or uncomfortable. So far they just looked hot.

Tim arrived and set up his electric clippers in our

shed. As well as shearing his own 200 ewes, he does contract shearing for other farmers and has a deservedly fine reputation as a skilled and deft shearer. Good shearers make it look effortless. They hold the sheep between their knees and appear to dance with it; the whirring clippers glide beneath the wool making it fall in a thick, luxuriant wave away from the sheep's body until it lies in one frothy piece on the shearing board and the sheep, pale and leggy, skips away like an embarrassed teenager.

Having had a couple of attempts at shearing I can tell you it is far from effortless. Sheep are quite heavy things for a start. My ewes probably weigh fifty kilograms or so; the more commercial mules will be closer to eighty kilograms. Just getting hold of one and tipping it on its back to start shearing is exhausting enough. And a sheep can spot an inexperienced shearer in an instant and will employ every possible wriggling and kicking tactic to get away.

There is a pattern to shearing, starting on the belly, with the sheep sitting on its hind quarters, one front leg tucked between the legs of the shearer, its head braced between the knees. Here you have to be mindful of not slicing off the teats or cutting the milk vein. Once the belly is clean, you shear around the tail, using your knees, feet and body weight to manoeuvre the sheep into position. The tail is fiddly and often encrusted in poo, just to make the task a little more challenging. Then it's up the back leg, following the contours in a series of 'blows' up to the backbone. A bit of fancy footwork and you start up the throat, neck and under the jawline. Suddenly the sheep is on her back, half the fleece is off, she is turned again and the final blows reveal her in all her naked glory. That's the theory anyway. My slow, clumsy attempts have left me aching and sweaty, the poor ewe threadbare in some places, patchy and tufty in others.

As if Tim didn't have enough shearing to do, he had also entered himself into a local shearing match. Ludo and I had never been to a shearing match before so when Tim asked if I would be in charge of his pen, I happily agreed, even though I wasn't quite sure what it entailed.

The shearing match was being held at a farm a few miles away and we parked our truck behind a row of other mud-encrusted farm vehicles that were squeezed against the hedge on the narrow lane. Inside the shearing shed it was more like a party; people standing in gaggles, nursing big mugs of tea or munching on burgers. At one end there was a stage with a line of pens at the back and the shearing rigs all lined up at the front. Four men were shearing as we came in.

'There's Russ, look!' said Tim. Russ, who had lent us the Badger Face ram, was shearing a sheep with hand clippers, the old way. 'There are classes for all styles of shearing,' said Tim. 'I've entered the speed shearing.'

Russ won his class and his wife, who was one of only four women who had entered a class, won hers.

'Feel inspired? Going to enter next year?' asked Tim.

'Umm,' I said. 'It might take rather longer than that before I reach that standard. Anyway, you've sheared all my sheep. I've got nothing to practise on unless I try the dogs.'

The stage was set for the speed class. Six sheep were put in each of the pens. The first four competitors climbed up onto the stage, shears at the ready. Each competitor had an assistant, someone who would tip each sheep on its back and have it waiting at the gate of the pen for the shearer to grab it the moment he had finished shearing the last one. The winner would be the person who sheared the six sheep fastest and cleanest and the job of the assistant was crucial.

'That's what you'll be doing,' said Tim. I looked at him, aghast.

'You'll be fine!' he laughed, but instantly my stomach was tight with nerves. It was an incredible thing to watch; sweat, wool and clippers flying. All too quickly the first round was over and it was Tim's turn. We eyed up the competition.

'I'll never beat him,' said Tim, nodding at a young man who had taken to the stage with bare feet. 'He's been working in New Zealand, shearing hundreds of sheep a day. He's one of the best.'

I stood in the pen, sheep at the ready. The whistle blew. Tim grabbed the sheep and started. In almost the time it took me to catch another sheep and get her turned on her back he was ready for her. There was no time to watch; he sheared all six sheep in a little over five minutes. And he didn't win. As Tim predicted, the bare-footed shearer went home with the prize, having sheared all his sheep in under four and half minutes. 'Never mind,' said Tim. 'Next year I'll do your pen and you can have a go.'

Adam Henson called about the Dorsets. 'The breeder is called Jim Dufosee. He's very well respected. He's got ewes of various ages that he is happy for you to come and look at. They are all in lamb and have been scanned, so that saves you having to find a ram for the time being.'

As I'd learnt from the Beavans, sheep, as a rule, come into season and are able to breed only as the day length shortens and the weather starts to get colder. Sometime around September a biological trigger is twitched which says 'right, now's the time to get pregnant' – which explains the very distinct 'lambing season' from January to May.

But there are a couple of breeds that don't follow this rule and will happily mate at any time of year. The Portland is one and another is the Dorset, which explains why Jim had ewes in lamb in summer. It was another reason we were keen on them as a breed to show people who came to do our smallholder or sheep courses.

We could have gone the easy route and chosen the more commonly kept polled Dorset, which also breeds at any time of year, but, like Adam, we were keen to champion rare breeds. The luxury of being a small-holder is that you don't have to make choices based purely on commercial terms. Smallholding is not something you go into to make money; the reward of having a smallholding is not financial, it is the satisfaction of being able to produce your own food – whether it is a bit of veg and a few eggs, or for the more adventurous, meat, milk, cheese and honey. Smallholders can therefore play an important role in supporting traditional breeds that are now classed as rare because they have been superseded by more commercial breeds.

Jim Dufosee's farm spans a beautiful valley on the edge of Salisbury Plain. His flock of newly shorn Dorsets stood out bright white against the green grass. Jim sent his dog around to gather them up and drive them towards us. They are solid-looking sheep, broad faced, with horns like racing bike handlebars.

'They produce a lot of wool,' said Jim. 'If you had seen them before we sheared them you would see they grow wool from the tips of their noses right down to their toes.'

'That'll keep you busy!' Tim whispered to me.

The ewes Jim had set aside for me to look at were in the barn. 'I've chosen a few of mixed ages,' said Jim. 'It's good to have a flock of different ages so they don't all die at the same time!'

We checked their teeth, their eyes, their legs and most importantly their udders. 'What you don't want,' Adam had told me, 'is a ewe that is in lamb but has a problem that means she can't feed the lambs when they are born.'

We picked out four, one youngster expecting a single lamb, and three more mature ewes all due to have twins. Jim and I finished the paperwork and we loaded them into the trailer. 'They are due anytime from mid September,' said Jim. 'Let me know if you have any problems.'

The break in the weather didn't last long. 'I hope to God we don't get done by the Trades Description Act,' I said gloomily, as Ludo and I drove into the farmyard in sheeting rain on the morning of our 'Wild Taste of Summer' foraging and cooking course. When we had been planning our timetable of courses in preparation for the launch of the website, we thought a summer forage on a balmy, fragrant day in June would be the perfect course to start with; something that showcased the farm and the glorious Monmouthshire countryside. On this midsummer day, the farm should have been the very epitome of a bucolic idyll. Newly shorn sheep should have been relishing the release of the woolly warmth and weight of their fleeces. The sows should be stretched out on their sides in a blissful sun-drenched trance; calves and lambs skipping and gambolling in green meadows. Instead everything was huddled miserably behind hedges or in their shelters and the farm was awash. Gateways had become quagmires, drainage ditches raging torrents, the lane a lake and even the geese were beginning to look uncomfortable.

'There is some news that will cheer you up,' said Tim, as we sloshed up to the barn, wearing, ludicrously for a summer's day, thermals and head-to-toe Gore-Tex, still sodden and mud-covered from the previous day. 'Denty has won Myf over. I caught them at it yesterday and I've just been out to check them. They're in the ark, lying together, spooning!'

At the Smallholders' Show, Liz had introduced us to Chris Impey, a prison officer with a passion for Berkshire pigs. He had agreed to lend us his champion Berkshire boar, Denty – so called because he has a dent in his side from a run-in with an older boar when he was just a youngster. Myfanwy had settled in very contentedly and we all adored her. There had been a nerve-racking couple of days when she had first been introduced to Blackberry. Pigs may not like to be on their own, but Blackberry was not going to let just any old pig share her paddock. At first meeting both sows eyed each other suspiciously. Myf hung back, feeling shy. Blackberry, perhaps sensing Myf's unease, decided to take full advantage of the situation and galloped over – as much as something with quite short legs and quite a big belly can gallop – and gave Myf a bit of a shove. Myf lashed out and that was it. Blackberry launched an attack that had both pigs spinning around, mouths agape, trying to take chunks out of each other. I was terrified. Liz Shankland had warned me that it was quite usual for sows to have a bit of a scrap when they are first put together, but she also told me that her much-treasured sow had been killed in one such encounter. The fight broke up; Myf retreated, leaving Blackberry looking triumphant. 'They'll work it out,' said Tim. 'I'll check on them last thing.'

It took a few days. Myf refused to go into the ark if Blackberry was in it, so we put another one in the field and fed them well apart from each other. As time went on we would find them grazing in the same part of the field, basking within a few feet of each other, and then came the happy morning that Tim was able to report he'd found them both in the same ark. Bob Stevenson had been up to see them and pronounced them both in perfect condition and more than ready to be introduced to the boar.

The last time Blackberry had been to a boar she had failed to conceive. Myfanwy hadn't had a litter for over two years. Bob warned that despite Denty's championship credentials, there was no guarantee that either sow would get in pig. Chris had said Denty could stay for a few months to give them the best chance, but we all knew that if either sow failed to get pregnant there was little point in keeping them. We would have to prepare ourselves to eat an awful lot of sausages. So it was indeed news to make us smile that Denty and Myf had worked out the best way to while away a wet day.

Cars started to arrive at the farm; gallant souls in wellies, raincoats and hats came dripping into the barn. Kather, who would be demonstrating how to cook with the wild ingredients we hoped they'd find, had made an orange and poppy-seed cake with poppy syrup as a summery welcome to go with their coffee.

'Perhaps I should have made porridge?' she said, only half joking, as the rain, whipped into a frenzy by a gale-force wind, slammed into the tin barn making conversation almost impossible. Nonetheless Liz Knight, whose irrepressible enthusiasm for the joys of wild food and the culinary secrets to be unearthed in every garden and hedgerow, was not going to be put off by the deluge. She led our game course-goers out into the downpour and returned, well over an hour later, all of them soaked to the skin, but buzzing with excitement, bags and baskets full. Kather showed them how to make flat breads to dip in olive oil and a heady mix of wild seeds and spices, which they added to a spirit-lifting lunch of lamb tagine, couscous with rose petals and honeysuckle sorbet. After lunch, with no let-up in the weather, we turned up the heaters in an attempt to replicate some summer warmth, and Liz demon-strated how to make rose-petal syrup and a wildflower vinegar with the ingredients they had foraged in the morning.

'They seemed to enjoy themselves, despite the weather,' said Ludo. I was so limp with exhaustion, so worn down by the noise of the rain, that I had no idea whether it had been a success or not. If it had, it was thanks to Liz and Kather's boundless energy and inven-tiveness, which had saved it from being a washout.

'If we do it again, we'll need to call it something different.'

'What about "How to Forage in a Monsoon"?' suggested Ludo.

'Perfect,' I said, 'no one could quibble with that.'

It was Roosevelt who said 'nothing in the world is worth having or worth doing unless it means effort, pain, difficulty' – a rather joyless, if accurate sentiment, as we were beginning to discover. Jane Howorth, I'm sure would agree, as it was largely thanks to a decade of effort, pain and difficulty on her part that I found myself sitting at an M4 service station outside Cardiff the day after our soggy forage. I had been instructed to avoid the main car park and pull over in a quieter area around the side. I was early. There was no one about and I sat in the truck listening to the radio and waiting. Half an hour later another vehicle, this one towing a trailer, pulled into the same area and drew to a halt beside my truck. I got out, greeted the other driver, handed over the money. The cover was lifted off the trailer and a crate taken from the back and loaded into my truck. With a short final exchange we parted company, driving off in opposite directions.

This transaction, suspicious though it must have looked to anyone watching from the sidelines, was meticulously planned and entirely legal. As a result we became the proud owners of twelve new hens. That morning Lucy, a volunteer from the British Hen Welfare Trust, had picked up several hundred commercial layers from a farm in Cornwall. As I had learnt at the Lewis's farm, commercial layers – whether free-range, barn or caged – have a short life. They are kept until they are about ten months old, then, as their productivity starts to wane, they are sent for slaughter and replaced by new stock. The layers I had picked up from the Lewis farm earlier in the year had proved a great success, consistently outlaying their rather more pedigree coun-terparts.

These new birds were for the smallholding at the farm and, we hoped, would become advocates for would-be chicken owners to consider taking on ex-commercial layers. Up until this point, these hens had spent all their laying life in cages. Battery cages – bare wire cages big enough to contain a hen but not big enough for it to move – were banned in the UK in January 2012.

My birds would have been kept in what are called enriched cages – larger cages holding up to ninety birds each with perches, a scratching area and a nest box to allow a certain amount of natural behaviour. The reason they didn't go to slaughter, the reason battery cages are no longer legal in Britain, is thanks in no small part to the tireless work of Jane Howorth.

Jane is the champion of the commercial layer. I had read about her, seen her on television, but never met her. Almost a decade ago she started the British Hen Welfare Trust and her pragmatic, sensible approach has made her a real force for change. She, like many of us, would like to see caged egg production banned altogether and for all eggs to be free range. 'But', she explained, standing in our farmyard with Tim and Sarah's chickens pecking around her feet, 'the onus is not simply on farmers. As long as businesses and consumers still demand cheap eggs, we will have caged birds. And I would rather they were eggs from British farms. If we ban caged egg production in Britain altogether, businesses will simply get their eggs abroad where welfare standards might be much worse.'

As well as educating consumers and persuading businesses like Hellmann's to use only free-range eggs, she runs an extensive re-homing programme. She works with about fifty farms around the country and with a national network of dedicated volunteers has found new homes for over 30,000 birds to date. 'It's hugely rewarding for people to take on these scruffy hens and see their gradual transformation into happy, healthy, free-range birds.'

Our birds were certainly scruffy. With their wonky beaks, overgrown claws and bald patches, they were not, as Tim pointed out as we unloaded them from the crate, going to win a beauty contest any time soon. Jane had warned me they would take a day or two to adjust to their new surroundings and although some of them ventured to the open door of their house and looked out at the grass, none of them was quite brave enough to make the leap.

But early the next morning a text came through from Tim. 'Chickens are out. You've even got some eggs!' I emailed Jane. 'Hens all doing well and I've had an idea.' It was an idea that had come to me as I was driving my bedraggled cargo back down the M4. I had had to pick up my chickens from the service station because there was no re-homing centre in our part of Wales.

'Would the farm be any good?' I suggested to Jane.

Her reply came straight back. 'Thank you!!! Yes please!'

Chapter 19

Don't Fence Me In

'Right,' said Tom, bringing up a new slide that made us all wince. 'Sucking chest wounds. Who knows what they are and what to do if someone you're with gets one?'

In just over a week I would be leaving Wales and flying to Afghanistan, which was why I was sitting in a classroom in Herefordshire doing what is cheerfully described as a Hostile Environments Course. Tom, an ex-Special Forces medic, had been teaching us what to do with compound fractures, severed arteries, gunshot wounds and heart attacks. When we were not wrestling with Sam splints and triangular bandages with Tom we were hanging out with the slightly humourless Hamish, who told us what to do under mortar fire and how to behave in a minefield. All of which would probably have been very useful if I was going to try and out-burka John Simpson and head for the front line, but I was going to Afghanistan to film sheep.

I was heading for the Wakhan Corridor, a thin finger of mountainous land in the far north-east of the country, bordered by Tajikistan to the north, China to the east and Pakistan to the south. The BBC had commissioned a series about the evolution of herding. The domestication of sheep gave human beings a rich and wonderful resource. In the days before global markets, mass urbanisation and spiralling population figures, a family might have had a few sheep, principally for their milk and wool, or to trade and only very occasionally to eat. In the modern world herding has had to change and adapt to allow it to be something that is purely commercial, and herders are at the whim and mercy of factors well beyond their control. We planned to start the series with the shepherds of the Wakhan corridor, who live with their small herds in a way probably little changed for hundreds if not thousands of years. We would complete the series at the other end of the spectrum in Australia, where herding is done on a vast scale and where shepherds can no longer go and check their livestock on foot, but need planes, helicopters and motorbikes.

My phone vibrated on the desk. Tom had moved on to CPR. Surreptitiously I opened the text. It was from Tim. 'First Dorset about to lamb.'

Jim Dufosee, who I had bought my four Dorset ewes

from, had told us they were due sometime around mid September and it seemed his estimate was spot on. Over the last few weeks, the three expecting twins had got broader and broader, until they resembled cider barrels on legs, and their udders began to swell. Now the first one was about to lamb any minute and I was stuck inside giving mouth to mouth to a plastic torso. 'Keep me posted,' I texted back. 'I'll get out of here as soon as I can.'

We spent the afternoon in the woods, orienteering. The historian Dan Snow, who was about to go to Syria, was on my team. As soon as we worked out the next set of coordinates I would race off.

'Bloody hell, Humble,' said Dan, 'what's the rush? The pub doesn't open for hours yet!'

Another text came through from Tim. 'No lambs yet.' One final first-aid training scenario involving multiple fractures and concussion and I was away.

I drove straight to the farm. Tim had left to pick Sarah up from work so I rushed out to the field to see what was happening. The ewe was now in the late stages of labour; restless, pawing the ground, getting up and down, but there was no sign that the lamb was imminent. I left her in peace, and did the rounds, feeding the piglets, bringing in the goats, shutting in the chickens. I checked her again. She was on her side, straining. I walked slowly towards her, just to make sure that everything looked all right. She was one of the older ewes and had had lambs before, so I wasn't expecting her to need my help. But as I got closer I realised something was wrong. The head of a lamb was out, but it was still in the water bag, which hadn't broken, and if I didn't act immediately it would suffocate. The ewe stayed put as I broke the bag and pulled the lamb out as quickly as possible. There was no sign of life. I cleared the mucus from around its nose, rubbed its sides and then picked it up by the back legs and swung it. A snort, a splutter. 'Come on!' I willed it. Nothing. I swung it again, rubbed the chest and just as I was about to lose hope, miraculously it took its first breath. I laid it in the grass in front of its mum and she started to lick it. I delivered the twin and then sat back in the warm evening sunshine to watch mum and lambs bond.

Tim and Sarah came running across the field. 'I can't believe I missed it,' said Tim. 'Everything all right?'

'Had to do a bit of first aid,' I said, grinning, 'but they're doing OK now.'

While the Dorsets were lambing, the rest of Tim's flock and my Badger Faced Welsh Mountains were only now starting to come into season. Tim, along with every sheep farmer in the country, was starting to plan ahead for the following spring. He had also been working on some new ideas for the farm and the first thing he wanted to try was an idea that had come to him after our first impromptu meeting of the Pig Owners' Club.

The club had come about in a fairly haphazard way. Liz Shankland had suggested we get some weaners for the smallholder courses. Smallholders who are interested in keeping pigs, particularly if they have limited land, will often go down the route of buying a couple of weaners which they keep for six months or so until they reach slaughter weight. They will then have a freezer full of delicious home-reared pork that will keep them going for months.

We agreed it would be a good idea and decided on

two different rare breeds, notable both for their placid temperaments and also, of course, for the taste of their meat. We carried the three Berkshires and three Middle Whites into the Byre, now beautifully restored, light and airy with a bank of solar panels on the roof. 'That's going to be an awful lot of pork,' commented Ludo as he watched them rolling about delightedly in the straw.

'Well, why don't we keep them here, but offer them for sale?' I said. 'Then people who don't have the land or time to keep a pig themselves can own a pig, pay all the costs involved, visit it when they want, but we look after it day to day and take it to the abattoir when the time is right. They then end up with lots of delicious pork, and know exactly where it has come from and how it has been looked after. And we make a bit of much-needed cash.'

So we put up some notices in the classroom at the farm and sent emails to our friends and the mailing list. We had no idea what response we would get, whether this was the sort of idea that anyone would take up. A few people expressed an interest, made polite noises about it being a good idea, but didn't take it any further. Then the Peacocks, a family who moved to Monmouthshire at about the same time as we did and have become great friends, said they would love to buy a pig. The four of them came to the farm and chose a Middle White. I have never eaten Middle White, but Liz said that in blind taste tests it almost always comes out the favourite. They are strange-looking pigs, often referred to as the Ugly Pigs because their squashed, crumpled snouts and pink-rimmed eyes give them a rather gremlin-like appearance, but the Peacocks were very taken with theirs, as was the delightful Scottish ex-international rugby player who came to the farm to present one to his Polish wife for her birthday. Kather bought one for her father's seventieth birthday and encouraged a fellow mum at her son's school to think about buying one too. Tracey thought a whole pig would be too much for their family alone so joined forces with two other local families and they all turned up, en masse, one Sunday, to choose one of the Berkshires. It was one of those lovely, unplanned, spur-of-the-moment days when the sun shone and the farm looked beautiful. The kids, a great mob of them all under ten years old, and full of the spirit of adventure, ran around the fields, climbed trees, cuddled the goats, tickled Duffy and Delilah, the KuneKune sows, and went with Tim to meet the newborn calf. The Pig Owners' Club had been successfully inaugurated.

'I was wondering,' said Tim the next morning, as I was mucking out the goats and he was feeding the piglets, 'given that people are obviously interested in buying meat straight from the farm, and being able to visit the animals with their kids, what you would think about getting some bull calves from a dairy farm to raise here for meat.'

Veal still has uncomfortable connotations in this country. Veal is calf meat – most often a bull calf of a dairy cow – and traditionally was produced by keeping calves in very small crates and feeding them a milk-only diet to keep the meat white and soft. A UK campaign in the 1980s highlighting the way veal was produced resulted in a crash in sales. Veal crates were banned in the UK in 1990, but veal has never made a comeback.

The problem is that the dairy industry still produces bull calves that now have no use or value, so tens of thousands are killed every year at just a few days old. Not only that, dairy farmers, already under huge financial pressure thanks to the drop in milk prices, have to pay to have the calves dispatched and removed. Farmers and foodies like Jimmy Doherty and Hugh Fearnley-Whittingstall believe there is a simple solution to what is undeniably a waste of a perfectly good animal. They are championing what is known as rose veal – meat from calves which have been reared along RSPCA guidelines, on a more natural, mixed diet with plenty of space to move around. The meat, rather than being the rather white, anaemic-looking stuff that the word veal conjures up, is pink and looks more like beef.

I thought it was a great idea. 'I'll phone Robert Brook.'

Robert and his wife Eileen have a dairy farm just down the road. They have a herd of 100 Jersey cows, sell some of the milk to the Milk Board and the rest they keep to produce ice cream.

'Twenty years ago,' said Robert, 'when milk prices came under pressure again, we decided to try and add value to our milk by using it ourselves to make another product.' The ice cream they make has been a huge success, but Robert, like many dairy farmers, still has to take a hit when it comes to his bull calves. 'It costs me to have them killed and taken away and yet these are animals that should have a value. I'd be delighted for you to have our bull calves, but remember they are Jerseys. Not your ideal meat breed. I'll ring you when the next one is born.'

Robert phoned a couple of days before I was leaving for Afghanistan. Tim and I drove down to his farm to go and pick up the calf that had been born just a few days before. He was tiny, with the scrawny conformation typical of his breed, but with a rich, warm, caramel-coloured coat and big dark liquid eyes. We carried him to the trailer and put him alongside a Hereford cross heifer calf that Tim had just bought for £200 as an addition to his herd. She will grow up to become what is known as a suckler cow, breeding more calves that can be sold on either for breeding or beef – both valued products that in turn give her a value.

'He looks like a little deer!' said Sarah as she came to see the new arrivals. We had put both calves together in a big, airy pen, with a thick bed of straw and the goats as neighbours. The heifer calf curled up in the straw, but the Jersey skipped and pranced, fell over and got up again, until, worn out, he too settled down.

'It's ridiculous isn't it,' I said, looking at him. 'We've got one ten-day-old calf that is worth a couple of hundred quid and another that is worth nothing, simply because it is the bull calf of a dairy cow.' Tim nodded. 'Well, maybe this calf can do something to start changing that.'

There was one other pressing issue that had to be dealt with before I went away, that of Myfanwy and Blackberry. They had been living in a happy threesome with Denty the boar for several months. There was plenty of evidence that Denty had been doing his job, but so far, every pregnancy test that Bob Stevenson had done had proved negative. Pigs are expensive to keep and with winter approaching we had to think practically. Feeding two sows incapable of breeding throughout the winter would be an enormous waste of money. Before I could bring myself to make the decision I phoned Bob.

There is nothing unusual about a pig lying stretched out in a state of muddy bliss on a warm afternoon, but Myfanwy seemed to be spending more time than usual lying down. That morning, when I went to check on them, Blackberry and Denty were happily rooting around, but Myfanwy was lying down again. She seemed perfectly content, just a little more lethargic than usual.

'I know it is extremely unlikely after all this time that Myf is pregnant,' I said to Bob, 'but she's behaving a bit differently and maybe . . .'

When a pig is four weeks pregnant or more the blood that runs through the uterine artery starts to flow differently. It is a symptom known as 'fremitus'; the blood flows with a running pulse and using ultrasound, it is possible to hear it and ascertain whether a pig is pregnant.

Bob shook his head. 'There's nothing,' he said.

My heart sank.

'I'll do an internal check, just to make sure, but there doesn't appear to be any sign of pregnancy.'

I stroked Myfanwy's face, hoping against hope that Bob might detect something that would change the fate that by now seemed inevitable.

'That artery I told you about is enlarged. The blood flow is not in fremitus, but it could mean she is in the very early stages of pregnancy. I'll come back and test her while you're in Afghanistan. Hopefully there will be some good news when you come home.'

It wasn't until I got back to Kabul after three tough but inspiring weeks with the shepherds of the Wakhan Corridor that a text message, sent some days before, came through from Ludo. 'Bob confirmed Myf is pregnant. Could be due within a month.' I had my first bath in three weeks to celebrate.

The gestation period of a pig is three months, three weeks, three days. Tim had used straw bales to create a maternity wing in the barn and Myfanwy, now in the final weeks of her pregnancy, had moved in.

'Your suspicions proved to be right!' said Bob with a big smile as we watched Myfanwy stretch out in the straw for a nap.

'Female intuition,' I laughed. 'If I was expecting a litter of up to twelve piglets, I suspect I'd like to do a lot of lying around too!'

My delight that Myfanwy was pregnant was tempered only by the fact that I was about to go away again, this time to Australia, and was likely to miss the birth. But one morning, just a week before I was leaving, Tim told me that she had started to produce milk.

'Bob said it is only when she begins building a nest that the birth is really imminent,' he said, 'but if she's got milk, I reckon it could happen in the next two or three days.'

October's shortening days make some animals fly south, some prepare to sleep away the winter and some to think about sex. The woods around the farm echoed with the throaty roars of stags all trying to out-bellow each other, secure territory and, most importantly, impress the does. As evening fell the tawny owls took over. 'Teer-witt!' cried the males, followed by an anxious silence, the heavy pause before an answering 'ter-woo' told them they'd caught the attention of a female. And out in the fields the rams had been put to work.

We were hoping that with all this romance in the air the two goats, Biscuit and Honey, would be distracted from thinking about how to break out and get into the feed bin, or better still, the orchard, which they had managed to do only a few days after they arrived.

'Don't tell Ludo,' texted Sarah, who despite her better judgement had become rather fond of them, 'but they escaped and have eaten three of the five crab apples you planted behind the house.' Ludo, of course, found out, and walked around with his I-told-you-so face for several days, but the goats stayed and now I was keen to breed from them. Neither had bred before and finding the right husband was proving a bit of a challenge. They are not pure bred, but a cross between a Boer goat and a Guernsey. As we were interested in trying to raise goats for meat, and Boer goats are principally a meat breed, I was on the lookout for a Boer billy. I trawled the internet and tracked down Jo Murphy, who lives not far from the farm and had just started rearing Boer goats. 'Come and see them!' she said.

Jo and her husband Ian have about twelve acres of land on which they keep chickens and turkeys, a flock of sheep and of course the goats. Jo milks some of them and is experimenting with making cheese, but her real interest is building up a Boer herd for the meat. Boer goats are small and stocky. Like sheep, they too come into season in the autumn and Axil, their Billy goat, was strutting around the field with his harem of ladies looking very pleased with himself indeed.

'We don't want to lend you Axil, because he's going to be busy here,' said Jo, 'but come and meet his son Alex. If you like him we are happy for you to have him.'

'My only concern', I said, as we stood in the field assessing Honey and Biscuit's potential partner, 'is that he is quite a bit shorter than they are. The Guernsey in them means they are quite long-legged. Do you think he'll manage?'

Jo laughed. 'I think he'll find a way!'

Alex arrived on the farm the day the bee inspector called. I had registered with the National Bee Unit when I first acquired a beehive, and as a result got free inspections and advice. The bee inspector said that worryingly, two diseases – European Foul Brood and American Foul Brood – had been reported in the area and he needed to come and inspect the hives. If he found American Foul Brood in any of the hives they would have to be destroyed. I could hardly bear to think that we might lose our bees again. We'd had to wait until late July for there to be enough of a let-up in the weather for Tony Davies to come and deliver our new bees. He'd arrived at the farm, the boot of his car full of buzzing boxes.

'I won't open the window,' he said, shouting through the glass, 'some of them have escaped.'

He wasn't exaggerating. The whole car was full of bees. Tony, who had driven fifteen miles, presumably with the bees flying around his head for most of the journey, was unconcerned.

'I'll just drive across the field to where the hives are and deal with it there.'

'OK,' I shouted back. 'Don't get stuck. It's muddy out there. . .'

Tony emerged unscathed and the bees were transferred to the five hives placed amongst the trees and shrubs of a little copse, which Tim had fenced to protect it from curious livestock. 'You'll need to feed them for a while,' said Tony, 'it is still so cold and wet they won't be flying much, but hopefully they'll start to establish. You won't get any honey this year, but then I don't suppose many of us will.'

The bees, largely thanks to Tim, who, having never kept bees before, became mildly obsessed with them, all survived and slowly the colonies started to grow. We kept feeding them and by the time the bee inspector came one mercifully warm and dry autumn evening, each hive had eggs and brood in several frames of the brood box, and had even managed to store some honey for the winter.

'It's a great spot for them,' said the inspector, approvingly, as he climbed over the stile and zipped up his bee-suit. Tim and I held our breath as the inspector opened the first hive.

'They're very calm and quiet,' he said, sounding grateful.

'I think that's thanks to Tony,' I said. 'He obviously has a knack for raising gentle queens.'

The temperament of the queen will dictate the temperament of the whole colony and Tony's bees all seem to be particularly laid back, which was why, when the inspector opened one of the hives and the bees seemed agitated he suspected something was amiss.

'All your hives are free of disease' (I let myself breath again) '. . . but the behaviour of these bees makes me think they might have lost their queen.'

We went through the frames, looking either for the long-bodied queen or newly laid eggs that would indicate she was still in residence. We found neither.

'It's too late in the year to introduce a new queen,' said the inspector, 'so I suggest you try and merge this colony with one that has a queen. It might not work, but it's worth a go.'

The next morning Tim and I walked back out to the hives clutching an old newspaper. On the inspector's advice we put a sheet of newspaper on top of the brood box of the hive with the queen, poked a few holes in the paper and put the brood box of the queenless hive on top of it. Each colony of bees has its own distinct odour and bees will identify and fight with bees from outside their own colony. But the newspaper method forces the bees to chew through the paper to mix, by which time the odours of each colony have combined and they believe they are one big happy family. A few days later we went back to see what had happened. The newspaper was in ribbons and the bees seemed perfectly content.

Meanwhile, Myf's milk had appeared to dry up and she showed no further signs that she was about to give birth. I had to accept the fact that I was almost certainly going to miss it. But then, a couple of days before I was due to leave, Tim met us on the yard with the news that her milk had come back and there was lots of it. There was no change during the day, but Tim promised as we left the farm that evening to text us as soon as anything started to happen. At eleven o'clock that night my phone bleeped. 'Myf's started nesting.' We slung sleeping bags and the dogs into the camper van and drove straight to the farm.

Tim was in the barn when we arrived. According to Bob's instructions he had sectioned off a corner of the farrowing pen for the piglets and he was busy rigging up a heat lamp. Myf was on her feet, gathering mouth-fuls of straw and carrying them carefully to one corner of the barn, piling them up into a huge unruly nest. She fiddled and fussed, pawed at the straw, carried more over until finally she was satisfied and then lay down on her side with a contented grunt and closed her eyes. We took our cue from her and went to bed. I lay in the campervan, listening to her gentle snores and grunts, hardly daring to fall asleep in case anything might happen. We checked her at 3 a.m. but she was firmly asleep and was still asleep when we checked her again at 6 a.m. She got up briefly for a drink but wasn't interested in breakfast.

'She's in the first stage of labour,' said Bob when we gave him a progress report. 'Typically she'll be very still and quiet. Things get a bit noisier in the second stage. She'll grunt a bit, and strain, her back leg will kick out and her tail will twitch. Then the next thing you'll know there'll be a piglet.'

'Her tail's twitching,' I whispered urgently to Ludo. By now it was half past eleven in the morning and she had been showing all the signs Bob said she would for some time. Then silently, without any fanfare at all, a small, shiny black piglet slipped onto the straw from under the twitching tail. Fifteen minutes later there was another; ten minutes later a third. Within moments their velvety coats were dry and they were latched onto a teat without any intervention from mum or from us. By 4 p.m. she had given birth to nine piglets; two stillborn, which, said Bob, who had been there throughout, was not unusual, but the other seven strong and healthy and quite the most adorable things I'd ever seen. We all sat in a row on the bales grinning.

'I've never seen a pig being born,' I said to Bob.

He smiled. 'I've seen hundreds of farrowings and I never get bored of them. It's magical, isn't it?'

It was something of a milestone: our first piglets born at the farm. Alex, in the meantime, did not seem to be having much success with Honey and Biscuit, who greeted his arrival with barely suppressed scorn. It may be a while before we can celebrate the birth of our first new generation of goats. But the night of the piglets' birth marked another even more significant milestone. Tim and Sarah had their housewarming. They had finally been able to move into the farmhouse. The holiday cottage was finished too, and the first booking was made by the man from North Lancashire who had been on our very first hedge-laying course. He came with his wife and two sons and despite truly awful weather had loved being in the midst of a working farm.

'I can't believe how much you've done since we first came here,' said Kate Beavan, who together with Jim, and a huge crowd of neighbours, friends and family, had come to help Tim and Sarah celebrate their escape from the caravan.

And I suppose it did look very different from the way it was after a year of standing abandoned and awaiting its fate. Very different from the day when the phone call came to tell us the farm was ours, and we stood at its chained and padlocked gate on a chilly November afternoon surveying the empty fields, the fences sagging, the gates hanging, hedges overgrown and full of brambles, the farmyard and Ros and Arthur's vegetable patch a riot of weeds, the house black with damp, wind echoing through the barns, making the rusting corrugated iron rattle and bang. But repairing buildings, re-hanging gates, clearing weeds and planting trees only goes a little way to making a farm feel alive again. The real transformation came when there were animals back in the fields and farmers back in the house. It was what we had set out to do; somehow keep the legacy of this little piece of land intact. For a hundred years and more it had supported three generations of Winnie's family and then Ros and Arthur. It had, coaxed by skill, knowledge and sheer hard work, provided a livelihood for those families and produced food for the community and far beyond. And now it is Tim and Sarah's turn; the start of a new phase in the life of this land.

So is Ludo's and my job done? The truth is, it has

barely started. It isn't just that we are still to realise many of our original plans and ideas. The apple press awaits its first apples; the honey extractor is still on the shopping list. The local primary school braved the mud and the rain and became what we hope will be the first of many enthusiastic, noisy and joyful school visits. We still have the main barn to restore, and a distant plan to transform the mud and rubble of the courtyard into an edible garden, as long as we can find a way to make it goat-proof. We hope our day as a re-homing centre for the British Hen Welfare trust – 300 chickens now have happy new lives in and around Monmouthshire – will be the first of many. I still harbour dreams of breeding an animal worthy of the show-ring and maybe even training a sheepdog, although Ludo remains sceptical that any dog I own will ever do anything other than take up residence alongside Badger and Bella on the sofa in front of the fire. It is more that our lives have changed exponentially; we have become rooted in a way neither of us has felt rooted before. I was never homesick when I travelled. Now I feel an insistent pull, as if I'm straining on a chain anchored firmly in the stony clay of Monmouthshire, and get increasingly impatient for the heart-lifting moment I always feel as I cross back over the ever-changing waters of the Severn, heading west over the old bridge.

The last year has been a series of challenges and neither of us of has any doubts that there are plenty more to come. Every day is a lesson; sometimes a tough one, even, on occasion, heartbreaking. We've seen the not-so-nice side of human nature, but also some of the best. We had a CV from someone called Rachael who lives just a mile from the farm and, unperturbed when we said we had no office, no phone, no internet and no income, told us she wanted to work with us anyway – and she, along with a whole host of extraordinary people that we have been lucky enough to come across, have helped turn what was once a pretty business plan with no numbers on it into something akin to our wild, unfettered imaginings. Along the way, I've cried tears of fury, frustration and anger, but also of sheer, unadulterated joy. I've done battle with strangers, but joined hands with others to encircle Old Man Oak, all of us laughing, delighted by something as simple as hugging a tree. And it is all those things that have helped to consolidate a realisation that has crept up on me over the last twelve months: that when your life is wrapped up in the land, each becomes intrinsic to each other. We had only wanted a few more acres; we had got a whole new life.

There is a song by Cole Porter that, if I were ever invited on *Desert Island Discs*, would be on my list of must-haves, alongside the Elgar cello concerto and the theme from *The Muppets*. Under a sky full of stars, I hummed it to myself as I drove Tim's tractor around a field in the pitch dark one late summer night. Badger lay across my knees, Bella sat up at my side, looking out of the windscreen. Sarah was on the trailer at the back and Tim and Ludo were walking alongside, picking up bales of hay and throwing them up to her. The rumble of tractors could be heard in every direction, despite the lateness of the hour, as farmers all over the county made the most of a dry night to get their hay undercover before the next deluge hit. I felt supremely, madly, gloriously happy.

'Just give me land, lots of land and the starry skies above. Don't fence me in!' I sang, tunelessly. Badger jerked awake and gave me a look of barely suppressed irritation from under his unruly eyebrows.

'You can head to the middle of the field now!' yelled Tim. 'The last of the bales are up there.'

I hauled the heavy steering wheel around, serenading the dogs. 'Let me ride through the wide-open spaces that I love! Don't fence me in!'

Bella jumped out of the open door in search of mice. Badger gave a long-suffering sigh, rested his nose on his paws and went back to sleep.

Acknowledgments

Writing a book is something I've wanted to do for a very long time, but never quite had the nerve to start. Thank you, Rosemary Scoular at United Agents, and Wendy Millyard, for your unwavering belief that I could find 80,000 words and string them into something that made sense.

To Sarah Emsley and all the Headline team, thanks goes to you, not just for believing Rosemary, but also for your invaluable support and encouragement along the way.

I owe a huge debt to Polly Morland, my friend and neighbour-across-the-river who was just finishing her wonderfully titled book *The Society for Timid Souls* as I was starting mine. She had an unerring knack of sending a funny email, bolstering text or invitation to the pub at just the right time.

My husband Ludo has spent the last year realising what it is like to be married to someone trying to write a book. Ludo, I don't know how or why you put up with me, but you know I couldn't have done it without you, and in my defence, my mum did warn you . . .

And finally to Badger and Bella, without whom this book would have been written much more quickly, but who always provided welcome distraction.

Kate Humble
February 2013

Picture Credits

All photos © Ludo Graham except for:

Section 1; p1, p2, p3 (top right), p4 (bottom left), p6, p7 (centre right), p8; Section 2; p1, p2, p3 (top right), p4, p5, p6, p7 (top left), p8 © Clare Richardson

Section 1; p3 (centre left), p7 (Humble the Lamb) © Sarah Gibbs; p4 (bottom right) © Sam Beavan

Index